For

Peter Barkworth is one of Britain's best-known actors. He has appeared many times on the West End stage, on television and in films, twice winning the BAFTA Best Actor Award. His stage and television appearances have included *Crown Matrimonial*, *Shadowlands*, *Hidden Laughter*, *Professional Foul* and *Telford's Change*. He has also written a slice of autobiography called *First Houses* and *The Complete About Acting*, based on classes he gave at the Royal Academy of Dramatic Art in London.

FOR ALL OCCASIONS

Poems, prose and party pieces
for reading aloud

COMPILED
BY
Peter Barkworth

Methuen

Published by Methuen 1999

5 7 9 10 8 6

First published in hardback in the United Kingdom
in 1997 by Methuen Publishing Limited

This paperback edition was first published in 1999
by Methuen Publishing Limited
215 Vauxhall Bridge Road, London SW1V 1EJ

Compilation copyright © 1997 Peter Barkworth

For copyright in individual pieces see the acknowledgement pages.

Peter Barkworth has asserted his right under the Copyright, Designs
and Patents Act, 1988, to be identified as the author of this work.

Methuen Publishing Limited Reg. No. 3543167

A CIP catalogue record for this book is available
from the British Library

ISBN 0 413 72650 9

Phototypeset in 11/13pt Bembo by Intype London Ltd
Printed and bound in Great Britain by CPD Wales, Ebbw Vale

TO MY FRIENDS AND ACQUAINTANCES WHO HAVE SENT ME SOME OF THEIR FAVOURITE PIECES

Simon Brett, The Reverend Philip Buckler, The Reverend Alan Burroughs, Ray Connolly, Tom Conti, Steve Cook and Magmasters Sound Studios, John Cunningham, David Daiches, Robert Daws, Tricia Eddington, Derek Fowlds, Michael Frayn, Christopher Fry, Hannah Gordon, Rupert Hart-Davis, Robin Hawdon, Tim Heath, Wendy Hiller, Thelma Holt, Gerald Isaaman, Peter Jeffrey, Wyn Jones, Penelope Keith, Andrew Maclean, Alec McCowen, Leo Marks, Aylwin Mayhew, The Very Reverend Michael Mayne, Lee Montague, Nanette Newman, Geoffrey Palmer, Edward Petherbridge, Robert Powell, Michael Redington, Ruth Rendell, Ian Richardson, James Roose-Evans, Prunella Scales, Mark Shivas, Donald Sinden, Rosemary Anne Sisson, Stephen Sondheim, Amanda Waring, Keith Waterhouse, Samuel West, Timothy West, Simon Williams and Canon Frank Wright.

Contents

ix

EASTER

ARMISTICE DAY

THEATRE BENEFITS

CHURCH CONCERTS

CHARITY DO'S

MUSICAL EVENINGS

LUNCHES AND DINNERS

CHRISTENINGS

WEDDINGS

xiv

THE FOUR SEASONS

SHOW-OFF POEMS

Introduction

I've been getting up and doing my bit at carol concerts for a long time now and, because they have tended to be at the same places every year, I've had to be constantly on the look-out for new pieces which, hopefully, nobody has heard before. Easier said than done. Gradually, however, and with a good deal of trial and error, my list grew longer.

It was only when I was confronted with having to arrange a full evening's concert in midsummer with a group of singers that I realised how impoverished the rest of my repertoire still was. The conductor and I had hit upon the idea, which we thought was enormously witty, of *The Four Seasons, But Not Vivaldi,* and having laughed at the thought of it on posters round the town we couldn't let it go. So suddenly I was saddled with having to find three-quarters of an hour's worth of poignant, interesting or funny pieces whose themes would complement those of the songs the singers found.

It was then that the idea of compiling a book of pieces for all occasions occurred to me. I could have done with one, and there hadn't been one. Of course there are anthologies galore, but not one, that I could find, which concentrated on those pieces which go well when read aloud.

So the question I have asked myself about each piece I have included here is, 'Would I want to do it?' The result is, I daresay, a most idiosyncratic selection, top-heavy with some of my favourite authors. I couldn't help including lots of John Betjeman, Noël Coward and Joyce Grenfell because they wrote such perfect party pieces: felicitous, easy to understand, full of grace and truth, witty and sad by turns. I've tried to include as many little-known things as possible and avoid the hackneyed. However, there remain a few golden oldies which I felt I could not possibly leave out.

Ideally, I suppose, pieces should last between three and five minutes. Of course they can be shorter (happily so at memorial services and christenings) or longer when you think you can risk it. The longest one here is a slightly cut-down version of *The Selfish Giant* by Oscar Wilde; I have not removed anything of substance, but the cuts reduce the reading time from twelve minutes to a more pleasurable ten. Alec McCowen's choice of the story of the burning fiery furnace is on the long side too, but I haven't cut a word of that. Incidentally, whenever I have edited a piece I have said so in my introduction to it.

The introductions are there primarily to help you introduce the pieces to an audience, if you want to. I have noticed that, even at the most formal of concerts, audiences seem to welcome a word or two about why you chose a particular piece, or, if it's an excerpt from a book or a play, where it comes in the story, or even, occasionally, what it's about! Not a speech; a word or two. Cavafy's *Ithaca* and Keats's *Ode to Autumn* are just two poems which can benefit greatly from a short explanation. After all, you, the reader, will have had several goes through them while you've been prac-tising, whereas the audience has to rely on only one hearing.

How well should you know the words? Of course there are no rules, and it's bound to vary a lot from piece to piece, but it will certainly make it easier if you are reasonably familiar with them. You will understand them more completely and deliver them more clearly. You will be able to lift your eyes from the page from time to time, and that is always a desirable thing to do: it will make you and the people in the audience feel that you are communi-cating with them and not merely reading to them. And you will be able to gauge more accurately the amount of projection and clarity of speech you need in order to reach those at the back of the room, hall, church, theatre or wherever you are.

One of the greatest pleasures I've had from compiling this book has been in receiving suggestions for it from friends and acquaintances. Occasionally I've sensed an understandable reluctance to let go of something which has been a secret treasure for a long time, merely to have it put in a book so that everybody else can have a go at it. I've felt this myself a bit with some of what I thought were my specials, like *A Child's View of Christmas* which, as far as I know, nobody else has ever done. So I am extremely grateful to all the people who have allowed me to publish their secrets. And what secrets some of them are! The poems of U. A. Fanthorpe, Phyllis McGinley and N. F. Simpson, for example, were new to me and I feel enriched for having been introduced to them. 'Poetry is life,' wrote John Betjeman, 'and you can't do without it. It makes life worth living.'

Peter Barkworth
London
April 1997

Acknowledgements

The compiler has taken all possible care to trace the copyright of all the pieces reprinted in this volume, and to make acknowledgement of their use. If any errors have accidentally occurred, they will be corrected in subsequent editions, provided notification is sent to the publisher.

Exley Publications Ltd for extracts from *A Child's View of Christmas*, edited by Richard and Helen Exley.

Magmasters Sound Studios Ltd for 'Twenty Tactful Phrases to Help a Voice-Over Artiste Feel at Home'.

Eurotunnel for children's poems from *Connexions*.

Kent County Council Arts and Libraries, for children's poems from *From Cover to Cover* and *Time to Write*.

New English Bible, copyright © 1961, 1970 Oxford University Press and Cambridge University Press, for parts of Chapters 31 and 32 from *Ecclesiasticus*, and 'A Letter of James', Chapter 2, verses 14 to 26.

Adscene Kent Newspapers, for the leading article from the *Folkestone, Hythe & District Herald*, 6 June, 1944.

Reality Press, c/o Centerprise Trust Ltd for 'A Crabbit Old Woman', published in *Elders*, 1973, alternatively known as 'Look Closer' by Phyllis McCormack.

Dame Janet Baker for the excerpt from *Full Circle*, published by Penguin Books.

The Peters Fraser and Dunlop Group Ltd for 'Tarantella' by Hilaire Belloc; 'The Fight of the Year' by Roger McGough; the extract from *I, An Actor* by Nicholas Craig; the extract from *Cider with Rosie* by Laurie Lee and the extract from *The Letters of Evelyn Waugh* by Mark Amory on behalf of copyright © Weidenfeld and Nicolson.

John Murray for 'Christmas', 'Back from Australia' and 'Autumn 1964' from *Collected Poems*, 'Advent 1955' from *Uncollected Poems* and 'Blame the Vicar' and 'Churchyards' from *Church Poems* by John Betjeman; and 'The Highwayman' from *Collected Poems* by Alfred Noyes.

Desmond Elliott, the Administrator of the Estate of Sir John Betjeman, for 'Electric Light and Heating' and 'Summer'.

The Estate of C. P. Cavafy for 'Ithaca' from *The Complete Poems of C. P. Cavafy*, translated by Rae Dalven, published by Chatto and Windus.

Ray Connolly for the excerpt from *Lost Fortnight*, a radio play about Raymond Chandler in Hollywood.

Alan Brodie Representation Ltd for 'Mrs Worthington, Don't Put Your Daughter on the Stage' and an extract from 'Star Quality' by Noël Coward.

David Daiches for 'On the Twelfth Day of Christmas I Screamed'.

Guardian News Service Ltd for an article in the *Observer* about Armistice Day by Geoff Dyer.

Faber and Faber Ltd for 'Skimbleshanks: the Railway Cat' and 'Journey of the Magi' from *The Complete Poems and Plays* by T. S. Eliot; 'Advertisement' and 'A Nursery Rhyme' from *Making Cocoa for Kingsley Amis* and 'Valentine' and 'The New Regime' from *Serious Concerns* by Wendy Cope; 'Baby Song' from *Jack Straw's Castle* by Thom Gunn; and an extract from *Siegfried's Journey* by Siegfried Sassoon.

Crown Publishing Co. for 'A Prayer' from *The Desiderata of Happiness* by Max Ehrmann.

Peterloo Poets for 'Patience Strong' from *Side Effects* (1978), 'What the Donkey Saw' from *Poems for Christmas*, 'BC:AD' from *Standing To* (1982), and 'The Sheepdog' from *Voices Off* (1984) by U. A. Fanthorpe; and 'The Adoration of the Magi' from *Poems for Christmas* (1982) by Christopher Pilling.

David Higham Associates for 'Mrs Malone' from *Silver Sand and Snow* by Eleanor Farjeon, published by Michael Joseph; 'The

Innkeeper's Wife', 'The Poem I'd Like to Write' and 'Snow-flakes' by Clive Sansom; 'Sonnet XXXII' from *The Sonnets of Michelangelo* translated by Elizabeth Jennings, published by Carcanet Press Ltd; and the extract from 'Memories of Christmas' from *Quite Early One Morning* by Dylan Thomas, published by J. M. Dent.

Reed Consumer Books Ltd for 'Value for Money' and 'An Occasion of this Nature' from *Listen to This* by Michael Frayn, published by Methuen; 'Do I Believe', 'The Boy Actor', 'Irene Vanbrugh Memorial Matinee: The Epilogue', 'This is to Let You Know', 'Lie in the Dark and Listen', 'Social Grace', 'When I Have Fears' and 'I'm Here for a Short Visit Only' from *Collected Verse* by Noël Coward, published by Methuen London; the extract from *Sheppey* by W. Somerset Maugham, published by William Heinemann Ltd; the extract from *Shirley Valentine* by Willy Russell, published by Methuen; and 'The King's Breakfast' from *When We Were Very Young* by A. A. Milne, published by Methuen Children's Books.

Christopher Fry for 'Blind Children' and 'For a Tree-Planting'.

Victor Gollancz Ltd for 'Prayer for Michaelmas' from *Dedication* by Viola Garvin.

HarperCollins Publishers Ltd for 'Christmas Thank You's' by Mick Gowar; extracts from *The Towers of Trebizond* by Rose Macaulay; 'So Many Different Lengths of Time' by Brian Patten; and 'Love's Insight' by Robert Winnett.

Richard Scott Simon Ltd for 'Time', 'Opera Interval', 'Nativity Play', 'There's Nothing New To Tell You', 'If I Should Go Before the Rest of You', 'Christmas Eve' and No. 3 of 'Speeches', all from *Turn Back the Clock* by Joyce Grenfell, published by Futura Books, copyright © Joyce Grenfell, 1977, 1978, Joyce Grenfell Memorial Trust, 1983.

Tom Kempinski for the extract from his play *Duet for One*.

Laurence Pollinger Ltd and the Estate of Frieda Lawrence Ravagli for 'Peace and War' and 'When I Read Shakespeare' by D. H. Lawrence.

Andrew Maclean for 'TV. OD.' from *See Base of Can*.

Penguin USA for poems by Phyllis McGinley: 'Origin of Species' from *Times Three*, and 'Paterfamilias' and 'Love Note to a Play-wright' from *The Love Letters of Phyllis McGinley*.

Leo Marks for his poem 'The Life That I Have'.

Aylwin Mayhew for 'A Letter Written on November 11, 1920', by Dorothy Mary Mayhew.

Carcanet Press Ltd for 'Instructions to an Actor' from *Collected Poems* by Edwin Morgan.

Curtis Brown Ltd for 'The Boy Who Laughed at Santa Claus', copyright © 1942 by Ogden Nash, renewed; and 'Snow in Suburbia' by David Lodge.

Peter Newbolt for 'Fidele's Grassy Tomb' from *Selected Poems of Henry Newbolt*.

Nanette Newman for 'Christmas Cheating' from *The Christmas Cookbook*.

John Julius Norwich for 'The Twelve Days of Christmas'.

Glenys Ormond for 'Cathedral Builders' by John Ormond.

Gerald Duckworth and Company Ltd for the extract from 'A Telephone Call' and 'Sympton Recital' by Dorothy Parker.

Julian de Sola Pinto for 'Love Poem' by V. de Sola Pinto.

Scholastic Ltd for 'Christmas Dinner' from *Quick Let's Get Out of Here* by Michael Rosen. Text copyright © Michael Rosen, 1983, first published by André Deutsch Children's Books.

George Sassoon for 'December Stillness', 'To Any Dead Officer', 'The Hero', 'Everyone Sang' and the extract from *The Weald of Youth* by Siegfried Sassoon.

The Royal Mail for the extract from *The Springtime Presentation Pack 1995* by Tim Shackleton.

Macmillan General Books for 'The Other Little Boats: July 1588' by Edward Shanks.

N. F. Simpson for his poem 'One of our St Bernard Dogs is Missing'.

Rosemary Anne Sisson for 'Go Cheerful' from *Rosemary for Remembrance*, published by The Radcliffe Press.

The National Poetry Foundation for 'Consumer Complaint' from *Turn Any Stone* by C. Marjorie Smith.

The Estate of the late Dodie Smith, c/o Laurence Fitch Ltd, for the extract from *Dear Octopus*.

Hodder and Stoughton Ltd for 'Christmas is really for the Children' from *Up to Date* by Steve Turner.
Canon W. H. Vanstone for 'Joseph's Easter'.
Keith Waterhouse Ltd for 'How Long, O Lord . . .?'
Waterhall Productions Ltd for 'The Father of the Bride' by Keith Waterhouse and Willis Hall.
The Estate of Virginia Woolf for the excerpt from *A Room of One's Own*, published by Chatto and Windus.

Christmas

THIS IS the big one. And as the years go by it seems to get bigger. And longer. Mail order catalogues start arriving at the end of July, shop windows are certainly ready by the middle of November, and carol concerts start soon after that.

'You can get awfully tired of Hallelujah,' whispered the woman next to me towards the end of a grand but over-long carol concert in London a year or so ago.

'And you can get awfully tired of standing,' her husband hissed across her as we rose to sing the last of the longest carols they could find. We'd stood for all six of them and for the *Hallelujah Chorus* and, for the first time in my experience, for the Bible readings. The programme had actually said it: 'Reading, all stand.' So all you do is stand and look around and not listen to a word.

Anyway, stand or not, there's usually plenty of Bible in carol concerts in the form of lessons read by clergymen or dignitaries; so apart from a short piece from *A Child's Bible* I've resisted it here. The thing about Christmas is that, although it is wonderful, the story at the heart of it can be told so briefly and is repeated so often that anything which is off the beaten track is profoundly welcome. You could well find some pieces in the sections on Winter and New Year in this book: and Valentine's Day could provide you with some apt poems about love. Funny pieces work especially well and, because they're such a relief from the solemnity of the rest of it, they bring spontaneous and somewhat surprised laughter from grateful audiences.

Mummer's Song

ANONYMOUS

This is a nice little fanfare with which to herald the beginning of
a carol concert.

> Now welcome, welcome Christmas
> With a right good cheer.
> Away dumps, away dumps
> Nor come you not here.
> And I wish you a merry Christmas
> And a Happy New Year.

Christmas

JOHN BETJEMAN

I suppose this has become the most famous Christmas poem in the English language. Well, it is the perfect party piece: succinct, colourful, of ideal length, easy to understand and easy to speak if you just keep the rhythm of the lines and know where the rhymes are but don't emphasise them. Then it will travel effortlessly from the village church on a rainy night, to the industrial town in the provinces, to London, and thence to the poignant and repeated question: 'And is it true?'

It was only when I was preparing this book that I realised that, in spite of having done the poem umpteen times over the years, I'd never bothered to find out what Hooker's Green was. Who was Hooker? Why did he have a Green named after him? In spite of asking around a lot, I still haven't found out. A spokesperson for Winsor and Newton, who still produce the colour, was confidently vague: 'We have always assumed he was an artist of some sort.'

But at least I know what sort of green it is. Originally a mixture of Prussian Blue and Gamboge, it is now produced, as a watercolour, in two shades: one yellowish, one blueish, both rather olive in tone.

> The bells of waiting Advent ring,
>   The Tortoise stove is lit again
> And lamp-oil light across the night
>   Has caught the streaks of winter rain
> In many a stained-glass window sheen
> From Crimson Lake to Hooker's Green.

The holly in the windy hedge
    And round the Manor House the yew
Will soon be stripped to deck the ledge,
    The altar, font and arch and pew,
So that the villagers can say
'The church looks nice' on Christmas Day.

Provincial public houses blaze
    And Corporation tramcars clang,
On lighted tenements I gaze
    Where paper decorations hang,
And bunting in the red Town Hall
Says 'Merry Christmas to you all'.

And London shops on Christmas Eve
    Are strung with silver bells and flowers
As hurrying clerks the City leave
    To pigeon-haunted classic towers,
And marbled clouds go scudding by
The many-steepled London sky.

And girls in slacks remember Dad,
    And oafish louts remember Mum,
And sleepless children's hearts are glad,
    And Christmas-morning bells say 'Come!'
Even to shining ones who dwell
Safe in the Dorchester Hotel.

And is it true? And is it true,
    This most tremendous tale of all,
Seen in a stained-glass window's hue,
    A Baby in an ox's stall?
The Maker of the stars and sea
Become a Child on earth for me?

And is it true? For if it is,
    No loving fingers tying strings
Around those tissued fripperies,

The sweet and silly Christmas things,
Bath salts and inexpensive scent
And hideous tie so kindly meant,

No love that in a family dwells,
    No carolling in frosty air,
Nor all the steeple-shaking bells
    Can with this single Truth compare –
That God was Man in Palestine
And lives today in Bread and Wine.

Advent 1955

JOHN BETJEMAN

Although this doesn't have quite the charisma of the previous poem, it's a nice blend of the serious and the cynical, and has the advantage of being considerably less well-known.

Betjeman said, 'A really natural poem should need no punctuation: it should punctuate itself by the natural cadence of its words.' You will see here there's no punctuation during lines four to eight inclusive.

'Take it easy and just let the lines happen,' I try to say to myself whenever I do a poem of his. And one of the reasons why there are so many in this book is that they are so enjoyable to do!

> The Advent wind begins to stir
> With sea-like sounds in our Scotch fir,
> It's dark at breakfast, dark at tea,
> And in between we only see
> Clouds hurrying across the sky
> And rain-wet roads the wind blows dry
> And branches bending to the gale
> Against great skies all silver-pale.
> The world seems travelling into space,
> And travelling at a faster pace
> Than in the leisured summer weather
> When we and it sit out together,
> For now we feel the world spin round
> On some momentous journey bound –
> Journey to what? to whom? to where?
> The Advent bells call out 'Prepare,

Your world is journeying to the birth
Of God made Man for us on earth.'
    And how, in fact, do we prepare
For the great day that waits us there —
The twenty-fifth day of December,
The birth of Christ? For some it means
An interchange of hunting scenes
On coloured cards. And I remember
Last year I sent out twenty yards,
Laid end to end, of Christmas cards
To people that I scarcely know —
They'd sent a card to me, and so
I had to send one back. Oh dear!
Is this a form of Christmas cheer?
Or is it, which is less surprising,
My pride gone in for advertising?
The only cards that really count
Are that extremely small amount
From real friends who keep in touch
And are not rich but love us much.
Some ways indeed are very odd
By which we hail the birth of God.
We raise the price of things in shops,
We give plain boxes fancy tops
And lines which traders cannot sell
Thus parcell'd go extremely well.
We dole out bribes we call a present
To those to whom we must be pleasant
For business reasons. Our defence is
These bribes are charged against expenses
And bring relief in Income Tax.
Enough of these unworthy cracks!
'The time draws near the birth of Christ',
A present that cannot be priced
Given two thousand years ago.
Yet if God had not given so

He still would be a distant stranger
And not the Baby in the manger.

From *A Child's Bible*

SHIRLEY STEEN

Shirley Steen has simplified and shortened the stories of the New Testament; and when you compare her version of the birth of Jesus with the original, in St Luke 2, verses one to twenty, you realise just how adroitly she has done it.

When it was nearly time for Mary's child to be born, a law was announced by Augustus Caesar that all the people in the world should be registered and everybody had to go to the town where they had been born for this registration to take place. Joseph and Mary went from Nazareth to Bethlehem.

Although they looked everywhere for a room to stay, the town was full so they had to sleep in a stable and here Mary's baby was born, and she wrapped him up and laid him in a manger.

Not far away there were some shepherds looking after their flocks of sheep throughout the night. And suddenly an angel appeared before them and there was a great brilliance, and the shepherds were very frightened.

And the angel said: 'Do not be afraid. I bring you wonderful news. Today in David's city a Saviour has been born for you. He is Christ the Lord. You will find him wrapped up and lying in a manger.'

At once there appeared with the angel a great throng of angels saying: 'Glory to God in Heaven and on earth peace towards men who are good.'

Then the angels left the shepherds, and the shepherds said

to each other: 'Let's hurry to Bethlehem and see this thing for ourselves.'

And they travelled quickly and found Mary and Joseph, and the baby lying in the manger. And having seen the baby they told everybody what had been told to them about the child, and then returned to their work marvelling at what had happened. And Mary cherished these memories in her heart.

Journey of the Magi

T. S. ELIOT

One of Eliot's recurring themes is the hardship which was suffered by men of religion. This recollection by one of the three Magi (later called the Wise Men, later still the Kings) of their appalling journey from Persia to Bethlehem, by way of the 'temperate valley' of the Rivers Tigris and Euphrates, is a vivid example of it. The journey itself was nothing, however, compared to the deeper and more permanent suffering they endured when they got home. Now that they had seen the birth of a new religion, they found it impossible to live with the old, with its outmoded customs and the 'alien people clutching their gods'.

Because it is conversational, the poem communicates easily. Because it is about suffering, it is a welcome relief from the rest of the Christmas euphoria.

'A cold coming we had of it,
Just the worst time of the year
For a journey, and such a long journey:
The ways deep and the weather sharp,
The very dead of winter.'
And the camels galled, sore-footed, refractory,
Lying down in the melting snow.
There were times we regretted
The summer palaces on slopes, the terraces,
And the silken girls bringing sherbet.
Then the camel men cursing and grumbling
And running away, and wanting their liquor and
    women,

And the night-fires going out, and the lack of shelters,
And the cities hostile and the towns unfriendly
And the villages dirty and charging high prices:
A hard time we had of it.
At the end we preferred to travel all night,
Sleeping in snatches,
With the voices singing in our ears, saying
That this was all folly.

    Then at dawn we came down to a temperate valley,
Wet, below the snow line, smelling of vegetation,
With a running stream and a water-mill beating the
    darkness,
And three trees on the low sky.
And an old white horse galloped away in the meadow.
Then we came to a tavern with vine-leaves over the
    lintel,
Six hands at an open door dicing for pieces of silver,
And feet kicking the empty wine-skins.
But there was no information, so we continued
And arrived at evening, not a moment too soon
Finding the place; it was (you may say) satisfactory.

    All this was a long time ago, I remember,
And I would do it again, but set down
This set down
This: were we led all that way for
Birth or Death? There was a Birth, certainly,
We had evidence and no doubt. I had seen birth and
    death,
But had thought they were different; this Birth was
Hard and bitter agony for us, like Death, our death.
We returned to our places, these Kingdoms,
But no longer at ease here, in the old dispensation,
With an alien people clutching their gods.
I should be glad of another death.

The Adoration of the Magi
CHRISTOPHER PILLING

I always like it when reading sounds like talking. It's hard to do, but any attempt is worthwhile. It's a triumph if, when you launch into a poem having introduced it in your own words, the audience can't hear the join. A poem like this, which is even more conversational than the previous one, will give you a head start. What about, for example, in a *poem*, the two lines:

> 'And what were we to make of
> was it angels falling through the air'!

But then it is, after all, a soldier speaking. And doubting. And marvelling.

> It was the arrival of the kings
> that caught us unawares;
> we'd looked in on the woman in the barn,
> curiosity you could call it,
> something to do on a cold winter's night;
> we'd wished her well –
> that was the best we could do, she was in pain,
> and the next thing we knew
> she was lying on the straw
> – the little there was of it –
> and there was this baby in her arms.
>
> It was, as I say, the kings
> that caught us unawares . . .
> Women have babies every other day,
> not that we are there –

let's call it a common occurrence though,
giving birth. But kings
appearing in a stable with a
'Is this the place?' and kneeling,
each with his gift held out towards the child!

They didn't even notice us.
Their robes trailed on the floor,
rich, lined robes that money couldn't buy.
What must this child be
to bring kings from distant lands
with costly incense and gold?
What could a tiny baby make of that?

And what were we to make of
was it angels falling through the air,
entwined and falling as if from the rafters
to where the gaze of the kings met the child's
— assuming the child could see?

What would the mother do with the gift?
What would become of the child?
And we'll never admit there are angels

or that somewhere between
one man's eyes and another's
is a holy place, a space where a king could be
at one with a naked child,
at one with an astonished soldier.

What the Donkey Saw

U. A. FANTHORPE

It was Michael Mayne, the now retired Dean of Westminster, who introduced me to the delights of U. A. Fanthorpe. This is the first of several of her poems he sent me. It's short, but irresistible, and I love the nudge, nudge, wink, wink of the last two lines.

No room in the inn, of course,
And not that much in the stable,
What with the shepherds, Magi, Mary,
Joseph, the heavenly host —
Not to mention the baby
Using our manger as a cot.
You couldn't have squeezed another cherub in
For love or money.

Still, in spite of the overcrowding,
I did my best to make them feel wanted.
I could see the baby and I
Would be going places together.

The Innkeeper's Wife

CLIVE SANSOM

This poem was sent to me by Prunella Scales, who said, 'It was first suggested to me many years ago, and I've done it often. It goes well.'

A lovely piece for women, it needs a sureness of touch to make clear the difference between the inner, unvoiced thoughts, those bits without quotation marks, and the instructions and reminiscences to the visiting carpenter. Many years have elapsed since the birth of Jesus, which the Innkeeper's wife still can't help remembering, even though its significance remains unknown to her. It's a poem about remembering; and remembering things is a gift for a performer because, properly done, it makes everything seem so personal. This is one of those pieces where a good knowledge of the words would be helpful. Then you can talk to the carpenter, see the stable, and remember. Not too much, though! I mean, not too much acting!

> I love this byre. Shadows are kindly here.
> The light is flecked with travelling stars of dust.
> So quiet it seems after the inn-clamour,
> Scraping of fiddles and the stamping feet.
> Only the cows, each in her patient box,
> Turn their slow eyes, as we and the sunlight enter,
> Their slowly rhythmic mouths.
>   'That is the stall,
> Carpenter. You see it's too far gone
> For patching or repatching. My husband made it,
> And he's been gone these dozen years and more . . .'

Strange how this lifeless thing, degraded wood
Split from the tree and nailed and crucified
To make a wall, outlives the mastering hand
That struck it down, the warm firm hand
That touched my body with its wandering love.
'No, let the fire take them. Strip every board
And make a new beginning. Too many memories lurk
Like worms in this old wood. That piece you're
    holding –
That patch of grain with the giant's thumbprint –
I stared at it a full hour when he died:
Its grooves are down my mind. And that board there
Baring its knot-hole like a missing jig-saw –
I remember another hand along its rim.
No, not my husband's, and why I should remember
I cannot say. It was a night in winter.
Our house was full, tight-packed as salted herrings –
So full, they said, we had to hold our breaths
To close the door and shut the night-air out!
And then two travellers came. They stood outside
Across the threshold, half in the ring of light
And half beyond it. I would have let them in
Despite the crowding – the woman was past her time –
But I'd no mind to argue with my husband.
The flagon in my hand and half the inn
Still clamouring for wine. But when trade slackened,
And all our guests had sung themselves to bed
Or told the floor their troubles, I came out here
Where he had lodged them. The man was standing
As you are now, his hand smoothing that board –
He was a carpenter, I heard them say.
She rested on the straw, and on her arm
A child was lying. None of your creased-faced brats
Squalling their lungs out. Just lying there
As calm as a new-dropped calf – his eyes wide open,
And gazing round as if the world he saw

In the chaff-strewn light of the stable lantern
Was something beautiful and new and strange.
Ah well, he'll have learnt different now, I reckon,
Wherever he is. And why I should recall
A scene like that, when times I would remember
Have passed beyond reliving, I cannot think.
It's a trick you're served by old possessions:
They have their memories too — too many memories.
Well, I must go in. There are meals to serve.
Join us there, Carpenter, when you've had enough
Of cattle-company. The world is a sad place,
But wine and music blunt the truth of it.'

BC:AD and *The Sheepdog*

U. A. FANTHORPE

Normally I don't like doing 'groups' of things, and I prefer it when singers and instrumentalists don't, but these two poems go well together, and thereby make a rather more substantial party piece: the sublimity of the first followed by the incredibly obedient Yorkshire dog of the second.

BC:AD

This was the moment when Before
Turned into After, and the future's
Uninvented timekeepers presented arms.

This was the moment when nothing
Happened. Only dull peace
Sprawled boringly over the earth.

This was the moment when even energetic Romans
Could find nothing better to do
Than counting heads in remote provinces.

And this was the moment
When a few farm workers and three
Members of an obscure Persian sect

Walked haphazard by starlight straight
Into the kingdom of heaven.

The Sheepdog

After the very bright light,
And the talking bird,
And the singing,
And the sky filled up wi' wings,
And then the silence,

Our lads sez
We'd better go, then.
Stay, Shep. Good dog, stay.
So I stayed wi' t' sheep.

After they cum back,
It sounded grand, what they'd seen:
Camels, and kings, and such,
Wi' presents – human sort,
Not the kind you eat –
And a baby. Presents wes for him.
Our lads took him a lamb.

I had to stay behind wi' t' sheep.
Pity they didn't tek me along too.
I'm good wi' lambs,
And the baby might have liked a dog
After all that myrrh and such.

From *Shirley Valentine*

WILLY RUSSELL

I got the idea of including this from Hannah Gordon, who played Shirley Valentine after Pauline Collins. They were both wonderfully good in it in their different ways. Pauline Collins used the Liverpool accent intended by Willy Russell, while Hannah chose to do it as a Glaswegian. She told me afterwards that Russell had been very wary about this to start with, but when he saw that it worked rather well, he admitted he'd got the idea of the play from a stand-up performance by Billy Connolly! 'I just wondered if I could make a play out of one person talking to the audience, the way *he* did,' he said. It's a relief to know that, following Hannah's example, you don't have to impose an accent which doesn't sit comfortably: it's far better, for this party piece, to use one in which you feel at home.

Unlike the film, the play is a one-woman show, in which Shirley talks to the wall in her kitchen – a delightful invention of Willy Russell's to allow her to talk straight to the audience – 'Hey, wall, remember the nativity play? Oh God. Our Brian was only about eight or nine an' the school had given up with him.'

You may think it's a bit long, so I've marked three possible cuts ([ ]) which don't seem to spoil it at all.

[Well, when Brian learned he'd got the part of Joseph he was made up with himself. All the time he's rehearsin' this nativity play his behaviour is fantastic; the headmaster's made up with him. I'm made up with him, the teachers are made up with him. An' he's made up with himself. He's practisin', every night in his room –

(*on one note*)
'We are weary travellers on our way to Bethlehem an' my wife is having a baby and we need rest at the inn for the night.'] Well, the day of the show, I got down to the school, the play started an' it was lovely, y'know, all the little angels come on an' they all have a sly little wave to their mams. Then it was our Brian's entrance; he comes on an' he's pullin' this donkey behind him – it's like this hobby-horse on wheels. An' perched on top of it is this little girl, takin' the part of the Virgin Mary an' she's dressed beautiful, y'know, her mother's really dolled her up to be the part. [An' she's givin' a little wave to her mam. So Brian gives the donkey a bit of a tug because he's takin' it dead serious an' he doesn't believe they should be wavin' to their mams. He's up there, he's actin' like he might win the Oscar – y'know, he's mimin' givin' hay to the donkey an' he's pattin' it on the head. Well, the headmaster turned round an' smiled at me. I think he was as proud of our Brian as I was.] Well, Brian gets to the door of the inn and he goes 'Knock, knock, knock' an' the little Innkeeper appears. Our Brian starts 'We are weary travellers on our way to Bethlehem an' my wife is havin' a baby an' we need to rest for the night at the inn.' So the little feller playin' the Innkeeper pipes up: 'You cannot stay at the inn because the inn is full up an' there is no room in the inn.' An' then our Brian is supposed to say somethin' like: 'Well, we must go an' find a lowly cattle shed an' stay in there.' Then he's supposed to go off pullin' the donkey an' the Virgin Mary behind him. But he didn't. Well, I don't know if it's the Virgin Mary, gettin' up our Brian's nose, because she's spent the whole scene wavin' to her mother, or whether it was just that our Brian suddenly realized that the part of Joseph wasn't as big as it had been cracked up to be. But whatever it was, instead of goin' off pullin' the donkey, he suddenly turned to the little Innkeeper an' yelled at him: 'Full up? Full up? But we booked!' Well, the poor little Innkeeper didn't know what day of the week it was.

23

He's lookin' all round the hall for someone to rescue him an' his bottom lip's beginnin' to tremble an' our Brian's goin', 'Full up? I've got the wife outside, waitin' with the donkey. She's expectin' a baby any minute now, there's snow everywhere in six-foot drifts an' you're tryin' to tell me that you're full up?' [Well, the top brass on the front row are beginnin' to look a bit uncomfortable – they're beginnin' to turn and look at the headmaster an' our Brian's givin' a perfect imitation of his father, on a bad day; he's beratin' anythin' that dares move.] The little Innkeeper's lip is goin' ten to the dozen an' the Virgin Mary's in floods of tears on the donkey. Well, the Innkeeper finally grasps that the script is well out of the window an' that he has to do somethin' about our Brian. So he steps forward an' he says, 'Listen mate, listen! I was only jokin'. We have got room really. Y'can come in if y'want.' An' with that the three of them disappeared into the inn. End of nativity play an' end of our Brian's actin' career. Me an' our Brian, we sometimes have a laugh about it now, but at the time I could have died of shame. It was all over the papers: 'Mary And Joseph Fail To Arrive in Bethlehem.' I was ashamed.

Nativity Play

JOYCE GRENFELL

Another very different version of the same thing. I saw the solo performance given by Joyce Grenfell at the Theatre Royal, Haymarket, in 1963 and this, more than any other monologue she did, has stuck in my memory. I can still hear her saying, 'Oh, you're a *cattle*, are you? And you're going to *low.*' She was bright and smiley and motherly and kindly and bright, and she swooped mercilessly on to operative words: 'Mary and Joseph were *friends.*'

In her book, *In Pleasant Places*, she wrote: 'In my series of nursery school sketches I always introduced a five-year-old character called George. He is apparently misbehaving and in every sketch I admonish him in that high, bright adult voice that is used to divert attention from some undesirable behaviour . . . "George – don't do that . . ." The misdeed remains unspecified to this day.'

Hello, Mrs Binton. I'm so glad you could get along to see a rehearsal of our Nativity Play! Can you squeeze in there? I'm afraid our chairs are a wee bitty wee, as they say north of the border!

Now then, children. We are going to start our rehearsal. Where are my Mary and Joseph?

That's right, Shirleen, take Denis by the hand and come and sit nice and quietly on this bench in the middle.

Don't drag him. He'll come if you leave him alone!

Don't hit each other, Mary and Joseph were *friends.*

Now, who are my Wise Men?

You're a Wise Man, aren't you, Geoffrey?

Oh, aren't you? What are you then?

Oh, you're a cattle, are you? And you are going to low. Splendid! Go over to Miss Boulting, will you, please?

Miss Boulting . . . You are organising the animals and the angels? He is one of yours.

Now, my Wise Men here, please!

Billy, Peter and George.

And George, Wise Men never do that . . .

Now my Kings, please.

Of course, Mrs Binton, we know that by tradition the Wise Men and the Kings are one and the same, but we did want everyone in our Nursery School Nativity Play to have a chance, so we have taken a few liberties, and I don't think any one will mind.

Now Kings: Sidney, Neville, Cliff and Nikolas Anoniodes.

Four Kings, I'm afraid. We happen to have four lovely crowns, so it seemed a pity not to use them.

Sidney, put your crown on *straight* please, not over one eye. What have you got under your jersey?

That's not the place for a hamster, is it. Put him straight back in his little pen, please.

Sidney, which one have you got, Paddington or Harold Wilson?

Well, who's got Paddington?

Neville, put him back at once.

Poor Paddington and Harold Wilson, it isn't very Christmassy for them under your jersey.

Sidney, I think it serves you right if Harold Wilson bit you, and don't bite him back.

Because he's smaller than you are. Are you bleeding?

Then don't make such a fuss.

Cliff, put your crown on, please.

It's too big? Let's see. Ah, yes it is . . .

Where are you! Oh, there you are! Nice to see you again! Change with Nikolas.

Nikolas, you can manage a big crown, can't you?

You've got just the ears for it.

I think if you pull your ears down a bit that will hold it up. And lean back a bit. That's it.

Stay like that, dear. Don't move.

Wise Men and Kings, don't muddle yourselves with each other.

Now then, Shepherds.

Jimmy, you are my First Shepherd and not a racing car.

Yes, Caroline, you're a shepherd.

No, dear you can't wear your Little Bo-Peep costume: because there aren't any little girl shepherdesses in our play. They're all boy shepherds, and you are a girl being a boy shepherd.

Yes, it is rotten. But we just have to settle for it. I think if you are very good perhaps you can wear a lovely grey beard; wouldn't that be fun?

George, what do Wise Men never do?

Yes . . .

Jimmy, do you remember what you see up in the sky? Something lovely, isn't it?

No, not a baby. Try again.

It's a lovely silver star, and you are going to put your hand up and point to it. And what are you going to say when you do that?

No, Sidney, he isn't going to say, 'Please may I go to the bathroom?'

Children, that isn't funny; it's a perfectly natural function, and we might as well get used to it.

Come on, Jimmy. You are going to say, 'Behold!' aren't you?

Yes, you are, dear. You said it yesterday.

You'd rather say it tomorrow?

Perhaps you are right.

We have broken the back of the play, so you may as well get ready to go home. Hand in your crowns gently, please. No Sidney, you can't wear your crown home on the bus.

I think – I HOPE it will be all right on the night.

But you know, Mrs Binton, I think perhaps next year we might make do with a Christmas carol.

My Christmas Survey
LUCY WAINWRIGHT aged 12

The first of many poems and pieces by children, this is from a slim volume called *Time to Write*, published by the enterprising Arts and Libraries department of Kent County Council. The Head of Operations there, Michael Curtis, writes in the Introduction, 'Young people don't have a problem with poems. Their writing is characterised by originality and freshness, first time insight, first ever combinations of words.'

My Mum and Dad said, 'Lucy,
It's homework time for you!'
So here's my special survey
Of Christmas '92.

I went down to the high street
to see who I could find
to answer Christmas questions.
I hoped they wouldn't mind.

The friendly looking grandma
had lovely sparkling eyes.
She said that she liked Christmas cake
and hot Tesco mince pies.

The lady with the pushchair
and shopping bags in tow
said she'd like actor Richard Gere,
beneath her mistletoe.

The workman with the scruffy coat
had not a lot to say.
Christmas was a time off work,
And that was without pay.

The school boy had two pointed ears
And a very dirty face.
He said, 'Scotty beam me up!'
And vanished without trace.

And finally a postman
came walking up to me.
He said he liked the presents
around the Christmas tree.

I came home from my survey.
It seems quite sad to say
that no one mentioned Our Lord Jesus,
Born on Christmas Day.

Origin of Species

PHYLLIS McGINLEY

A few pieces, now, about Santa Claus. This first one was sent to
me by Michael Mayne, and was my introduction to the scintillating
light verse of this regular contributor to *The New Yorker*. She is
enormously popular in the States and hardly known at all here.
This poem appears in her book, *The Love Letters of Phyllis McGinley*.

St Nicholas, who became Santa Claus, the patron saint of
children, was Bishop of Myra, an ancient city in the province
of Lycia on the southern coast of Turkey, in the fourth century
AD.

> Nicholas, Bishop of Myra's See,
> Was holy a saint
> As a saint could be;
> Saved not a bit
> Of his wordly wealth
> And loved to commit
> Good deeds by stealth.
>
> Was there a poor man,
> Wanting a roof?
> Nicholas sheltered him weatherproof.
> Who lacked a morsel
> Had but to ask it
> And at his doorsill
> Was Nicholas' basket.
>
> O, many a basket did he carry.
> Penniless girls

Whom none would marry
Used to discover to their delight,
Into their windows
Tossed at night
(When the moon was old
And the dark was showry),
Bags of gold
Enough for a dowry.

People, I read,
Grew slightly lyrical,
Calling each deed
He did, a miracle.
Told how he calmed the sea for sailors
And rescued children
From awful jailors
Who, drawing lots
For the foul design,
Liked pickling tots
In pickle brine.

Nicholas, *circa*
Fourth cent AD,
Died in the odor of sanctity.
But fortune changes,
Blessings pass,
And look what's happened to Nicholas.

He who had feared
The world's applause
Now, with a beard,
Is Santa Claus.
A multiplied elf, he struts and poses,
Ringing up sales
In putty noses;
With Comet and Cupid
His constant partners,

Telling tall tales to kindergart'ners,
His halo fickle as
Wind and wave.

While dizzily Nicholas
Spins in his grave.

Yes, Virginia, there is a Santa Claus

FRANCIS P. CHURCH

I found *Norman Rockwell's Christmas Book* in New York a couple of years ago and delighted in my discovery of this piece. 'Aha!' I thought, 'at last: something new, something unknown at home! Nobody will have heard of it!'

But when I tried it out the following Christmas many people in the audience had seen, only the day before, a film on television called *Yes, Virginia, There is a Santa Claus!* They told me about it. 'It starred Charles Bronson and was very touching. It's very well known,' they said. Ah well.

Nevertheless the piece has gone straight into my top ten for Christmas: it's so exactly right and deep, with that tingling sentence, 'The most real things in the world are those that neither children nor men can see'.

Virginia O'Hanlon wrote to the Editor of the *New York Sun*:

Dear Editor, I am 8 years old.
Some of my little friends say there is no Santa Claus.
Papa says 'If you see it in *The Sun* it's so.'
Please tell me the truth; is there a Santa Claus?

The New York Sun printed this reply on September 21, 1897:

Virginia, your little friends are wrong. They have been affected by the skepticism of a skeptical age. They do not believe except they see. They think that nothing can be which is not comprehensible by their little minds. All minds, Virginia, whether they be men's or children's, are little. In

33

this great universe of ours man is a mere insect, an ant, in his intellect, as compared with the boundless world about him, as measured by the intelligence capable of grasping the whole of truth and knowledge.

Yes, Virginia, there is a Santa Claus. He exists as certainly as love and generosity and devotion exist, and you know that they abound and give to your life its highest beauty and joy. Alas! How dreary would be the world if there were no Santa Claus! It would be as dreary as if there were no Virginias. There would be no childlike faith then, no poetry, no romance to make tolerable this existence. We should have no enjoyment, except in sense and sight. The eternal light with which childhood fills the world would be extinguished.

Not believe in Santa Claus! You might as well not believe in fairies! You might get your papa to hire men to watch in all the chimneys on Christmas Eve to catch Santa Claus, but even if they did not see Santa Claus coming down, what would that prove? Nobody sees Santa Claus, but that is no sign that there is no Santa Claus. The most real things in the world are those that neither children nor men can see.

No Santa Claus! Thank God, he lives, and he lives forever. A thousand years from now, Virginia, nay, ten times ten thousand years from now, he will continue to make glad the heart of childhood.

The Boy who Laughed at Santa Claus

OGDEN NASH

A less well-known habit of Santa Claus, when on his flights around the world, laden with presents for all the children who are good, is to carry close to his chest a Book of Sins and punish those who are naughty. The extremely savage punishment meted out to Jabez Dawes is surprising from someone who was, after all, a saint; but then, I suppose the boy had committed the worst of all possible sins.

Along with the previous piece, I found this in Norman Rockwell's beautifully illustrated book. I have included it here because, as far as I know, it has not been published previously in this country. And I bet I'm wrong about that, too. It's a little long, I think; and I think I prefer it with the suggested cuts I have marked.

In Baltimore there lived a boy.
He wasn't anybody's joy.
Although his name was Jabez Dawes,
His character was full of flaws.
In school he never led the classes,
He hid old ladies' reading glasses.
His mouth was open while he chewed,
And elbows to the table glued.
He stole the milk of hungry kittens
And walked through doors marked No Admittance.

[He said he acted thus because
There wasn't any Santa Claus.
Another trick that tickled Jabez

Was crying 'Boo' at little babies.]
He brushed his teeth, they said in town,
Sideways instead of up and down.
Yet people pardoned every sin
And viewed his antics with a grin
Till they were told by Jabez Dawes,
'There isn't any Santa Claus!'

Deploring how he did behave
His parents quickly sought their grave.
They hurried through the portals pearly,
And Jabez left the funeral early.
Like whooping cough, from child to child
He sped to spread the rumour wild:
'Sure as my name is Jabez Dawes
There isn't any Santa Claus!'
[Slunk like a weasel or a marten
Through nursery and kindergarten,
Whispering low to every tot,
'There isn't any, no, there's not!]
No beard, no pipe, no scarlet clothes,
No twinkling eyes, no cherry nose,
No sleigh, and furthermore, by Jiminy
Nobody coming down the chimney!'

The children wept all Christmas Eve
And Jabez chortled up his sleeve.
[No infant dared to hang up his stocking
For fear of Jabez' ribald mocking.]
He sprawled on his untidy bed,
Fresh malice dancing in his head,
When presently with scalp a-tingling
Jabez heard a distant jingling;
He heard the crunch of sleigh and hoof
Crisply alighting on the roof.
What good to rise and bar the door?
A shower of soot was on the floor.

Jabez beheld, oh, awe of awes.
The fireplace full of Santa Claus!
Then Jabez fell upon his knees
With cries of 'Don't' and 'Pretty please.'
He howled, 'I don't know where you read it.
I swear some other fellow said it!'
'Jabez,' replied the angry saint,
'It isn't I, it's you that ain't.
Although there *is* a Santa Claus,
There isn't any Jabez Dawes!'
Said Jabez then with impudent vim,
'Oh yes there is; and I am him!
Your language don't scare me, it doesn't − '
And suddenly he found he wasn't!
From grinning feet to unkempt locks
Jabez became a Jack–in–the–Box.
An ugly toy in Santa's sack,
Mounting the flue on Santa's back.
The neighbours heard his mournful squeal;
They searched for him, but not with zeal.
No trace was found of Jabez Dawes,
Which led to thunderous applause,
And people drank a loving cup
And went and hung their stockings up.
All you who sneer at Santa Claus,
Beware the fate of Jabez Dawes,
The saucy boy who told the saint off;
The child who got him, licked his paint off.

Reindeer Report

U. A. FANTHORPE

I don't quite know where this would go in your carol concert.
It's just a little extra piece. An encore perhaps. Part of a preamble.
A post script. A summing up.

> Chimneys: colder.
> Flightpaths: busier.
> Driver: Christmas (F)
> Still baffled by postcodes.
>
> Children: more
> And stay up later.
> Presents: heavier.
> Pay: frozen.
>
> Mission in spite
> Of all this
> Accomplished.

Christmas Eve

JOYCE GRENFELL

The first stanza is full of panic and irritation and can go as quickly
as you like. The words 'dazing' and 'deliberately' help to capture
this feeling. Then you can see yourself standing 'on an island in
mid-traffic.' You are still there in the second stanza, but calmer
now, and realising, after all, that it is Christmas. So you can go as
slowly as you like.

Today with a list of jobs to be done
As long as my arm,
And too many people in too many places pushing,
Christmas has lost its charm.
What with neon signs blazing and dazing
As they changed,
And nothing left in the shops . . .
No wrapping paper, tags or scarlet string,
Not a *thing* left . . .
And the wear and tear
Of trying to get from A to B
And no time to spare for transit –
Oh, I lost sight of Christmas.
'Well, it's not for me anyway,' I said,
'It's for the children.'
And I waited, tapping my foot,
On an island in mid-traffic,
While the lights deliberately stuck
To prevent me or anybody else
Getting anywhere.

'Oh Lor',' I said,
'Look at that terrible pink, plastic duck
In a sailor's hat
Going by under a woman's arm.
What's that a manifestation of?
Thank heaven there are no more shopping days to
    Christmas.'

Christmas?
Oh, Christmas. I'd forgotten.
I looked along the busy city thoroughfare.
The holly colours in a hundred rear lamps
Made their small contribution.
Red buses rumbled by, loaded with individuals
And their packages and private plans for tomorrow.
A street band blew a carol.
The pink glow above the city
Hid the star,
But the street was bright with more than electricity
And through a crack in a man-made world
I caught a glimpse of the glory
And the good of Christmas.

From *A Child's View of Christmas: 1*
Edited by RICHARD & HELEN EXLEY

I found this colourful little book in Birmingham soon after it was published in 1980 and unhappily I have never seen it in any bookshop since. The little pieces are a joy to do: the funny ones really funny and the poignant ones effortlessly telling, bringing a lovely silence into the church or hall or wherever you are.

I'm always suspicious of little books of children's sayings, with their cute illustrations and wobbly handwriting, wondering if children themselves had anything to do with them: but as Helen Exley explains in her introduction, 'All the work is absolutely genuine and by children – even the spelling mistakes.'

I've made two selections from it for this book, and they are numbers one and two in my top ten for Christmas. Here's the first.

Loraine Cook, aged 12:
> I was so excited on Christmas Eve that I couldn't get to sleep. All night I kept getting out of bed and brushing my teeth just for an excuse. I don't know how many times I brushed my teeth but I know my gums were sore.

Jayne Roberts, aged 5:
> I think Father Christmas is a kind old man taking toys to boys and girls all over the world. I saw him down the town and he showed me sellotape on his beard.

Claire Senior, aged 7:
> One day at Xmas Eve we put out some sherry for Santa

Claws and wrote a letter and he replied in my Mummys handwriting.

Sophia Jones wrote to Santa Claus:
Dear Santa, Please can I have just one teddy bear this christmas, nothing else but a teddy bear,
                                        from Sophia
PS. Please can teddy have a portable TV to keep teddy amused when I'm at school?

Tracey O'Leary, aged 7, started her letter:
Dear Santa, I am sorry that I have not written all year around but Mummy says you are only in at Christmas.

Diana Upcraft, aged 11:
I like everyone saying 'That's just what I wonted,' and all the 'ooos' and 'ahhhs' and 'you shouldn't haves'.

Charlotte Beattie, aged 10:
Somehow you know that giving should be more fun than receiving but it isn't.

Joanne Hayes, aged 6:
I like Christmas because it is Jesus's birthday. He has the birthday we get the presents.

Nicola Channon, aged 9:
Christ came to earth to teach us to believe in God and not to be naughty.

Samantha Oxford, aged 7, wonders what the Queen probably does on Christmas Day:
The Queen probably puts up decorations like we do, but instead of tinsel she probably puts up gold and silver. She would have a feast like a big, big Christmas cake and a big, big trifle and a big plate full of chipsticks and crisps and

sausages and things like that. If I was the Queen at Christmas I would go out in my golden coach saying happy new year to the poor people. And I would go round the shops and see how people are working. If they aren't working properly I shall say you're not working properly and say your finished. I would take my golden coach, fill it with presents, and go round and give them to the poor children. I would not put chocolate on the tree I would put rubies and diamonds on the christmas tree to you, that's what I would do. And I would give mummy a ring and I would give the rest 5000 pounds.

Arun Stobbert, aged 11:

When I wake up on Christmas morning I usually just lie in bed and think about all those poor children who have no mother or father. They probably won't even have a Christmas turkey or any presents. Then there's all those poor men who are made to go to war, to fight for their country, they won't get a Christmas either.

After that I lie in bed and think about what I will get for Christmas: maybe I will get some clothes, or plenty of sweets, or chocolates in boxes or maybe lots of games like Cluedo, Monopoly, battleships and lots of other games. But then while I'm lying in bed it all keeps coming back about those poor people who won't have Christmas.

Donna Smith, aged 10:

I like christmas because You think about things.

And finally, here's 'My Wish For You,' by Katie Mitchell, aged 14:

> I wish you joy
> Love with your friends,
> Happiness in your work,
> Fortune with your salary,
> Pleasure in your walks,

Well being in your dwelling,
Health in your body,
Beauty in yourself,
Delight in all,
Kindness from your friends,
Excellence in all you do,
Courage to do all well,
Determination to get things right,
And tender love from all.

From *A Child's View of Christmas: 2*

Edited by RICHARD & HELEN EXLEY

Iain Whitaker, aged 12:
> I can't wait for Christmas. I count the days, hours and even minutes. And when it comes a tingley feeling comes all over me. Even the word Christmas makes me feel different inside.

Sally Anderson, aged 6, wrote a pre-Christmas letter to her mother:
> Dear Mummy
> Thank you very much for the kind presents that you always give me and I like them very much, and I like my guinea pig and it makes me go to sleep and I like you very much and I hope you love me as well, and you are very kind to me when I am poorly and you make me happy. You are very lovely indeed and I am looking forward to Christmas.
> Love Sally.

Penny Knight Hamilton, aged 12:
> To be happy is the secret of life. To wake up on Christmas morning and know that you are loved makes you very happy.

Stephen Shears, aged 12:
> Christmas time is a very happy time. Even Adults are happy at Christmas.

Linda Dickinson, aged 10:
> Christmas is mum's saying don't fight this is the season of good will.

Mark Harvey, aged 8:
Really it is one big birthday party for Jesus but as he is not here to give him presents we give them to the people we love instead.

Elizabeth Lamb, aged 13:
Unhappiness is weight watching at Christmas.

Philip Luck, aged 12, wrote:
The Christmas pudding's on the table,
Eat some more if you are able;
Plenty there so help yourself,
Alka-seltzer on the shelf.

Emma Goble, aged 8:
I fed my Christmas Pudding to my cat because I do not like it, and I only wanted the money. My poor cat was sick.

Richard Coelho wrote:
Every year my mum usually told me a Christmas story from the Bible. Every year it was just as if I had heard the story for the first time and it was never old or something like 'I have heard that before'.

However this year it was a very sad year because one year ago my grandfather died and my mother was naturally very quiet.

We were busy putting presents around the Christmas tree, when we suddenly found our mum was upstairs so my sister and I went up and found our mum crying. I immediately thought of the message Christ tried to teach us – always be mild and humble and think, and Christmas should be a time of giving and not of receiving.

My sister and I put our arms around our mother, and tried in our small way to comfort her by telling her that our Christmas gift to her was our love. She smiled and said it was the loveliest Christmas gift she had ever received.

Trina Rust, aged 11:

I was made an orphan in February. I can't get used to the fact that my parents are dead. I'll never see them again.

Although the Matron sends us all a present which says From Mum and Dad, it's not the same, you know it's not really from them. We all get a visit from the butcher dressed up as Santa but even though his beard falls off like Daddy's used to do, it's not the same.

I hope I'll soon be adopted, then presents really *will* be 'from Mum and Dad,' and not Matron. If I'm adopted then Christmas will be all normal, like everybody else.

John, aged 7:

The only thing I don't like about Christmas is getting presents because I can only play with my dad and he's usually talking.

Shirin Syed, aged 12, wrote a poem called *Christmas in the Life of an Old Woman*:

> I see their happy little faces
> As they bundle down the street.
> Their scarves and little woolly bobble hats.
> I see them singing carols
> With lanterns that light up the night
> Their little mouths opening for every word,
> And their eyes twinkling bright.
> I watch them go home over the hills
> Their lanterns fading dim
> I look at myself by the fire
> And wish I was as happy as them.

Jason Webb, aged 8:

I want it to snow. On Christmas Eve and on Christmas Day and Boxing Day and every day. I want it six feet deep. I want a blizzard and a snowstorm and frost underneath as well.

And finally, Gail Wilson, aged 11:

> Every November God collects all the white goodness from Heaven and throws it down on to the world. If you wonder why snow does not snow so much as it used to it is because there is not enough goodness.

From *Cider With Rosie*

LAURIE LEE

'I am made uneasy by any form of writing which cannot readily be spoken aloud,' wrote Laurie Lee, and the ease with which this carol-singing episode lifts from the page is largely why it has become so popular. In its entirety it is too long for a party piece, so I have made considerable cuts which reduce it to about five minutes. All the best bits are intact, though.

If it's at a carol concert you could ask to have 'As Joseph Was A-walking' sung immediately afterwards. It has a haunting tune, which could even be played or hummed during the last paragraph.

The time is the early 1920s, the setting the remote village of Slad in the Cotswolds. *Cider with Rosie* is the first volume of Laurie Lee's autobiographical trilogy, completed by the marvellous *As I Walked Out One Midsummer Morning* and *A Moment of War*.

The week before Christmas, when snow seemed to lie thickest, was the moment for carol-singing; and when I think back to those nights it is to the crunch of snow and to the lights of the lanterns on it. Carol-singing in my village was a special tithe for the boys, the girls had little to do with it.

We were the Church Choir. For a year we had praised the Lord out of key, and as a reward for this service we now had the right to visit all the big houses, to sing our carols and collect our tribute.

Eight of us set out that night. Our first call as usual was the house of the Squire, and we trouped nervously down his drive. We arranged ourselves shuffling around the big front door, then knocked and announced the Choir. 'Let's give 'em "Wild Shepherds",' said Jack. We began in confusion, plunging into a wreckage of keys, of different words and tempo; but we gathered our strength; he who sang loudest took the rest of us with him, and the carol took shape if not sweetness.

As we sang 'Wild Shepherds' we craned our necks, gaping into that lamplit hall which we had never entered, until suddenly, on the stairs, we saw the old Squire himself standing and listening with his head on one side. He didn't move until we'd finished; then slowly he tottered towards us, dropped two coins in our box with a trembling hand, scratched his name in the book we carried, gave us each a long look with his moist blind eyes, then turned away in silence.

As though released from a spell, we took a few sedate steps, then broke into a run for the gate. We squatted by the cowsheds, held our lanterns over the book, and saw that he had written 'Two Shillings'. This was quite a good start. No one of any worth in the district would dare to give us less than the Squire.

Steadily we worked through the length of the valley, going from house to house, visiting the lesser and the greater gentry – the farmers, the doctors, the merchants, the majors, and other exalted persons. The snow blew into our faces, into our eyes and mouths, soaked through our puttees, got into our boots, and dripped from our woollen caps. But we did not care. The collecting-box grew heavier, and the list of names in the book longer and more extravagant, each trying to outdo the other.

We approached our last house high up on the hill, the place of Joseph the farmer. For him we had chosen a special carol, which was about the other Joseph, so that we always felt that singing it added a spicy cheek to the night.

We grouped ourselves round the farmhouse porch. The sky cleared, and broad streams of stars ran down over the valley and away to Wales. Everything was quiet; everywhere there was the faint crackling silence of the winter night. We started singing, and we were all moved by the words and the sudden trueness of our voices. Pure, very clear, and breathless we sang:

> As Joseph was a-walking
> He heard an angel sing;
> 'This night shall be the birth-time
> Of Christ the Heavenly King.
>
> He neither shall be bornèd
> In Housen nor in hall,
> Nor in a place of paradise
> But in an ox's stall . . .'

And two thousand Christmases became real to us then; the houses, the halls, the places of paradise had all been visited; the stars were bright to guide the Kings through the snow; and across the farmyard we could hear the beasts in their stalls. We were given roast apples and hot mince-pies, in our nostrils were spices like myrrh, and in our wooden box, as we headed back for the village, there were golden gifts for all.

From *Memories of Christmas*
DYLAN THOMAS

This abridged excerpt is one of Timothy West's favourites, and I was glad to have it as it provides a nice alternative to the Laurie Lee. It covers the same period (Dylan Thomas was born in 1914, in Swansea), but it is spookier and funnier and very do-able. It was written as one of a series of autobiographical talks, published under the title *Quite Early One Morning*, which he read for BBC radio in the late 'thirties and during the war.

It was always snowing at Christmas; December, in my memory, is white as Lapland, though there were no reindeers. And I remember that on the afternoon of Christmas Day, I would go out, school-capped and gloved and mufflered, with my bright new boots squeaking, into the white world on the seaward hill, to call on Jim and Dan and Jack and to walk with them through the silent snowscape of our town.

We went paddling through the streets, leaving huge deep footprints in the snow, on the hidden pavements.

'Once upon a time,' Jim said, 'there were three boys, just like us, who got lost in the dark in the snow, near Bethesda Chapel, and this is what happened to them. . . .' It was the most dreadful happening I had ever heard.

And I remember that we went singing carols once, a night or two before Christmas Eve, when there wasn't the shaving of a moon to light the secret, white-flying streets. At the end of a long road was a drive that led to a large house, and we stumbled up the darkness of the drive that night, each one of us afraid, each one holding a stone in his hand in case, and all of us too brave to say a word. The wind made through the drive-trees noises as of old and unpleasant and maybe web-footed men wheezing in caves. We reached the black bulk of the house.

'What shall we give them?' Dan whispered.

' "Hark the Herald"? "Christmas comes but Once a Year"?'

'No,' Jack said: 'We'll sing "Good King Wenceslas." I'll count three.'

One, two, three, and we began to sing, our voices high and seemingly distant in the snow-felted darkness round the house that was occupied by nobody we knew. We stood close together, near the dark door.

> Good King Wenceslas looked out
> On the Feast of Stephen.

And then a small, dry voice, like the voice of someone who has not spoken for a long time, suddenly joined our singing: a small, dry voice from the other side of the door: a small, dry voice through the keyhole. And when we stopped running we were outside *our* house; the front room was lovely and bright; the gramophone was playing; we saw the red and white balloons hanging from the gas-bracket; uncles and aunts sat by the fire; I thought I smelt our supper being fried in the kitchen. Everything was good again, and Christmas shone through all the familiar town.

'Perhaps it was a ghost,' Jim said.

'Perhaps it was trolls,' Dan said, who was always reading.

'Let's go in and see if there's any jelly left,' Jack said. And we did that.

From *Dear Octopus*

DODIE SMITH

This after-dinner speech is the climax of Dodie Smith's most successful and popular play. I was Nicholas in a television production in 1972. Nora Swinburne and Cyril Luckham were the grandparents celebrating their Golden Wedding, and it was directed by one of TV's greats: Joan Kemp-Welch. This version of the speech, which was the one we used, is slightly abridged.

The place is a country house in Essex, the time a Sunday evening in the late autumn of 1938. Four generations of the Randolph family sit round the table. Fifteen people. Nicholas's great-nephew, a new-born baby, is asleep upstairs. The meal is just over. Nicholas rises.

Nicholas: We are an abstemious family, both in drink and speeches. We make one speech and drink one family toast – at Christmas, at New Year and at all our family gatherings. So we have always done, right back, I believe, into Great-grandfather's day. But tonight, wondering what I should say to you, it seemed to me another toast was called for. None of my generation remembers a Golden Wedding in this house and, indeed, I think they are rarer throughout the world, in these days of later marriage and earlier divorce. It is a great occasion for us all, and one, I felt, which could well warrant a break with our tradition. And so I planned a separate toast for Father and Mother on their Golden Wedding day.

And then I knew this could not be. For they *are* the family and never, for my occasion, shall they be separated from it in our thoughts. We have already given them our presents, good wishes and our love, which, indeed, is always theirs, and now this Golden Wedding is no longer theirs alone, but ours to share with them. And so, once more I shall propose Grand Toast to our family.

One hears so many jokes against families, of family quarrels, family jealousies, we hear on every hand that family ties are slackening – and yet, we pack the trains at Christmas going home. A sense of duty only? I wonder. (*Slight pause.*) We are a very ordinary family. We own no crests, no heirlooms, and our few ancestors are very badly painted. I wonder what they would think of us, Great-grandfather with his twinkle and Grandmamma, who wasn't quite as fierce as that. (*He looks up at the portrait.*) But she *was* a little fierce. I think she might shake her head and say, 'The family isn't what it was.' And there, most honoured Grandmamma, lies its strength. It is, like nearly every British institution, adaptable. It bends, it stretches – but it never breaks. And so I give you our toast. From that young man upstairs who has had the impudence to make me a great-uncle – to Mother and Father on their Golden Wedding; through four generations of us; and to those who have gone, and those who are to come. To the family – that dear octopus from whose tentacles we never quite escape nor, in our inmost hearts, ever quite wish to. Ladies and Gentlemen, Grand Toast.

Christmas Dinner

MICHAEL ROSEN

A very different dinner. I love this self-explanatory poem: you can
see it all.

We were all sitting round the table.
There was roast turkey
there were roast potatoes
there were roast parsnips
there were broccoli tips
there was a dishful of crispy bacon off the turkey
there was wine, cider, lemonade
and milk for the youngsters.
Everything was set.
It was all on the table.
We were ready to begin.
Suddenly there was a terrible terrible scream.
Right next to the turkey was a worm.
A dirty little worm wriggling about like mad.

For a moment everyone looked at it.
Someone said very quietly, 'Oh dear.'
And everyone was thinking things like –
'How did it get there?'
'If that came out of the turkey,
I don't want any of it.'
or
'I'm not eating any Christmas dinner. It could be full of
dirty little wriggly worms.'

Now – as it happens.
I don't mind wriggly worms.
There was plenty of room for it
at the table.
It was just that . . . that . . .
no-one had asked it to come over
for Christmas dinner.
So I said,
'I don't think it came out of the turkey. I think –
It came off the bottom of the milk bottle.'
And I picked up the worm,
and put it out the door to spend Christmas day
in a lovely patch of wet mud.
Much nicer place to be –
for a worm.

From *Sketches by Boz*

CHARLES DICKENS

If you want a traditional piece about a traditional Christmas this is it.

Christmas time! That man must be a misanthrope indeed, in whose breast something like a jovial feeling is not roused – in whose mind some pleasant associations are not awakened – by the recurrence of Christmas. There are people who will tell you that Christmas is not to them what it used to be; that each succeeding Christmas has found some cherished hope, or happy prospect, of the year before, dimmed or passed away; that the present only serves to remind them of reduced circumstances and straitened incomes – of the feasts they once bestowed on hollow friends, and of the cold looks that meet them now, in adversity and misfortune. Never heed such dismal reminiscences. There are few men who have lived long enough in the world, who cannot call up such thoughts any day in the year. Then do not select the merriest of the three hundred and sixty-five for your doleful recollections, but draw your chair nearer the blazing fire – fill the glass and send round the song – and if your room be smaller than it was a dozen years ago, or if your glass be filled with reeking punch, instead of sparkling wine, put a good face on the matter, and empty it off-hand, and fill another, and troll off the old ditty you used to sing, and thank God it's no worse . . .

Who can be insensible to the outpourings of good feeling, and the honest interchange of affectionate attachment which abound at this season of the year. A Christmas family-party! We know nothing in nature more delightful! There seems a magic in the very name of Christmas. Petty jealousies and discords are forgotten; social feelings are awakened, in bosoms to which they have long been strangers; father and son, or brother and sister, who have met and passed with averted gaze, or a look of cold recognition, for months before, proffer and return the cordial embrace, and bury their past animosities in their present happiness. Kindly hearts that have yearned towards each other but have been withheld by false notions of pride and self-dignity, are again reunited, and all is kindness and benevolence! Would that Christmas lasted the whole year through!

Christmas in Sarajevo

BONNIE LAVEROCK, aged 11

'Christmas makes you think of all the people who can't enjoy it because of war, or poverty, or loneliness, or homelessness.' Children often write from the heart about this. There are many examples in *A Child's View of Christmas*, quoted earlier. Here's another, from a book called *Connexions*, which has poems by young writers in England and France, and is published by Eurotunnel.

We will see the trees with lights glittering
and presents in colourful paper.
They will see dead people in the streets
as the huge tanks go by,
shooting bullets at everything.

We will hear carols and laughter
when, at Christmas dinner,
we share jokes with each other.
They will hear the bombs of hatred falling
and the cries of mothers
as they look at their dead children.

We will taste chicken, mince pies,
sweets and chocolate from our stockings.
They will taste nothing but the dirty,
sooty smoke of bombs that have fallen.

We will smell turkey in the oven
and candles burning.
They will smell the smoke of

bombs and bullets as tanks go by.

We will feel grandma's jumper
    as we hug her
and the presents newly opened.
They will feel concrete as they lie
    on the streets, staring at
a scene of destruction.
The only present they get
    is war and hatred.

Christmas Truce

CAPTAIN R. J. ARMES

While compiling this book I have tried as much as possible to steer clear of other anthologies. Very difficult, as so many of them are so beguiling; and impossible in the case of *The Christmas Reader*, edited by Godfrey Smith. I have raided it for its best pieces over the years. This is one of them. It's a perfect party piece for when you want to be serious: perfect length, intriguing content and a real letter. Captain Armes, a thirty-eight-year-old regular officer with the 1st Division North Staffs wrote to his wife on Christmas Eve, 1914, from the trenches in Northern France.

I have just been through one of the most extraordinary scenes imaginable. Tonight is Xmas Eve and I came up into the trenches this evening for my tour of duty in them. Firing was going on all the time and the enemy's machine guns were at it hard, firing at us. Then about seven the firing stopped.

I was in my dugout reading a paper and the mail was being dished out. It was reported that the Germans had lighted their trenches up all along our front. We had been calling to one another for some time Xmas wishes and other things. I went out and they shouted 'no shooting' and then somehow the scene became a peaceful one. All our men got out of the trenches and sat on the parapet, the Germans did the same, and they talked to one another in English and broken English. I got on the top of the trench and talked German and asked them to sing a German *Volkslied* [folk song], which they did, then our men sang quite well and each side clapped and cheered the other.

I asked a German who sang a solo to sing one of Schumann's songs, so he sang 'The Two Grenadiers' splendidly. Our men were a good audience and really enjoyed his singing.

Then Pope and I walked across and held a conversation with the German officer in command. One of his men introduced us properly, he asked my name and then presented me to his officer. I gave the latter permission to bury some German dead who were lying in between us, and we agreed to have no shooting until 12 midnight tomorrow. We talked together, 10 or more Germans gathered round. I was almost in their lines within a yard or so. We saluted each other, he thanked me for permission to bury his dead, and we fixed up how many men were to do it, and that otherwise both sides must remain in their trenches.

Then we wished one another good night and a good night's rest, and a happy Xmas and parted with a salute. I got back to the trench. The Germans sang *Die Wacht am Rhein*, it sounded well. Then our men sang quite well 'Christians Awake', it sounded so well, and with a good night we all got back into our trenches. It was a curious scene, a lovely moonlight night, the German trenches with small lights on them, and the men on both sides gathered in groups on the parapets.

At times we heard the guns in the distance and an occasional rifle shot. I can hear them now, but about us is absolute quiet. I allowed one or two men to go out and meet a German or two halfway. They exchanged cigars, a smoke and talked. The officer I spoke to hopes we shall do the same on New Year's Day. I said 'yes, if I am here'. I felt I must sit down and write the story of this Xmas Eve before I went to lie down. Of course no precautions are relaxed, but I think they mean to play the game. All the same, I think I shall be awake all night so as to be on the safe side. It is weird to think that tomorrow night we shall be at it hard again. If one gets through this show it will be a Xmas time to live in one's memory. The German who sang had a really fine voice.

Am just off for a walk round the trenches to see all is well. Good night.

The Selfish Giant

OSCAR WILDE

This has long been my favourite of Oscar Wilde's short stories; it is also, conveniently, the shortest. Nevertheless, as I said in the Introduction, I have reduced it further by about two minutes so that its reading time is about ten. That's still long for an ideal party piece. 'It's a bit of a risk,' I said to the audience when I ended a Christmas concert with it once; but there were many handkerchiefs wiping many eyes afterwards, and someone said, 'Where was the risk?'

Every afternoon, as they were coming from school, the children used to go and play in the Giant's garden.

It was a large lovely garden, with soft green grass. Here and there over the grass stood beautiful flowers like stars, and there were twelve peach-trees that in the spring-time broke out into delicate blossoms of pink and pearl, and in the autumn bore rich fruit. The birds sat on the trees and sang so sweetly that the children used to stop their games in order to listen to them. 'How happy we are here!' they cried to each other.

One day the Giant came back. He had been to visit his friend the Cornish ogre, and had stayed with him for seven years. After the seven years were over he had said all that he had to say, for his conversation was limited, and he determined to return to his own castle. When he arrived he saw the children playing in the garden.

'What are you doing here?' he cried in a very gruff voice, and the children ran away.

'My own garden is my own garden,' said the Giant; 'anyone can understand that, and I will allow nobody to play in it but myself.'

So he built a high wall all round it, and put up a notice-board.

TRESPASSERS WILL BE PROSECUTED

He was a very selfish Giant.

The poor children had now nowhere to play. They tried to play on the road, but the road was very dusty and full of hard stones, and they did not like it. They used to wander round the high walls when their lessons were over, and talk about the beautiful garden inside. 'How happy we were there!' they said to each other.

Then the Spring came, and all over the country there were little blossoms and little birds. Only in the garden of the Selfish Giant it was still winter. The birds did not care to sing in it as there were no children, and the trees forgot to blossom. The only people who were pleased were the Snow and the Frost. 'Spring has forgotten this garden,' they cried, 'so we will live here all the year round.' Then they invited the North Wind to stay with them, and he came. He was wrapped in furs, and he roared all day about the garden, and blew the chimney-pots down.

'I cannot understand why the Spring is so late in coming,' said the Selfish Giant, as he sat at the window and looked out at his cold, white garden; 'I hope there will be a change in the weather.'

But the Spring never came, nor the Summer. The Autumn gave golden fruit to every garden, but to the Giant's garden she gave none. 'He is too selfish,' she said.

One morning the Giant was lying awake in bed when he heard some lovely music. It was really only a little linnet singing outside his window, but it was so long since he had heard a bird sing in his garden that it seemed to him to be the most beautiful music in the world. 'I believe the Spring has come at last,' said the Giant; and he jumped out of bed and looked out.

What did he see?

He saw a most wonderful sight. Through a little hole in the wall the children had crept in, and they were sitting in the branches of the trees. In every tree that he could see there was a little child. And the trees were so glad to have the children back again that they had covered themselves with blossoms. The birds were flying about and twittering with delight, and the flowers were looking up through the green grass and laughing. It was a lovely scene, only in one corner it was still winter. It was the farthest corner of the garden, and in it was standing a little boy. He was so small that he could not reach up to the branches of the tree, and he was wandering all round it, crying bitterly. 'Climb up! little boy,' said the Tree, and it bent its branches down as low as it could; but the boy was too tiny.

And the Giant's heart melted as he looked out. 'How selfish I have been!' he said: 'now I know why the Spring would not come here.'

So he crept downstairs and opened the front door quite softly, and went out into the garden. But when the children saw him they were so frightened that they all ran away. Only the little boy did not run for his eyes were so full of tears that he did not see the Giant coming. And the Giant stole up behind him and took him gently in his hand, and put him up into the tree. And the tree broke at once into blossom, and the birds came and sang on it, and the little boy stretched out his two arms and flung them round the Giant's neck, and kissed him. And the other children when they saw that the Giant was not wicked any longer, came running back. 'It is your garden now, little children,' said the Giant, and he took a great axe and knocked down the wall. And when the people were going to market at twelve o'clock they found the Giant playing with the children in the most beautiful garden they had ever seen.

All day long they played, and in the evening they came to the Giant to bid him good-bye.

'But where is your little companion?' he said: 'the boy I put into the tree.' The Giant loved him the best because he had kissed him.

'We don't know,' answered the children: 'he has gone away.'

'You must tell him to be sure and come tomorrow,' said the Giant. But the children said that they did not know where he lived and had never seen him before; and the Giant felt very sad.

Years went over, and the Giant grew very old and feeble. He could not play about any more, so he sat in a huge armchair, and watched the children at their games, and admired his garden. 'I have many beautiful flowers,' he said: 'but the children are the most beautiful flowers of all.'

One winter morning he looked out of his window as he was dressing.

Suddenly he rubbed his eyes in wonder and looked and looked. It certainly was a marvellous sight. In the farthest corner of the garden was a tree quite covered with lovely white blossoms. Its branches were golden, and silver fruit hung down from them, and underneath it stood the little boy he had loved.

Downstairs ran the Giant in great joy, and out into the garden. He hastened across the grass, and came near to the child. And when he came quite close his face grew red with anger, and he said, 'Who hath dared to wound thee?' For on the palms of the child's hands were the prints of two nails, and the prints of two nails were on the little feet.

'Who hath dared to wound thee?' cried the Giant, 'tell me, that I may take my big sword and slay him.'

'Nay,' answered the child: 'but these are the wounds of Love.'

'Who art thou?' said the Giant, and a strange awe fell on him, and he knelt before the little child.

And the child smiled on the Giant, and said to him, 'You

let me play once in your garden, today you shall come with me to my garden, which is Paradise.'

And when the children ran in that afternoon, they found the Giant lying dead under the tree, all covered with white blossoms.

The Twelve Days of Christmas – A Correspondence

JOHN JULIUS NORWICH

This rightly famous Christmas piece was suggested to me by many people, including Robert Daws and Amanda Waring. They do it as a duet: she reads Emily's letters and he reads the one by G. Creep. And together they sing the appropriate line of the original carol before each one. Well, with or without the music, it's a winner.

25th December

My dearest darling,
That partridge, in that lovely little pear tree! What an enchanting, romantic, poetic present! Bless you and thank you.

Your deeply loving Emily

26th December

My dearest darling Edward,
The two turtle doves arrived this morning and are cooing away in the pear tree as I write. I'm so touched and grateful.

With undying love, as always, Emily

27th December

My darling Edward,
You do think of the most original presents; whoever thought of sending anybody three French hens? Do they really come all the way from France? It's a pity that we have no chicken

70

coops, but I expect we'll find some. Thank you, anyway, they're lovely.

Your loving Emily

28th December

Dearest Edward,

What a surprise — four calling birds arrived this morning. They are very sweet, even if they do call rather loudly — they make telephoning impossible. But I expect they'll calm down when they get used to their new home. Anyway, I'm very grateful — of course I am.

Love from Emily

29th December

Dearest Edward,

The postman has just delivered five most beautiful gold rings, one for each finger, and all fitting perfectly. A really lovely present — lovelier in a way than birds, which do take rather a lot of looking after. The four that arrived yesterday are still making a terrible row, and I'm afraid none of us got much sleep last night. Mummy says she wants to use the rings to 'wring' their necks — she's only joking, I think; though I know what she means. But I *love* the rings. Bless you.

Love, Emily

30th December

Dear Edward,

Whatever I expected to find when I opened the front door this morning, it certainly wasn't six socking great geese laying eggs all over the doorstep. Frankly, I rather hoped you had stopped sending me birds — we have no room for them and they have already ruined the croquet lawn. I know you meant well, but — let's call a halt, shall we?

Love, Emily

71

31st December

Edward,

I thought I said no more birds; but this morning I woke up to find no less than seven swans all trying to get into our tiny goldfish pond. I'd rather not think what happened to the goldfish. The whole house seems to be full of birds – to say nothing of what they leave behind them. Please, please STOP.

Your Emily

1st January

Frankly, I think I prefer the birds. What am I to do with eight milkmaids – AND their cows? Is this some kind of a joke? If so, I'm afraid I don't find it very amusing.

Emily

2nd January

Look here Edward, this has gone far enough. You say you're sending me nine ladies dancing; all I can say is that judging from the way they dance, they're certainly not ladies. The village just isn't accustomed to seeing a regiment of shameless hussies with nothing on but their lipstick cavorting round the green – and it's Mummy and I who get blamed. If you value our friendship – which I do less and less – kindly stop this ridiculous behaviour at once.

Emily

3rd January

As I write this letter, ten disgusting old men are prancing about all over what used to be the garden – before the geese and the swans and the cows got at it; and several of them, I notice, are taking inexcusable liberties with the milkmaids. Meanwhile the neighbours are trying to have us evicted. I shall never speak to you again.

Emily

4th January

This is the last straw. You know I detest bagpipes. The place has now become something between a menagerie and a madhouse and a man from the Council has just declared it unfit for habitation. At least Mummy has been spared this last outrage; they took her away yesterday afternoon in an ambulance. I hope you're satisfied.

5th January

Sir,

Our client, Miss Emily Wilbraham, instructs me to inform you that with the arrival on her premises at half-past seven this morning of the entire percussion section of the Liverpool Philharmonic Orchestra and several of their friends she has no course left open to her but to seek an injunction to prevent your importuning her further. I am making arrangements for the return of much assorted livestock.

I am, Sir, Yours faithfully,

G. CREEP

Solicitor-at-Law

On the Twelfth Day of Christmas I Screamed

A LETTER FROM HIS GIRL TO A G.I. IN TOKYO

DAVID DAICHES

Prunella Scales had wanted to send me this but couldn't find it. 'Some base person has nicked it from my files,' she said. So I got it from David Daiches himself, and am very grateful for a poem of such quivering anguish.

'It first appeared,' he said, 'in *The New Yorker* in the late 1940s.'

> Now April's here, what ever can I do
> With those fantastic gifts I got from you?
> Spring's in the air, but, honey, life is hard:
> The three French hens are picking in the yard,
> And the turtledove, the turtledove
> (One of them died) —
> Ah, love, my own true love, you have denied
> Me nothing the mails or the express could bring.
> But look: we're into spring;
> The calling birds are calling, calling;
> The pear tree's leaves are slowly falling;
> I sit here with those cackling geese
> And never know a moment's peace.
> My memories are mixed and hazy,
> The drumming drummers drive me crazy,
> The milking maids enjoy canasta,

The lords are leaping ever faster,
The pipers — God in Heaven knows
I've more than had enough of those.

My love, you do such wondrous things
(Who else would think of *five* gold rings?)
I know you send me all you can
Of spoils of occupied Japan,
But you remain on alien shore
And waiting here is such a bore.
My love, the lively lords are leaping:
Some things will not improve with keeping.

Now April's here, the weary days go by;
I watch that wretched dove attempt to fly;
The partridge smells; the geese are getting hoarse;
My diction's growing positively coarse.
You must forgive my gestures of rejection —
I'm crazed with all your tokens of affection.
Enough's enough; next time be less romantic
And don't send gifts that drive a lady frantic.
Send me a postcard with a pretty view
And I shall look at it and think of you.

Christmas Thank You's

MICK GOWAR

This is one of those useful comic pieces which get funnier as they go along. Sometimes I've been disappointed by what I thought was a muted reaction from the audience, until I realised I was doing it too slowly. You need to get a move on after 'Dear Auntie,' 'Dear Uncle,' and the rest.

Dear Auntie
Oh, what a nice jumper
I've always adored powder blue
and fancy you thinking of
orange and pink
for the stripes
how clever of you

Dear Uncle
The soap is
terrific
So
useful
and such a kind thought and
how did you guess that
I'd just used the last of
the soap that last Christmas brought

Dear Gran
Many thanks for the hankies
Now I really can't wait for the flu
and the daisies embroidered

in red round the 'M'
for Michael
how
thoughtful of you

Dear Cousin
What socks!
and the same sort you wear
so you must be
the last word in style
and I'm certain you're right that the
luminous green
will make me stand out a mile

Dear Sister
I quite understand your concern
it's a risk sending jam in the post
But I think I've pulled out
all the big bits
of glass
so it won't taste too sharp
spread on toast

Dear Grandad
Don't fret
I'm delighted
So *don't* think your gift will
offend
I'm not at all hurt
that you gave up this year
and just sent me
a fiver
to spend

New Year

Christmas pieces look back; New Year pieces look forward.

Christmas pieces are about the story in the Bible, the way it has been celebrated over the years, and the myths and traditions which have grown up around it. New Year pieces are about starting again, making resolutions, and trying to make a better job of things this time round.

Nevertheless, with only a week between them, the two festivals have merged. Merry Christmas and a Happy New Year. So the few pieces here can happily be included in your merry carol concerts.

From *In Memoriam AHH*

ALFRED, LORD TENNYSON

Arthur Henry Hallam, a friend of Tennyson's at Trinity College, Cambridge, died suddenly on September 15, 1833, in Vienna, while on a European tour with his father. He was twenty-two years old. Over the next twelve years, Tennyson wrote a series of elegies in memory of 'The man I held as half-divine.' This is number 106, and is one of only a handful of great poems about New Year. It is splendid to do, making clear, as it does, what is past – 'Ring out' – and what is hopefully to come – 'Ring in'. Note especially, 'the grief . . . for those that here we see no more.'

Ring out, wild bells, to the wild sky,
　　The flying cloud, the frosty light:
　　The year is dying in the night;
Ring out, wild bells, and let him die.

Ring out the old, ring in the new,
　　Ring, happy bells, across the snow:
　　The year is going, let him go;
Ring out the false, ring in the true.

Ring out the grief that saps the mind,
　　For those that here we see no more;
　　Ring out the feud of rich and poor,
Ring in redress to all mankind.

Ring out a slowly dying cause,
　　And ancient forms of party strife;

Ring in the nobler modes of life,
With sweeter manners, purer laws.

Ring out the want, the care, the sin,
  The faithless coldness of the times;
  Ring out, ring out my mournful rhymes,
But ring the fuller minstrel in.

Ring out false pride in place and blood,
  The civic slander and the spite;
  Ring in the love of truth and right,
Ring in the common love of good.

Ring out old shapes of foul disease;
  Ring out the narrowing lust of gold;
  Ring out the thousand wars of old,
Ring in the thousand years of peace.

Ring in the valiant man and free,
  The larger heart, the kindlier hand;
  Ring out the darkness of the land,
Ring in the Christ that is to be.

A Prayer

MAX EHRMAN

Lee Montague sent me a slightly shortened version of this, which he found in the new Prayer Book used by the Liberal Jewish community. This is the complete poem, as published by Souvenir Press in a book called *The Desiderata of Happiness*.

To my chagrin, I have not been allowed to reproduce here the famous *Desiderata* itself (the one which begins, 'Go placidly amid the noise and haste') which Max Ehrmann wrote in 1927. 'Contractual stipulations' were blamed. It is a superb piece for New Year, and I have found that audiences lap it up. It is the only piece I have ever done which was once encored on the spot. Robin Hawdon wrote to me, when he knew I was wanting to include it, 'Wouldn't the world be a happier place if we could all abide by its advice!' All I can do here is commend it. Meanwhile:

> Let me do my work each day;
> and if the darkened hours
> of despair overcome me, may I
> not forget the strength
> that comforted me in the
> desolation of other times. May I
> still remember the bright
> hours that found me walking
> over the silent hills of my
> childhood, or dreaming on the
> margin of the quiet river,
> when a light glowed within me,
> and I promised my early God

to have courage amid the
tempests of the changing years.
Spare me from bitterness
and from the sharp passions of
unguarded moments. May
I not forget that poverty and
riches are of the spirit.
Though the world know me not,
may my thoughts and actions
be such as shall keep me friendly
with myself. Lift my eyes
from the earth, and let me not
forget the uses of the stars.
Forbid that I should judge others
lest I condemn myself.
Let me not follow the clamour of
the world, but walk calmly
in my path. Give me a few friends
who will love me for what
I am; and keep ever burning
before my vagrant steps
the kindly light of hope. And
though age and infirmity overtake
me, and I come not within
sight of the castle of my dreams,
teach me still to be thankful
for life, and for time's olden
memories that are good and
sweet; and may the evening's
twilight find me gentle still.

Procrastination

ENID BARRACLOUGH

Although this poem has strong echoes of the BT commercials in
which Bob Hoskins tells us, 'It's good to talk,' it is very persuasive
and, in its easy, conversational way, strikes right home. I include
it here because there's a New Year resolution in it somewhere!

It is difficult to pick up
A thing you have let go –
A ball – bouncing out of sight –
The string of a kite
That sails away in the wind,
But most of all a friend
Neglected, lost to view
And almost out of mind.
The writing pad is near at hand
The pen invites you but
You hesitate, it is so long –
How can you break the barrier
Of time you both have built?
Your hand is on the telephone,
It rings, and someone else's voice
Deters you from the link you
Would have forged. Days go by,
The thought still in your mind
At intervals, but you do not
Make the move. Sometimes you think
Why should I be the first
To bridge the gap? You thrust away

The instinct of a friend –
Or else you fear that
You may meet rebuff.
And so the overture
Is never made. How sad
That friendships die
For lack of nurture. So much
Love is wasted in the air.
It is difficult to pick up
A thing you have let go,
Hard to retrieve
So delicate a thing
Held by so tenuous a thread,
That gone beyond recall
It breaks –
You only had to lift the telephone.

Nothing But Stones

ELLA WHEELER WILCOX

I was flicking through the pages of *Poems of Life* and *Moments*, and thinking easy thoughts about how sentimental and predictable they all were, with titles like 'A Song of Life', 'Life and I', and 'Two Sunsets', when this poem and two others stopped me in my tracks. All three are in this book. They've all got arresting first lines and are curiously vivid and speakable. You can paint the pictures this one offers as clearly as you like: the stuffy people in the important church contrasting with the memory of a much-loved friend.

I think I never passed so sad an hour,
  Dear friend, as that one at the church tonight.
The edifice from basement to the tower
  Was one resplendent blaze of coloured light.
Up through broad aisles the stylish crowd was thronging,
  Each richly robed like some king's bidden guest.
'Here will I bring my sorrow and my longing,'
  I said, 'and here find rest.'

I heard the heavenly organ's voice of thunder,
  It seemed to give me infinite relief
I wept. Strange eyes looked on in well-bred wonder,
  I dried my tears: their gaze profaned my grief.
Wrapt in the costly furs, and silks and laces
  Beat alien hearts, that had no part with me.
I could not read, in all those proud cold faces,
  One thought of sympathy.

I watched them bowing and devoutly kneeling,
  Heard their responses like sweet waters roll.
But only the glorious organ's sacred pealing
  Seemed gushing from a full and fervent soul.
I listened to the man of holy calling,
  He spoke of creeds, and hailed his own as best;
Of man's corruption and of Adam's falling,
  But naught that gave me rest.

Nothing that helped me bear the daily grinding
  Of soul with body, heart with heated brain.
Nothing to show the purpose of this blinding
  And sometimes overwhelming sense of pain.
And then, dear friend, I thought of thee, so lowly,
  So unassuming, and so gently kind.
And lo! a peace, a calm serene and holy,
  Settled upon my mind.

Ah, friend, my friend! one true heart, fond and tender,
  That understands our troubles and our needs,
Brings us more near to God than all the splendour
  And pomp of seeming worship and vain creeds.
One glance of thy dear eyes so full of feeling,
  Doth bring me closer to the Infinite,
Than all that throng of worldly people kneeling
  In blaze of gorgeous light.

Patience Strong

U.A. FANTHORPE

Michael Mayne included this in his package of poems by U. A. Fanthorpe. I like the way she so lightly puts us in our place when we have sneering thoughts about the platitudes of Patience Strong. Or Ella Wheeler Wilcox, indeed.

> Everyone knows her name. Trite calendars
> Of rose-nooked cottages or winding ways
> Display her sentiments in homespun verse
> Disguised as prose. She has her tiny niche
> In women's magazines, too, tucked away
> Among the recipes or near the end
> Of some perennial serial. Her theme
> Always the same: rain falls in every life,
> But rainbows, bluebirds, spring, babies or God
> Lift up our hearts. No doubt such rubbish sells.
> She must be feathering her inglenook.
> Genuine poets seldom coin the stuff,
> Nor do they flaunt such aptly bogus names.
> Their message is oblique; it doesn't fit
> A pocket diary's page; nor does it pay.
>
> One day in epileptic out-patients,
> A working-man, a fellow in his fifties,
> Was feeling bad. I brought a cup of tea.
> He talked about his family and job:
> His dad was in the Ambulance Brigade;
> He hoped to join, but being epileptic,

They wouldn't have him. *Naturally,* he said,
With my disease, I'd be a handicap.
But I'd have liked to help. He sucked his tea,
Then from some special inner pocket brought
A booklet muffled up in cellophane,
Unwrapped it gently, opened at a page –
Characteristic cottage garden, seen
Through chintzy casement windows. Underneath
Some cosy musing in the usual vein,
And *See,* he said, *this is what keeps me going.*

The New Regime

WENDY COPE

This is the first of several poems by this wise and witty writer. In
the front of the book from which it comes, *Serious Concerns*, it
says, 'She . . . went to St Hilda's College, Oxford, where she
learned to play the guitar. After university she worked for fifteen
years as a primary school teacher in London.' She certainly has
the common touch.

Yes, I agree. We'll pull ourselves together.
We eat too much. We're always getting pissed.
It's not a bad idea to find out whether
We like each other sober. Let's resist.
I've got the Perrier and the carrot-grater,
I'll look on a Scotch or a pudding as a crime.
We all have to be sensible sooner or later
But don't let's be sensible all the time.

No more thinking about a second bottle
And saying 'What the hell?' and giving in.
Tomorrow I'll be jogging at full throttle
To make myself successful, rich and thin.
A healthy life's a great rejuvenator
But, God, it's going to be an uphill climb.
We all have to be sensible sooner or later
But don't let's be sensible all the time.

The conversation won't be half as trivial –
You'll hold forth on the issues of the day –
And, when our evenings aren't quite so convivial,

You'll start remembering the things I say.
Oh, see if you can catch the eye of the waiter
And order me a double vodka and lime.
We all have to be sensible sooner or later
But I refuse to be sensible all the time.

Valentine's Day

Valentine's Day is a useful peg on which to hang pieces about love. And yet there won't be much call for them on the day itself. There aren't many 'do's', they are mostly private parties, and at the few I've been to, or heard about, party pieces of the literary sort were the last things on anybody's mind.

No, these are poems and prose for the whole year round. They are an essential part of any performer's repertoire. They are in constant demand and give endless delight. They are truly for all occasions.

But it's still nice to have one day in the year which celebrates love. Hurrah for it!

Valentine

WENDY COPE

Clear and to the point, as always. No wasted words.

My heart has made its mind up
And I'm afraid it's you.
Whatever you've got lined up,
My heart has made its mind up
And if you can't be signed up
This year, next year will do.
My heart has made its mind up
And I'm afraid it's you.

Poem

CHARLES II

I was in a revival of *The Winslow Boy* during much of 1994, and one Sunday evening during its run some of the cast and I went to Leatherhead to help celebrate the 25th anniversary of the opening of the Thorndike Theatre. Hazel Vincent Wallace, its founder and long-time director, gave one of the most impressive speeches I have ever heard. Or seen. She reminisced in great detail without notes or script, and stood in the centre of the stage, absolutely still, making only the occasional expressive gesture. For our part, we did a shortened version of *The Hollow Crown*, and my favourite piece in it was this exquisitely troubled poem, with its to-ing and fro-ing of worry and delight. Or agony and ecstasy, indeed.

I pass all my hours in a shady old grove,
But I live not the day when I see not my love:
I survey every walk now my Phyllis is gone,
And sigh when I think we were there all alone.
    Oh then 'tis I think there's no hell
    Like loving too well.

But each shade and each conscious bow'r when I find,
Where I once have been happy, and she has been kind,
When I see the print left of her shape on the green,
I imagine the pleasure may yet come again.
    O then 'tis I think no joys are above
    The pleasures of love.

While alone to myself I repeat all her charms,

She I love may be lock'd in another man's arms;
She may laugh at my cares, and so false she may be,
To say all the kind thoughts she before said to me.
   O then 'tis O then, that I think there's no hell
   Like loving too well.

But when I consider the truth of her heart,
Such an innocent passion, so kind without art;
I fear I have wrong'd her, yet hope she may be
So full of true love to be jealous of me.
   O then 'tis I think that no joys are above
   The pleasures of love.

There is Nothing New to Tell You

JOYCE GRENFELL

Two love letters now. This one is actually a song, with music by
Richard Addinsell, but I think the mood of the words, which
float so lightly over deep and constant feelings, can be expressed
more poignantly without it.

> The stamp is on the envelope,
> I've written on your name –
> It's very nearly midnight,
> But I'm writing just the same.
>
> There is nothing new to tell you,
> The days go drifting by,
> And I hardly have to tell you,
>   just why.
>
> It was raining here this morning,
> It rained when first we met –
> So I like a rainy morning,
> And yet, it won't let me forget.
>
> I'm feeling fine but I wish you were here,
> I need you still, I always will,
>   my dear.
>
> There is nothing new to tell you,
> We've said it all before –
> But I thought I'd like to say it, once more
> You are all I adore.

This is to Let You Know

NOËL COWARD

A love letter from an unspecified place, but we know it's by the sea and 'two hours away'. Noël Coward said, 'I truly love writing both rhymed and unrhymed verse. It's complicated and exasperating, but rewarding when it comes off.' As it does here.

> This is to let you know
> That there was no moon last night
> And that the tide was high
> And that on the broken horizon glimmered the lights of
> ships
> Twenty at least, like a sedate procession passing by.
>
> This is to let you know
> That when I'd turned out the lamp
> And in the dark I lay
> That suddenly piercing loneliness, like a knife,
> Twisted my heart, for you were such a long long way away.
>
> This is to let you know
> That there are no English words
> That ever could explain
> How, quite without warning, lovingly you were here
> Holding me close, smoothing away the idiotic pain.
>
> This is to let you know
> That all that I feel for you
> Can never wholly go.

I love you and miss you, even two hours away,
With all my heart. This is to let you know.

Symptom Recital

DOROTHY PARKER

When I became a RADA student in 1946, we all had to learn at least two pieces a week for diction and voice production classes. We boomed out loads of Auden, Eliot and Dylan Thomas, who were all the rage then, so it was always a relief when someone found something different, like a girl did one day, surprising us all with this new poem by the newly-discovered Dorothy Parker.

> I do not like my state of mind;
> I'm bitter, querulous, unkind.
> I hate my legs, I hate my hands,
> I do not yearn for lovelier lands.
> I dread the dawn's recurrent light;
> I hate to go to bed at night.
> I snoot at simple, earnest folk.
> I cannot take the gentlest joke.
> I find no peace in paint or type.
> My world is but a lot of tripe.
> I'm disillusioned, empty-breasted.
> For what I think, I'd be arrested.
> I am not sick. I am not well.
> My quondam dreams are shot to hell.
> My soul is crushed, my spirit sore;
> I do not like me any more.
> I cavil, quarrel, grumble, grouse.
> I ponder on the narrow house.
> I shudder at the thought of men . . .
> I'm due to fall in love again.

A Telephone Call

DOROTHY PARKER

I have used only the top and the tail of this marvellous monologue in order to make it a good length for a party piece. I think it benefits from being shortened: it is only one joke – or one cry for help! – after all, and in the full version the repetition could easily pall. The join is three paragraphs from the end, between 'I mustn't be this way' and 'Look. Suppose he were someone I didn't know very well'. It's still on the long side but, taken at a good lick, it won't seem so.

Please, God, let him telephone me now. Dear God, let him call me now. I won't ask anything else of You, truly I won't. It isn't very much to ask. It would be so little to You, God, such a little, little thing. Only let him telephone now. Please, God. Please, please, please.

If I didn't think about it, maybe the telephone might ring. Sometimes it does that. If I could think of something else. If I could think of something else. Maybe if I counted five hundred by fives, it might ring by that time. I'll count slowly. I won't cheat. And if it rings when I get to three hundred, I won't stop; I won't answer it until I get to five hundred. Five, ten, fifteen, twenty, twenty-five, thirty, thirty-five, forty, forty-five, fifty. . . . Oh, please ring. Please.

This is the last time I'll look at the clock. I will not look at it again. It's ten minutes past seven. He said he would telephone at five o'clock. 'I'll call you at five, darling.' I think that's where he said 'darling.' I'm almost sure he said it there. I know he called me 'darling' twice, and the other time was when he said good-by. 'Good-by, darling.' He was busy, and he can't say much in the office, but he called me 'darling' twice. He couldn't have minded my calling him up. I know you shouldn't keep telephoning them – I know they don't like that. When you do that, they know you are thinking about them and wanting them, and that makes them hate you. But I hadn't talked to him in three days – not in three days. And all I did was ask him how he was; it was just the way anybody might have called him up. He couldn't have minded that. He couldn't have thought I was bothering him. 'No, of course you're not,' he said. And he said he'd telephone me. He didn't have to say that. I didn't ask him to, truly I didn't. I'm sure I didn't. I don't think he would say he'd telephone me, and then just never do it. Please don't let him do that, God. Please don't.

'I'll call you at five, darling.' 'Good-by, darling.' He was busy, and he was in a hurry, and there were people around him, but he called me 'darling' twice. That's mine, that's mine. I have that, even if I never see him again. Oh, but that's so little. That isn't enough. Nothing's enough, if I never see him again. Please let me see him again, God. Please. I want him so much. I want him so much. I'll be good, God. I will try to be better, I will, if You will let me see him again. If You let him telephone me. Oh, let him telephone me now.

Ah, don't let my prayer seem too little to You, God. You sit up there, so white and old, with all the angels about You and the stars slipping by. And I come to You with a prayer about a telephone call. Ah, don't laugh, God. You see, You don't know how it feels. You're so safe, there on Your throne, with the blue swirling under You. Nothing can touch you; no one can twist Your heart in his hands. This is suffering, God, this is bad, bad suffering. Won't You help me? For Your Son's sake, help me. You said You would do whatever was asked of You in His name. Oh, God, in the name of Thine only beloved Son, Jesus Christ, our Lord, let him telephone me now.

I must stop this. I mustn't be this way.

Look. Suppose he were someone I didn't know very well.

Suppose he were another girl. Then I'd just telephone and say, 'Well, for goodness' sake, what happened to you?' That's what I'd do, and I'd never even think about it. Why can't I be casual and natural, just because I love him? I can be. Honestly, I can be. I'll call him up, and be so easy and pleasant. You see if I won't, God. Oh, don't let me call him. Don't, don't, don't.

God, aren't You really going to let him call me? Are You sure, God? Couldn't You please relent? Couldn't You? I don't even ask You to let him telephone me this minute, God: only let him do it in a little while. I'll count five hundred by fives. I'll do it so slowly and so fairly. If he hasn't telephoned then, I'll call him. I will. Oh, please, dear God, dear kind God, my blessed Father in Heaven, let him call before then. Please, God. Please.

Five, ten, fifteen, twenty, twenty-five, thirty, thirty-five . . .

From *The Sonnets of Michelangelo*

ELIZABETH JENNINGS

This is Sonnet XXXII. I was introduced to it by Canon Frank Wright and read it in one of his *Meditation* programmes for Granada Television. I thought it difficult and unclear to start with, until I realised that its simple statement of the unbreakable strength of two equal loves needs, from the reader, plenty of emphasis on the words 'equal', 'equally', 'one', 'two', 'both', and 'same' whenever they occur.

> If love is chaste, if pity comes from heaven,
> If fortune, good or ill, is shared between
> Two equal loves, and if one wish can govern
> Two hearts, and nothing evil intervene;
> If one soul joins two bodies fast for ever,
> And if, on the same wings, those two can fly,
> And if one dart of love can pierce and sever
> The vital organs of both equally;
> If both love one another with the same
> Passion, and if each other's good is sought
> By both, if taste and pleasure and desire
> Bind such a faithful love-knot, who can claim,
> Either with envy, scorn, contempt or ire,
> The power to untie so fast a knot?

Love's Insight

ROBERT WINNETT

This is also from Frank Wright, and the simple statement this time
is 'Don't idealise me, please!'

Take me, accept me, love me as I am;
Love me with my disordered wayward past;
Love me with all the lusts that hold me fast
In bonds of sensuality and shame.
Love me as flesh and blood, not the ideal
Which vainly you imagine me to be;
Love me, the mixed-up creature that you see;
Love not the man you dream of but the real.
And yet they err who say that love is blind.
Beneath my earthy, sordid self your love
Discerns capacities which rise above
The futile passions of my carnal mind.
Love is creative. Your love brings to birth
God's image in the earthiest of earth.

Love Poem

V. de SOLA PINTO

After the comparative complexity of the two previous poems, the gentle simplicity of this one comes as a nice surprise. You will find that, whenever you do it, someone will come up to you afterwards and ask where they can get a copy. I got it originally from Rupert Hart-Davis. Vivian de Sola Pinto, a professor of English at Nottingham and Southampton universities, had been Siegfried Sassoon's second-in-command during the First World War.

His son, Oliver de Sola Pinto, who describes himself as 'a quasi-Italian farmer of sorts,' and lives near Siena, read this poem at his mother's funeral. 'For a couple who had lived together for a great many years it surely expresses an enviable sentiment,' he said.

As I sat at my old desk, writing
in golden evening sunshine,
my wife came in suddenly
and, standing beside me,
said, 'I love you'
(this year she will be sixty-three and I shall be sixty-eight)
Then I looked at her and saw
not the grey-haired woman but the girl I married in 1922:
poetry shining through that faithful prose,
a fresh flower in bloom.
I said. 'You are a rose'
(Thinking how awful it would have been if I had missed
   her)
and I kissed her.

Love and Age

THOMAS LOVE PEACOCK

As with the previous poem, love and age are combined in a poignant piece. Whenever I read this I am astonished by the ease with which it tells its complex and continually gripping story. T. L. Peacock was born in 1785 and died in 1866.

> I played with you 'mid cowslips blowing,
>   When I was six and you were four;
> When garlands weaving, flower-balls throwing,
>   Were pleasures soon to please no more.
> Through groves and meads, o'er grass and heather,
>   With little playmates, to and fro,
> We wandered hand in hand together;
>   But that was sixty years ago.
>
> You grew a lovely roseate maiden,
>   And still our early love was strong;
> Still with no care our days were laden,
>   They glided joyously along;
> And I did love you very dearly,
>   How dearly words want power to show;
> I thought your heart was touched as nearly;
>   But that was fifty years ago.
>
> Then other lovers came around you,
>   Your beauty grew from year to year,
> And many a splendid circle found you
>   The centre of its glittering sphere.
> I saw you then, first vows forsaking,

On rank and wealth your hand bestow;
Oh, then I thought my heart was breaking, —
    But that was forty years ago.

And I lived on, to wed another:
    No cause she gave me to repine;
And when I heard you were a mother,
    I did not wish the children mine.
My own young flock, in fair progression,
    Made up a pleasant Christmas row:
My joy in them was past expression; —
    But that was thirty years ago.

You grew a matron plump and comely,
    You dwelt in fashion's brightest blaze;
My earthly lot was far more homely;
    But I too had my festal days.
No merrier eyes have ever glistened
    Around the hearth-stone's wintry glow,
Than when my youngest child was christened, —
    But that was twenty years ago.

Time passed. My eldest girl was married,
    And I am now a grandsire grey;
One pet of four years old I've carried
    Among the wild-flowered meads to play.
In our old fields of childish pleasure,
    Where now, as then, the cowslips blow,
She fills her basket's ample measure; —
    And that is not ten years ago.

But though love's first impassioned blindness
    Has passed away in colder light,
I still have thought of you with kindness,
    And shall do, till our last good-night.
The ever-rolling silent hours

Will bring a time we shall not know,
When our young days of gathering flowers
Will be an hundred years ago.

A Leaf

ELLA WHEELER WILCOX

This is another poem about remembering. A half smile would be apt. And it needs to be spoken quite lightly and quickly; but give yourself time for pauses, when you want to dwell on something for a moment.

Somebody said, in the crowd, last eve,
   That you were married, or soon to be.
I have not thought of you, I believe,
   Since last we parted. Let me see:
Five long Summers have passed since then –
   Each has been pleasant in its own way –
And you are but one of a dozen men
   Who have played the suitor a Summer day.

But, nevertheless, when I heard your name,
   Coupled with someone's, not my own,
There burned in my bosom a sudden flame,
   That carried me back to the day that is flown.
I was sitting again by the laughing brook,
   With you at my feet and the sky above,
And my heart was fluttering under your look –
   The unmistakable look of Love.

Again your breath, like a South wind, fanned
   My cheek, where the blushes came and went;
And the tender clasp of your strong, warm hand
   Sudden thrills through my pulses sent.
Again you were mine by Love's own right –

Mine for ever by Love's decree:
So for a moment it seemed last night,
   When somebody mentioned your name to me.

Just for the moment I thought you mine –
   Loving me, wooing me, as of old.
The tale remembered seemed half divine –
   Though I held it lightly enough when told.
The past seemed fairer than when it was near,
   As 'Blessings brighten when taking flight';
And just for the moment I held you dear –
   When somebody mentioned your name last night.

Two Sonnets

WILLIAM SHAKESPEARE

The loved one is more beautiful and reliable than summer, the loved one is the means by which misfortunes and jealousies are forgotten. Those are the themes of these two wondrous pieces. As in all perfect sonnets the change of mood and direction occurs after the eighth line. They are numbers 18 and 29.

Shall I compare thee to a summer's day?
Thou art more lovely and more temperate:
Rough winds do shake the darling buds of May,
And summer's lease hath all too short a date:
Sometime too hot the eye of heaven shines,
And often is his gold complexion dimm'd;
And every fair from fair sometime declines,
By chance or nature's changing course untrimm'd;
But thy eternal summer shall not fade,
Nor lose possession of that fair thou owest;
Nor shall Death brag thou wander'st in his shade,
When in eternal lines to time thou grow'st:
   So long as men can breathe, or eyes can see,
   So long lives this, and this gives life to thee.

When, in disgrace with fortune and men's eyes,
I all alone beweep my outcast state,
And trouble deaf heaven with my bootless cries,
And look upon myself, and curse my fate,
Wishing me like to one more rich in hope,
Featured like him, like him with friends possess'd,

Desiring this man's art and that man's scope,
With what I most enjoy contented least;
Yet in these thoughts myself almost despising,
Haply I think on thee, and then my state,
Like to the lark at break of day arising
From sullen earth, sings hymns at heaven's gate;
    For thy sweet love remember'd such wealth brings
    That then I scorn to change my state with kings.

From *The Prophet*

KAHLIL GIBRAN

Another perfect utterance. This is an edited version of the original passage about love, which is just over three times as long. But it is the heart of the matter. It is a great favourite of Wyn Jones, who suggested it to me.

When love beckons to you, follow him,
Though his ways are hard and steep.
And when his wings enfold you, yield to him,
Though the sword hidden among his pinions may wound you.
If you would seek only love's peace and love's pleasure,
Then it is better for you that you cover your nakedness and pass out of love's threshing-floor,
Into the seasonless world where you shall laugh, but not all of your laughter, and weep, but not all of your tears.
But if you love and must needs have desires, let these be your desires:
To melt and be like a running brook that sings its melody to the night.
To know the pain of too much tenderness.
To be wounded by your own understanding of love;
And to bleed willingly and joyfully.
To wake at dawn with a winged heart and give thanks for another day of loving;
To rest at the noon hour and meditate love's ecstasy;
To return home at eventide with gratitude;
And then to sleep with a prayer for the beloved in your heart and a song of praise upon your lips.

I Do Not Love Thee

THE HON. MRS NORTON

Thumbing through the thick pages (thick paper, thick book) of my long-held and favourite anthology, *The Pageant of English Poetry*, published in 1909, this one made me stop. Ideal, I thought, for speaking aloud. Ideal for Valentine's Day. Ideal for the girls. Who is the Hon. Mrs Norton? The index lists her as Norton, Caroline Elizabeth Sarah (Lady Stirling-Maxwell) (1808–1877). That's all I know so far. But she's a pretty versifier!

> I do not love thee! – no! I do not love thee!
> And yet when thou art absent I am sad;
>   And envy even the bright blue sky above thee,
> Whose quiet stars may see thee and be glad.
>
>   I do not love thee! – yet, I know not why,
> Whate'er thou dost seems still well done, to me:
>   And often in my solitude I sigh
> That those I do love are not more like thee!
>
>   I do not love thee! – yet, when thou art gone,
> I hate the sound (though those who speak be dear)
>   Which breaks the lingering echo of the tone
> Thy voice of music leaves upon my ear.
>
>   I do not love thee! – yet thy speaking eyes,
> With their deep, bright, and most expressive blue,
>   Between me and the midnight heaven arise,
> Oftener than any eyes I ever knew.
>
>   I know I do not love thee! yet, alas!

Others will scarcely trust my candid heart;
    And oft I catch them smiling as they pass,
Because they see me gazing where thou art.

Answer

ANON (EIGHTEENTH CENTURY)

Compiling an anthology is a surprisingly complicated business, what with all the choosing and the research and the applications for permission and dealing with copyright, so in order to make life easier I decided to join The Society of Authors. The people who work there are helpful and welcoming, and at a party for new members I met the Chairman and prolific writer, Simon Brett. 'Why have you joined?' he asked, and I told him, and with characteristic generosity he said he would look out a few pieces which I might find useful. 'And they'll all be out of copyright,' he added brightly. This is one of them.

> Be quiet, Sir! begone, I say!
> Lord bless us! How you romp and tear!
> There!
> I swear!
> Now you have left my bosom bare!
> I do not like such boisterous play,
> So take that saucy hand away.
> Why now, you're ruder than before –
> Nay, I'll be hang'd if I comply –
> Fye!
> I'll cry!
> Oh, – I can't bear it – I shall die! –
> I vow I'll never see you more!
> But – are you sure you've shut the door?

The Lay of the Deserted Influenzed

H. CHOLMONDLEY PENNELL

This is also from Simon Brett; and by the time you get to the end
of it, you'll feel you've got a cold. Er – code!

Oh, doe, doe!
I shall dever see her bore!
Dever bore our feet shall rove
The beadows as of yore!
Dever bore with byrtle boughs
Her tresses shall I twide –
Dever bore her bellow voice
Bake bellody with bide!
Dever shall we lidger bore,
Abid the flow'rs at dood,
Dever shall we gaze at dight
Upod the tedtder bood!
Ho, doe, doe!
Those berry tibes have flow'd,
Ad I shall dever see her bore,
By beautiful! By owd!
Ho, doe, doe!
I shall dever see her bore,
She will forget be id a bonth –
Bost probably before.
She will forget the byrtle boughs,
The flow'rs we pluck'd at dood.
Our beetigs by the tedtder stars,
Our gazigs od the bood.

Ad I shall dever see agaid
   The Lily ad the Rose;
The dabask cheek! The sdowy brow!
   The perfect bouth ad dose!
            Ho, doe, doe!
   Those berry tibes have flow'd —
Ad I shall dever see her bore,
   By beautiful! By owd!!

If Thou Must Love Me

ELIZABETH BARRETT BROWNING

When I interviewed Prunella Scales for my book, *The Complete About Acting*, we got on to the subject of stresses when reading poetry. 'With classical texts it's easy to overstress,' she said. 'I've found that it's usually better to let subordinate clauses ride without stress or emphasis: just let the words themselves do the work for you. Without over-colouring.'

This sonnet by Elizabeth Barrett Browning, one of her *Sonnets from the Portuguese*, would certainly benefit from that approach. So here it is with suggested stresses underlined. Go gently for those, and throw the rest away.

> If thou must love me, let it be for nought
> Except for <u>love's</u> sake only. Do not say
> 'I love her for her <u>smile</u> . . . her <u>look</u> . . . her way
> Of speaking <u>gently</u>, . . . for a trick of <u>thought</u>
> That falls in well with <u>mine</u>, and certes brought
> A sense of pleasant <u>ease</u> on such a day' –
> For these things in <u>themselves</u>, Beloved, may
> Be <u>changed</u>, or change for <u>thee</u>, – and <u>love</u>, so wrought,
> May be <u>unwrought</u> so. Neither love me for
> Thine own dear pity's wiping my cheeks dry, –
> A creature might <u>forget</u> to weep, who bore
> Thy comfort long, and <u>lose</u> thy love thereby!
> But love me for <u>love's</u> sake, that evermore
> Thou mayst love <u>on</u>, through love's eternity.

Note: 'Certes' means 'assuredly', and is pronounced cĕrt′ĕs-z. Here is the poem again, unmarked!

If thou must love me, let it be for nought
Except for love's sake only. Do not say
'I love her for her smile . . . her look . . . her way
Of speaking gently, . . . For a trick of thought
That falls in well with mine, and certes brought
A sense of pleasant ease on such a day' –
For these things in themselves, Beloved, may
Be changed, or change for thee, – and love, so wrought,
May be unwrought so. Neither love me for
Thine own dear pity's wiping my cheeks dry, –
A creature might forget to weep, who bore
Thy comfort long, and lose thy love thereby!
But love me for love's sake, that evermore
Thou mayst love on, through love's eternity.

The Passionate Shepherd to his Love

CHRISTOPHER MARLOWE OR WILLIAM SHAKESPEARE

Well, what do you know? I found the Marlowe in *A Book of Beauty*, an anthology edited by John Hatfield, and the Shakespeare in *The Complete Works* as part of *The Passionate Pilgrim*.

As there are lots of little differences, I thought I'd include them both here. The Marlowe first:

> Come live with me and be my Love,
> And we will all the pleasures prove
> That valleys, groves, hills, and fields,
> Woods or steepy mountain yields.
>
> And we will sit upon the rocks,
> Seeing the shepherds feed their flocks
> By shallow rivers, to whose falls
> Melodious birds sing madrigals.
>
> And I will make thee beds of roses
> And a thousand fragrant posies;
> A cap of flowers, and a kirtle
> Embroidered all with leaves of myrtle;
>
> A gown made of the finest wool
> Which from our pretty lambs we pull;
> Fair linèd slippers for the cold,
> With buckles of the purest gold;
>
> A belt of straw and ivy-buds
> With coral clasps and amber studs;

And if these pleasures may thee move,
Come live with me and be my Love . . .

And now the Shakespeare:

Live with me, and be my love,
And we will all the pleasures prove
That hills and valleys, dales and fields,
And all the craggy mountains yields.

There will we sit upon the rocks,
And see the shepherds feed their flocks,
By shallow rivers, by whose falls
Melodious birds sing madrigals.

There will I make thee a bed of roses,
With a thousand fragrant posies,
A cap of flowers, and a kirtle
Embroidered all with leaves of myrtle;

A belt of straw and ivy buds,
With coral clasps and amber studs.
And if these pleasures may thee move,
Then live with me and be my love.

LOVE'S ANSWER

If that the world and love were young,
And truth in every shepherd's tongue,
These pretty pleasures might me move,
To live with thee and be thy love.

The Life That I Have

LEO MARKS

Derek Fowlds sent me this, but he didn't know who wrote it. He
had first heard it, he said, in the film *Carve Her Name with Pride*,
in which Virginia McKenna played Violette Szabo, a special agent
working in France during the last war. Derek said, 'I've never
forgotten it; and I've quoted it to every girl-friend I've ever had.'
Little bits of it had inevitably become changed over the years, so
I'm grateful to Leo Marks for sending me this correct version. He
was a Codemaster with SOE (Special Operations Executive), and
this poem, like all his others, was originally a code.

> The life that I have is all that I have
> And the life that I have is yours
>
> The love that I have
> Of the life that I have
> Is yours and yours and yours
>
> A sleep I shall have
> A rest I shall have
> Yet death will be but a pause
> For the peace of my years
> In the long green grass
> Will be yours and yours and yours.

Easter

Easter remains the most serious and 'religious' of all the festivals: the one least cluttered with commercialism and traditions. Here are just a few serious pieces.

To Keep A True Lent

ROBERT HERRICK

Another from Canon Frank Wright, this time from an Easter
programme in his 'Meditation' series for Granada Television.
Note: 'circumcise' means 'purify.'

Is this a Fast, to keep
The larder lean?
And clean
From fat of veals and sheep?

Is it to quit the dish
Of flesh, yet still to fill
The platter high with fish?

Is it to fast an hour.
Or ragg'd to go,
Or show
A down-cast look and sour?

No: 'tis a Fast to dole
Thy sheaf of wheat
And Meat
Unto the hungry Soul.

It is to fast from strife
And old debate.
And hate;
To circumcise thy life.

To show a heart grief-rent;

To starve thy sin,
Not bin;
And that's to keep thy Lent.

Christmas is Really for the Children

STEVE TURNER

This is exactly the sort of conversational poem which is a delight
to do; and there is a real teaser in the last line.

Christmas is really
for the children.
Especially for children
who like animals, stables,
stars and babies wrapped
in swaddling clothes.
Then there are wise men,
kings in fine robes,
humble shepherds and a
hint of rich perfume.

Easter is not really
for the children
unless accompanied by a
cream filled egg.
It has whips, blood, nails,
a spear and allegations
of body snatching.
It involves politics, God
and the sins of the world.
It is not good for people
of a nervous disposition.
They would do better to
think on rabbits, chickens

and the first snowdrop
of spring.
Or they'd do better to
wait for a re-run of
Christmas without asking
too many questions about
what Jesus did when he grew up
or whether there's any connection.

Joseph's Easter

W. H. VANSTONE

This poem, hitherto unpublished, was the big surprise among the many things sent to me by Michael Mayne. I especially like the way Canon Vanstone keeps it in the family: I mean, Joseph, Mary and Jesus.

'He's gone,' says Joseph: and, with Pilate's leave,
Eases the nails and lowers him from the tree,
Wraps him in reverent and tender thoughts
And lays him in the cave called Memory.

That cave is deeply hewn in Joseph's heart:
All that's within will always be his own:
In memory's cave the treasure of his past
Is safe for ever, walled and sealed by stone.

'He's safe,' says Joseph, 'safe in this cool place,
And no one now can take my Lord away:
In years to come I'll still see his dear face
As clearly as I saw it yesterday.'

'He's gone,' cries Joseph later, in despair.
But Mary says, 'He's left this word for you:
He cannot rest content to be your past –
So he has risen, to be your future too.'

From *The Towers of Trebizond*

ROSE MACAULAY

This is the first of two excerpts from one of my favourite books. Rose Macaulay's prose, with her prolific use of the word 'and', is eminently speakable, as Rohan McCullough proved recently when she performed a one-woman show of *The Towers of Trebizond* arranged by Hugh Whitemore.

What one feels in Jerusalem, where it all began, is the awful sadness and frustration and tragedy, and the great hope and triumph that sprang from it and still spring, in spite of everything we can do to spoil them with our cruelty and mean stupidity, and all the dark unchristened deeds of christened men. Jerusalem is a cruel, haunted city, like all ancient cities; it stands out because it crucified Christ; and because it was Christ we remember it with horror, but it also crucified thousands of other people, and wherever Rome (or indeed any one else) ruled, these ghastly deaths and torturings were enjoyed by all, that is, by all except the victims and those who loved them, and it is these, the crucifixions and the flayings and the burnings and the tearing to pieces and the floggings and the blindings and the throwing to the wild beasts, all the horrors of great pain that people thought out and enjoyed, which make history a dark pit full of serpents and terror, and out of this pit we were all dug, our roots are deep in it, and still it goes on, though all the time gradually less. And out of this ghastliness of cruelty and pain in Jerusalem on what we call Good Friday there sprang this Church that we have, and it inherited all that cruelty, which went on fighting against the love and goodness which it had inherited too, and they are still fighting, but sometimes it seems a losing battle for the love and goodness, though they never quite go under and never can. And all this grief and sadness and failure and defeat make Jerusalem heartbreaking for Christians, and perhaps for Jews, who so often have been massacred there by Christians, though it is more beautiful than one imagines before one sees it, and full of interest in every street, and the hills stand round it brooding.

Indifference

G. A. STUDDERT KENNEDY

The Reverend Geoffrey Anketell Studdert Kennedy was appointed
Chaplain to the Forces in 1915, served in the Somme Offensive,
and is famous for his book of verses about the First World War,
called *Rough Rhymes of a Padre*. I include two of them later in
the book. He had a voice like a foghorn, swore like a trooper, but
when he preached at a church parade 'every man was all attention,
and his sermons were the chief topic of conversation during the
ensuing week.' He handed out compassion, friendship, jollity and
cigarettes in equal measure. He was nicknamed Woodbine Willie.
Note: 'drave' is archaic for 'drove.'

When Jesus came to Golgotha they hanged Him on a tree,
They drave great nails through hands and feet, and made a
Calvary;
They crowned Him with a crown of thorns, red were His
wounds and deep,
For those were crude and cruel days, the human flesh was
cheap.

When Jesus came to Birmingham, they simply passed Him by,
They never hurt a hair of Him, they only let Him die:
For men had grown more tender, and they would not give
Him pain,
They only just passed down the street, and left Him in the
rain.

Still Jesus cried, 'Forgive them, for they know not what they
do,'

And still it rained the winter rain that drenched Him through
  and through;
The crowds went home and left the streets without a soul to
  see,
And Jesus crouched against a wall and cried for Calvary.

Churchyards

JOHN BETJEMAN

In spite of its many felicities ('English ploughboy faces' and 'Tomb-stones stacked round like playing cards') this is a strangely serious poem from Betjeman's slim volume, *Poems in the Porch*. Well, it's Easter, after all. Funnier ones from the same source are in the section devoted to Church Concerts.

Notes: 1. A 'vestry day' was a meeting of the rate-payers of a parish, usually held in the vestry.

2. 'Good King Edward' was Edward VII.

> Now when the weather starts to clear
> How fresh the primrose clumps appear,
> Those shining pools of springtime flower
> In our churchyard. And on the tower
> We see the sharp spring sunlight thrown
> On all its sparkling rainwashed stone,
> That tower, so built to take the light
> Of sun by day and moon by night,
> That centuries of weather there
> Have mellowed it to twice as fair
> As when it first rose new and hard
> Above the sports in our churchyard.
>   For churchyards then, though hallowed ground,
> Were not so grim as now they sound,
> And horns of ale were handed round
> For which churchwardens used to pay
> On each especial vestry day.
> 'Twas thus the village drunk its beer

With its relations buried near,
And that is why we often see
Inns where the alehouse used to be
Close to the church when prayers were said
And Masses for the village dead.
    But in these latter days we've grown
To think that the memorial stone
Is quite enough for soul and clay
Until the Resurrection Day.
Perhaps it is. It's not for me
To argue on theology.
    But this I know, you're sure to find
Some headstones of the Georgian kind
In each old churchyard near and far,
Just go and see how fine they are.
Notice the lettering of that age
Spaced like a noble title-page,
The parish names cut deep and strong
To hold the shades of evening long,
The quaint and sometimes touching rhymes
By parish poets of the times,
Bellows, or reaping hook or spade
To show, perhaps, the dead man's trade,
And cherubs in the corner spaces
With wings and English ploughboy faces.
    Engraved on slate or carved in stone
These Georgian headstones hold their own
With craftsmanship of earlier days
Men gave in their Creator's praise.
More homely are they than the white
Italian marbles which were quite
The rage in Good King Edward's reign,
With ugly lettering, hard and plain.
    Our churches are our history shown
In wood and glass and iron and stone.
I hate to see in old churchyards

Tombstones stacked round like playing cards
Along the wall which then encloses
A trim new lawn and standard roses,
Bird-baths and objects such as fill a
Garden in some suburban villa.
The Bishop comes; the bird-bath's blessed,
Our churchyard's now 'a garden of rest'.
And so it may be, all the same
Graveyard's a much more honest name.

Oh why do people waste their breath
Inventing dainty names for death?
On the old tombstones of the past
We do not read 'At peace at last'
But simply 'died' or plain 'departed'.
It's no good being chicken-hearted.
We die; that's that; our flesh decays
Or disappears in other ways.
But since we're Christians, we believe
That we new bodies will receive
To clothe our souls for us to meet
Our Maker at his Judgement Seat.
And this belief's a gift of faith
And, if it's true, no end is death.

Mid-Lent is passed and Easter's near
The greatest day of all the year
When Jesus, who indeed had died,
Rose with his body glorified.
And if you find believing hard
The primroses in your churchyard
And modern science too will show
That all things change the while they grow,
And we, who change in Time will be
Still more changed in Eternity.

Armistice Day

I like to have a lot of pieces ready for Armistice Day. Thoughts
of war and peace seem especially poignant as we approach the
Millenium, hoping against hope that the next century will be less
terrible than this one has been.

Peace and War

D. H. LAWRENCE

This astonishing poem is as apt today as ever it was. Think of the Middle East, think of Bosnia, think of Northern Ireland! The 'peace process' is always in operation whenever there is war about.

People always make war when they say they love peace.
The loud love of peace makes one quiver more than any
    battle-cry.
Why should one love peace? it is so obviously vile to make
    war.
Loud peace propaganda makes war seem imminent.
It is a form of war, even, self-assertion and being wise for
    other people.
Let people be wise for themselves. And anyhow
nobody can be wise except on rare occasions, like getting
    married or dying.
It's bad taste to be wise all the time, like being at a perpetual
    funeral.
For everyday use, give me somebody whimsical, with not
    too much purpose in life,
then we shan't have war, and we needn't talk about peace.

From *The Observer*, Sunday November 14, 1993

GEOFF DYER

I'm an inveterate cutter-outer of pieces from newspapers in the hope that they may come in useful one day. I was glad to find this one about the first two Armistice Days, in 1919 and 1920, because it told me all kinds of things which, if I'd ever known about them, I'd completely forgotten. I've done it several times, always to a pin-drop silence.

On 12 November 1919 the *Manchester Guardian* reported the previous day's silence: 'The first stroke of 11 produced a magical effect. The tram cars glided into stillness, motors ceased to cough and fume and stopped dead, and the mighty-limbed dray-horses hunched back upon their loads and stopped also, seeming to do it of their own volition. . . . Someone took off his hat, and with a nervous hesitancy the rest of the men bowed their heads also. Here and there an old soldier could be detected slipping unconsciously into the posture of attention. An elderly woman wiped her eyes and the man beside her looked white and stern. Everyone stood very still. . . .

'The hush deepened. It had spread over the whole city and become so pronounced as to impress one with a sense of audibility. It was . . . a silence which was almost pain. . . . And the spirit of memory brooded over it all.'

The following year the silence and the unveiling of the permanent Cenotaph were complemented by another even more emotive component of the ceremony of Remembrance: the burial of the Unknown Warrior.

Bodies from eight unmarked graves were exhumed from the most important battlefields of the war. Blindfolded, a senior officer selected one coffin at random. The rest were re-buried. In an elaborate series of symbol-packed rituals the body was carried through France with full battle honours and transported across the Channel in the destroyer *Verdun* (so that this battle and the role of France also found a place in the proceedings). On the morning of the eleventh the coffin was taken by gun carriage to Whitehall where, at 11 o'clock the permanent Cenotaph was unveiled.

The weather played its part. The sun shone through a haze of cloud and, on a windless day, flags, at half-mast, hung stock-still in folds as Big Ben struck the hour. 'In silence, broken only by a nearby sob', reported *The Times*, 'the great multitude bowed its head.' People held their breath lest they should be heard in the stillness.

From the Cenotaph, the carriage bearing the Unknown Warrior made its way to Westminster Abbey, where inside waited 1,000 widows and bereaved mothers; 100 nurses wounded or blinded in the war; and a guard of honour made up of 100 men who had won the Victoria Cross, 50 on each side of the nave. The highest ranking commanders from the war were among the pallbearers: Haig, French and Trenchard; the King, George V, scattered earth from France on to the coffin. 'All this,' commented one observer, 'was to stir such memories and emotions as might have made the very stones cry out.'

A Letter Written on November 11, 1920

DOROTHEA MARY MAYHEW

This letter, written largely on the spot to 'her husband or her father, we're not sure which,' was sent to me by the author's daughter-in-law, Aylwin Mayhew.

I have been wondering exactly where the barricade was erected. My guess is it was across Bridge Street at the Westminster Station end. From there she would have been able to see St Thomas's Hospital and the red sunrise over the River. And I guess when the gate was opened, and she managed to get through, she will have found a perch very near the corner of Whitehall and Parliament Square.

6.45 a.m.

It is just light enough to write – a wonderful pale dawn over St Thomas's. Big Ben's light has gone out, and the little lamps of the trams. I am settled on the pavement, my possessions around me, with my back against the barricade. Through a crack I can see all Parliament Square, swept and empty. The crowd, so far, is quiet.

I came with a handful of pleasant, grave, dark-clothed people – a man with obvious shell-shock, a father and mother with a little girl. The street hawkers are more various than usual. There are memorial cards, stools to stand on, 'words and music of the hymns,' and stacks of golden and white chrysanthemums. Every other person has an armful of flowers for the Cenotaph. As I wrote this, the police arrived. What a cheering sight they are. And the sunrise has turned red over the river. It's a good old world.

7.00 a.m.
Now chiming on Big Ben. Breakfast time.

7.20 a.m.
And a very good breakfast too. Scalding tea and tongue sandwiches and sweet biscuits. The crowd is getting big quickly now and people are beginning to ask which gate in the barrier will be opened. I don't care, I'm halfway between them. I wish you were here. London is at her best this morning.

8.40 a.m.
A bad business – very bad. At 8.15 they opened only one gate. People who had been behind the other gate all night never got in at all, and I – with them – was left stranded, while thousands went through who had only arrived at 8.00. I do wish the responsible authority would manage these things fairly and courteously. As it was, there was a bad cross rush, the police linking arms and pushing and being broken by the real insistence of the crowd. The worst way possible to begin Armistice Day. However I, with some six others, having at last burst through, took possession of some private steps with a more than average view. The sun is breaking through mists round the Abbey and the sense of space in Whitehall is wonderful. The Cenotaph is majestic, slung with great tasselled flags. The guns have just gone, so we shall not have long to wait.

Later, at home again
It was, I think, the most beautiful thing London has ever done. Partly because, after the first disaster, it was so well-ordered, so punctual, so disciplined. Partly because there is no tune in the world like the Chopin March when the Massed Guards band plays it.

Punctually then, far off, spread over the gorgeous width

of Whitehall, came the funeral procession. I could see the fluttering white of the choirboys round the Cenotaph hidden by the shifting mass of khaki as the guards closed round. Then there was a wait and then 'O God, our help' with the weight of the music lifted, as it always is at such times, by the shrillness of the nearer women's voices. And as Big Ben struck, the great flag drooped and fluttered from off the Cenotaph – and of all those hundreds of thousands of people clinging on every foothold, crowding on every roof, not one spoke or stirred during the silence. The only sound really was sobbing and crying here and there. One great brawny man next to us put his head in his hands and sobbed like a child when the Last Post broke the silence.

And immediately the mass of khaki shifted and broke and wheeled towards us, the great brass of the Guards soaring away with the Chopin, the people did begin to whisper and talk, which was a pity.

But nothing could spoil it or even get inside me at all. The gun carriage with its dirty flag and its Tommy's tin hat, and a sheaf of some scarlet blossoms on it, went past down the road to Westminster, surrounded by bishops and arch-bishops and princes and Kings and those that are in authority and, I doubt not, angels and archangels. And all of us felt He was overhead: and all, I think, were a little nicer to each other than we were before. And by some perfect device of wind and open doors the singing of the Abbey choir reached us faintly.

And so back to earth again – and home.

To *Any Dead Officer*

SIEGFRIED SASSOON

Siegfried Sassoon is another of those writers whose poems are ideal for reading aloud. They ring out easily, and the rhythms and rhymes tell you how to do them.

In a letter to Sassoon, dated June 8, 1960, John Betjeman wrote, 'I keep thinking of those things you said about poetry which are *exactly* my own sentiments:

(1) That you were almost led by the nose by sound.

(2) That if you had to choose between the startling word and the one that sounded well, you chose the latter.

(3) That poetry was meant to be said aloud.'

In 1986 I compiled a one-man show about Siegfried Sassoon and performed it all over the place for about a year. This is one of the poems I included in it, though I omitted the fourth stanza.

Well, how are things in Heaven? I wish you'd say,
    Because I'd like to know that you're all right.
Tell me, have you found everlasting day,
    Or been sucked in by everlasting night?
For when I shut my eyes your face shows plain;
    I hear you make some cheery old remark —
I can rebuild you in my brain,
    Though you've gone out patrolling in the dark.

You hated tours of trenches; you were proud
    Of nothing more than having good years to spend;
Longed to get home and join the careless crowd
    Of chaps who work in peace with Time for friend.

That's all washed out now. You're beyond the wire:
   No earthly chance can send you crawling back;
You've finished with machine-gun fire –
   Knocked over in a hopeless dud-attack.

Somehow I always thought you'd get done in,
   Because you were so desperate keen to live:
You were all out to try and save your skin,
   Well knowing how much the world had got to give.
You joked at shells and talked the usual 'shop,'
   Stuck to your dirty job and did it fine:
With 'Jesus Christ! when *will* it stop?
   Three years . . . It's hell unless we break their line.'

So when they told me you'd been left for dead
   I wouldn't believe them, feeling it *must* be true.
Next week the bloody Roll of Honour said
   'Wounded and missing' – (That's the thing to do
When lads are left in shell-holes dying slow,
   With nothing but blank sky and wounds that ache,
Moaning for water till they know
   It's night, and then it's not worth while to wake!)

Good-bye, old lad! Remember me to God,
   And tell Him that our Politicians swear
They won't give in till Prussian Rule's been trod
   Under the Heel of England . . . Are you there? . . .
Yes . . . and the War won't end for at least two years;
But we've got stacks of men . . . I'm blind with tears,
   Staring into the dark. Cheero!
I wish they'd killed you in a decent show.

The Hero

SIEGFRIED SASSOON

I also included this one.

'Jack fell as he'd have wished,' the Mother said,
And folded up the letter that she'd read.
'The Colonel writes so nicely.' Something broke
In the tired voice that quavered to a choke.
She half looked up. 'We mothers are so proud
Of our dead soldiers.' Then her face was bowed.

Quietly the Brother Officer went out.
He'd told the poor old dear some gallant lies
That she would nourish all her days, no doubt.
For while he coughed and mumbled, her weak eyes
Had shone with gentle triumph, brimmed with joy,
Because he'd been so brave, her glorious boy.

He thought how 'Jack', cold-footed, useless swine,
Had panicked down the trench that night the mine
Went up at Wicked Corner; how he'd tried
To get sent home, and how, at last, he died,
Blown to small bits. And no one seemed to care
Except that lonely woman with white hair.

From the *Yorkshire Evening Post,*
June 13, 1944

I found this in *A Year of Grace*, compiled by Victor Gollancz.

Mr and Mrs J. Gaines, of Fifteenth Avenue, Tong Road, Leeds, have received a letter from their son, Private Harry Gaines, who was wounded in the invasion and is in Worcester Royal Infirmary on this, his 19th birthday. He has wounds in both legs and the right arm.

He tells of the kindness of a German prisoner in a Red Cross hospital in Normandy in succouring him when he fell wounded: 'He carried me for 70 yards to the beach, then looked down at me, smiled, put a cigarette in my mouth, lit it, and put his lighter in my pocket. Then he took off his white shirt, tore it into shreds and dressed my wounds. Having done this, he kissed me, with tears in his eyes, and then walked away to attend to other wounded.'

Strange Meeting

WILFRED OWEN

This superb, deep, difficult poem about the encounter between a dead soldier and the enemy who killed him is one of two pieces chosen by Samuel West, who was such a splendid acting partner in Simon Gray's play, *Hidden Laughter*.

Strange, the assonance: the near-miss rhymes; strange, the searing vision of the dead man, who knows that while it is nations who 'trek from progress', it is individuals who bestow wisdom, compassion and healing.

I first encountered this poem in Benjamin Britten's great *War Requiem*. He used a slightly abridged version, and a passage towards the end is curiously different:

> 'I would go up and wash them from sweet wells.
> Even from wells we sunk too deep for war,
> Even the sweetest wells that ever were.
> I am the enemy you killed, my friend. . . .'

Strange, what happens to pieces when words get changed. While I've been compiling this anthology, I have been astonished at the number of pieces which have had words, spelling and punctuation altered as they've been handed from one person to another, and from one book to another. Peter Newbolt, Sir Henry Newbolt's grandson, with whom I corresponded about *Fidele's Grassy Tomb*, wrote, 'Sometimes the poems had been inaccurately transcribed from anthologies that had themselves been inaccurate, resulting in mistakes being perpetuated or even multiplied!'

I'm being so, so careful! But I bet there are some errors, still!

It seemed that out of battle I escaped
Down some profound dull tunnel, long since scooped
Through granites which titanic wars had groined.
Yet also there encumbered sleepers groaned,
Too fast in thought or death to be bestirred.
Then, as I probed them, one sprang up, and stared
With piteous recognition in fixed eyes,
Lifting distressful hands as if to bless.
And by his smile, I knew that sullen hall,
By his dead smile I knew we stood in Hell.
With a thousand pains that vision's face was grained;
Yet no blood reached there from the upper ground,
And no guns thumped, or down the flues made moan.
'Strange friend', I said, 'here is no cause to mourn.'
'None', said the other, 'save the undone years,
The hopelessness. Whatever hope is yours,
Was my life also: I went hunting wild
After the wildest beauty in the world,
Which lies not calm in eyes, or braided hair,
But mocks the steady running of the hour,
And if it grieves, grieves richlier than here.
For by my glee might many men have laughed,
And of my weeping something had been left,
Which must die now, I mean the truth untold,
The pity of war, the pity war distilled.
Now men will go content with what we spoiled.
Or, discontent, boil bloody, and be spilled.
They will be swift with swiftness of the tigress,
None will break ranks, though nations trek from progress.
Courage was mine, and I had mystery,
Wisdom was mine, and I had mastery;
To miss the march of this retreating world
Into vain citadels that are not walled.
Then, when much blood had clogged their chariot-
        wheels
I would go up and wash them from sweet wells,

Even with truths that lie too deep for taint.
I would have poured my spirit without stint
But not through wounds; not on the cess of war.
Foreheads of men have bled where no wounds were.
I am the enemy you killed, my friend.
I knew you in this dark; for so you frowned
Yesterday through me as you jabbed and killed.
I parried; but my hands were loath and cold.
Let us sleep now. . . .'

His Mate

G. A. STUDDERT KENNEDY

This poem is from the book called *Rough Rhymes of a Padre*, already referred to in the Easter section. It was sent to me by The Reverend Alan Burroughs, who runs a church and a charity in Folkestone. In an accompanying letter he wrote, 'I enclose an old, rather tatty copy of some Woodbine Willie poems from the First World War trenches: some, I feel, are devastating.' Like this one.

Thiepval (pronounced Tĭĕp'văl) is a small village in the valley of the River Somme. An integral part of the German defences, it was attacked in a massive raid by the 36th (Ulster) Division on July 1, 1916. Over 2,000 men of the division died and many more were injured in fourteen hours of terrible fighting. It was said that only bullet-proof men could have survived. Many people in Ulster still keep July 1 as a day of mourning.

Thiepval did not fall into British hands until late September, nearly three months after the initial attack. Today there are two memorials there: the Ulster Tower and the huge Thiepval Memorial, designed by Sir Edwin Lutyens. 'Here are recorded names of officers and men who fell on the Somme battlefields July 1915–February 1918 but to whom the fortune of war denied the known and honoured burial given to their comrades in death.'

> There's a broken battered village
>   Somewhere up behind the line,
> There's a dug-out and a bunk there,
>   That I used to say were mine.
>
> I remember how I reached them,

Dripping wet and all forlorn,
  In the dim and dreary twilight
    Of a weeping summer dawn.

All that week I'd buried brothers,
  In one bitter battle slain,
In one grave I laid two hundred.
  God! What sorrow and what rain!

And that night I'd been in trenches,
  Seeking out the sodden dead,
And just dropping them in shell holes,
  With a service swiftly said.

For the bullets rattled round me,
  But I couldn't leave them there,
Water-soaked in flooded shell holes,
  Reft of common Christian prayer.

So I crawled round on my belly,
  And I listened to the roar
Of the guns that hammered Thiepval,
  Like big breakers on the shore.

Then there spoke a dripping sergeant,
  When the time was growing late,
'Would you please to bury this one,
  'Cause 'e used to be my mate?'

So we groped our way in darkness
  To a body lying there,
Just a blacker lump of blackness,
  With a red blotch on his hair.

Though we turned him gently over,
  Yet I still can hear the thud,
As the body fell face forward,
  And then settled in the mud.

We went down upon our faces,

And I said the service through,
From 'I am the Resurrection'
    To the last, the great 'adieu.'

We stood up to give the Blessing,
    And commend him to the Lord,
When a sudden light shot soaring
    Silver swift and like a sword.

At a stroke it slew the darkness,
    Flashed its glory on the mud,
And I saw the sergeant staring
    At a crimson clot of blood.

There are many kinds of sorrow
    In this world of Love and Hate,
But there is no sterner sorrow
    Than a soldier's for his mate.

Lie in the Dark and Listen

NOËL COWARD

It is the hushed imaginings of what is going on in the loud
aeroplanes as they fly relentlessly overhead that make this poem so
special. The more hushed they are the better. Quiet thoughts
inspired by noise. This poem, one of my favourites, is yet another
where a good knowledge of the words is helpful. Then you can
look up.

Lie in the dark and listen,
It's clear tonight so they're flying high
Hundreds of them, thousands perhaps,
Riding the icy, moonlight sky.
Men, material, bombs and maps
Altimeters and guns and charts
Coffee, sandwiches, fleece-lined boots
Bones and muscles and minds and hearts
English saplings with English roots
Deep in the earth they've left below
Lie in the dark and let them go
Lie in the dark and listen.

Lie in the dark and listen
They're going over in waves and waves
High above villages, hills and streams
Country churches and little graves
And little citizen's worried dreams.
Very soon they'll have reached the sea
And far below them will lie the bays

And coves and sands where they used to be
Taken for summer holidays.
Lie in the dark and let them go
Lie in the dark and listen.

Lie in the dark and listen
City magnates and steel contractors,
Factory workers and politicians
Soft, hysterical little actors
Ballet dancers, 'Reserved' musicians,
Safe in your warm, civilian beds.
Count your profits and count your sheep
Life is flying above your heads
Just turn over and try to sleep.
Lie in the dark and let them go
Theirs is a world you'll never know
Lie in the dark and listen.

The Other Little Boats: July 1588

EDWARD SHANKS

This poem, with its ringing last line, is another treat to do.

A pause came in the fighting and England held her breath
For the battle was not ended and the ending might be death.
Then out they came, the little boats, from all the Channel
    shores,
Free men were these who set the sails and laboured at the
    oars.
From Itchenor and Shoreham, from Deal and Winchelsea,
They put out into the Channel to keep their country free.
Not of Dunkirk this story, but of boatmen long ago,
When our Queen was Gloriana and King Philip was our foe
And galleons rode the Narrow Sea, and Effingham and Drake
Were out of shot and powder, with all England still at stake.
They got the shot and powder, they charged their guns again,
The guns that guarded England from the galleons of Spain,
And the men who helped them to do it, helped them still to
    hold the sea,
Men from Itchenor and Shoreham, men from Deal and
    Winchelsea,
Looked out happily from Heaven and cheered to see the work
Of their grandsons' grandsons' grandsons on the beaches of
    Dunkirk.

From *The Folkestone, Hythe & District Herald*, D-day 6th June 1944: The Great Adventure

It is easy to forget what it was like living in a country at war, and this leading article, with its grandiose prose, is a tantalising reminder of the nation's faith in the rightness of the Allied cause, and its total hatred of the enemy and its 'hordes'. Everything we did was right and good, everything they did was wrong and evil. And God was certainly on our side.

D-Day was the biggest combined land, sea and air operation of all time. Several thousand ships crossed the Channel overnight and landed on the French coast from west of Cherbourg to le Havre. Airborne troops rained in from the sky, by parachute and glider.

June the 6th, 1944, will be remembered as long as Englishmen shall live as the day upon which the British Army, with its brothers in arms of the Empire and America, returned to France to free Europe from the tyranny of a ruthless oppressor, beneath whose despotism its people have suffered and endured and waited: waited for the coming of the Liberators.

Four years ago almost to the day the tragedy of Dunkirk was enacted; the British Expeditionary Force, left alone to face the overwhelming onslaught of the German hordes, was crowded along the bloodstained beaches of Dunkirk whilst behind it the town itself burned and blazed until it became a great cinder that glowed and smoked in the night.

We in Folkestone saw many of the big ships and the little ships that delivered our men from the hell of Dunkirk; we saw the destroyers and the colliers and the sailing boats draw in with their human cargoes crowding the decks, we saw the refugees who had fled from the horror that was being enacted but a few miles from our shores. And in the misery, the disappointment and the despair of Dunkirk was born a resolve, grim and implacable, that one day the British Army would go back to France, one day the might and power of British arms should grapple with and destroy the monstrous thing that evil minds and evil men had created to suppress, to terrify and to conquer peace-loving peoples.

That day has come. The waiting years have not been in vain; they have been filled with a purpose and a determination that have had but one outcome, the re-building and re-equipping of an army that will bring full, just and bitter retribution upon those who, in their mad ambition, have brought untold misery, sorrow and suffering upon the nations of Europe.

We await the outcome of the initial battles of the invasion of France with sober confidence, certain that our army and the armies of our allies will march forward to final victory.

Let each one of us pledge ourselves that we shall do nothing, absolutely nothing, that will in any way weaken the great efforts that our troops are making. A still tongue is more important than ever at this vital time. Whatever you may see, whatever you may hear by way of rumour, keep it to yourself. He or she who repeats rumours – and there have been many entirely false ones in Folkestone during the past week – is doing a disservice to the country and to the gallant men who are fighting and enduring on the coast of Normandy.

From a letter written by Evelyn Waugh to his wife Laura, from Glasgow on May 31, 1942

This was sent to me by Geoffrey Palmer who first heard it read by John Julius Norwich at a Platforms performance at the National Theatre. 'I'm particularly fond of this one,' wrote Geoffrey, 'having been in the Royal Marines myself, which looking at me now strikes me as not obvious casting. But how much less likely was E. Waugh as Royal Marine Commando material!'

. . . So No. 3 Cmdo were very anxious to be chums with Lord Glasgow so they offered to blow up an old tree stump for him and he was very grateful and said don't spoil the plantation of young trees near it because that is the apple of my eye and they said no of course not we can blow a tree down so that it falls on a sixpence and Lord Glasgow said goodness you are clever and he asked them all to luncheon for the great explosion. So Col. Durnford-Slater DSO said to his subaltern, have you put enough explosive in the tree. Yes, sir, 75 lbs. Is that enough? Yes sir I worked it out by mathematics it is exactly right. Well better put a bit more. Very good sir.

And when Col. D. Slater DSO had had his port he sent for the subaltern and said subaltern better put a bit more explosive in that tree. I don't want to disappoint Lord Glasgow. Very good sir.

Then they all went out to see the explosion and Col. D. S. DSO said you will see that tree fall flat at just that angle where it will hurt no young trees and Lord Glasgow said goodness you are clever.

So soon they lit the fuse and waited for the explosion and presently the tree, instead of falling quietly sideways, rose 50 feet into the air taking with it half an acre of soil and the whole of the young plantation.

And the subaltern said Sir I made a mistake, it should have been 7 and a half lbs not 75.

Lord Glasgow was so upset he walked in dead silence back to his castle and when they came to the turn of the drive in sight of his castle what should they find but that every pane of glass in the building was broken.

So Lord Glasgow gave a little cry and ran to hide his emotion in the lavatory and there when he pulled the plug the entire ceiling, loosened by the explosion, fell on his head.

This is quite true.

The Battle of Blenheim
ROBERT SOUTHEY

The Battle of Blenheim – a Bavarian village on the banks of the
Danube – was fought in 1704 and saved Vienna from the invading
French. It was a 'famous victory' for the 1ˢᵗ Duke of Marlborough,
who led the English, and Prince Eugene, who led the Austrians.
Blenheim Palace was named after the battle and given to the Duke
with the nation's thanks.

Ian Richardson introduced me to the poems of Robert Southey
(properly pronounced sow'dhĭ, though usually, inevitably, sŭ'dhĭ)
when he sent me the brilliant *How the Water comes Down at Lodore*
for the 'Show-off Poems' section.

It was a summer evening,
  Old Kaspar's work was done,
And he before his cottage door
  Was sitting in the sun,
And by him sported on the green
His little grandchild Wilhelmine.

She saw her brother Peterkin
  Roll something large and round,
Which he beside the rivulet
  In playing there had found;
He came to ask what he had found,
That was so large, and smooth, and round.

Old Kaspar took it from the boy,
  Who stood expectant by;
And then the old man shook his head,

And with a natural sigh,
'Tis some poor fellow's skull,' said he,
'Who fell in the great victory.'

'I find them in the garden,
    For there's many here about;
And often when I go to plough,
    The ploughshare turns them out!
For many thousand men,' said he,
'Were slain in that great victory.'

'Now tell us what 'twas all about,'
    Young Peterkin, he cries;
And little Wilhelmine looks up
    With wonder-waiting eyes;
'Now tell us all about the war,
And what they fought each other for.'

'It was the English,' Kaspar cried.
    'Who put the French to rout;
But what they fought each other for
    I could not well make out;
But everybody said,' quoth he,
'That 'twas a famous victory.

'My father lived at Blenheim then,
    Yon little stream hard by;
They burnt his dwelling to the ground,
    And he was forced to fly;
So with his wife and child he fled,
Nor had he where to rest his head.

'With fire and sword the country round
    Was wasted far and wide,
And many a childing mother then,
    And new-born baby died;
But things like that, you know, must be
At every famous victory.

'They say it was a shocking sight
　　After the field was won;
For many thousand bodies here
　　Lay rotting in the sun;
But things like that, you know, must be
　　After a famous victory.

'Great praise the Duke of Marlbro' won,
　　And our good Prince Eugene.'
'Why, 'twas a very wicked thing!'
　　Said little Wilhelmine.
'Nay . . . nay . . . my little girl,' quoth he,
'It was a famous victory.

'And everybody praised the Duke
　　Who this great fight did win.'
'But what good came of it at last?'
　　Quoth little Peterkin.
'Why, that I cannot tell,' said he,
'But 'twas a famous victory.'

The Soldier

RUPERT BROOKE

Yes, I want to include this. It is perfect, and it never fails. Rupert
Brooke, the 'celebrant of friendship, love, and laughter', enlisted
soon after the outbreak of the First World War and served with
the Royal Naval Division. After fighting at Antwerp, he sailed
for the Dardanelles, but died of blood-poisoning on the Greek
island of Skyros on April 23, 1915. He is buried there.

If I should die, think only this of me:
    That there's some corner of a foreign field
That is for ever England. There shall be
    In that rich earth a richer dust concealed;
A dust whom England bore, shaped, made aware,
    Gave, once, her flowers to love, her ways to roam,
A body of England's, breathing English air,
    Washed by the rivers, blest by suns of home.

And think, this heart, all evil shed away,
    A pulse in the eternal mind, no less
    Gives somewhere back the thoughts by England given;
Her sights and sounds; dreams happy as her day;
    And laughter, learnt of friends; and gentleness,
    In hearts at peace, under an English heaven.

Everyone Sang

SIEGFRIED SASSOON

This is how my one-man show about Siegfried Sassoon ended. The prose, the filling in the sandwich of the repeated poem, is from his autobiographical book, *Siegfried's Journey*.

Everyone suddenly burst out singing;
And I was filled with such delight
As prisoned birds must find in freedom,
Winging wildly across the white
Orchards and dark-green fields; on – on – and out of sight.

Everyone's voice was suddenly lifted;
And beauty came like the setting sun:
My heart was shaken with tears; and horror
Drifted away. . . . O, but Everyone
Was a bird; and the song was wordless; the singing will never
    be done.

One evening in the middle of April 1919, I was feeling dull-minded and depressed, for no assignable reason. It was a sultry spring night, and after sitting lethargically for about three hours after dinner, I came to the conclusion that there was nothing for it but to take my useless brain to bed.

    On the way from the arm-chair to the door I stood by the writing-table. A few words had floated into my head as though from nowhere. I picked up a pencil and wrote the words on a sheet of notepaper. Without sitting down, I added a second line. It was as if I were remembering rather than thinking. In this mindless, recollecting manner I wrote down my poem in a few minutes. I then went heavily upstairs and fell asleep without thinking about it again. *Everyone Sang* was composed without emotion, and needed no alteration afterwards. Yet it was essentially an expression of release, and signified a thankfulness for liberation from the war years which came to the surface with the advent of spring.

Everyone suddenly burst out singing;
And I was filled with such delight
As prisoned birds must find in freedom,
Winging wildly across the white
Orchards and dark-green fields; on – on – and out of sight.

Everyone's voice was suddenly lifted;
And beauty came like the setting sun:
My heart was shaken with tears; and horror
Drifted away. . . . O, but Everyone
Was a bird; and the song was wordless; the singing will never
    be done.

Theatre Benefits

Everybody always seems to get so nervous at theatre benefits. At least they always have at those I've been to. Perhaps it's the competition, perhaps it's the glitz. At a recent one at the Yvonne Arnaud theatre in Guildford we all paced about backstage, muttering to ourselves and dreading it. Then when we had done our pieces, and been clapped and congratulated, we wondered why we'd got so worked up about it, when it was all so obviously good and no trouble at all to do! 'Twas ever thus. . . .

After the whole thing was over, the party on the stage got very loud and eventually everybody was sufficiently psyched up to try and have a word with Virginia Bottomley. In fact a small queue formed. Over and over again the evening was pronounced a great success. And indeed it was: the theatre had been in deep trouble and, as James Barber, its Director, said a month or two later, 'The show raised £20,000. But fund-raising wasn't really what the evening was about. It attracted huge media coverage and turned a slightly troubling news story on page two of the local paper into a "cause". Thousands of letters were written to the Chairman of the Arts Council, the Heritage minister, MPs and the Regional Arts Board, and people started to send us money. A pretty good evening's work, I reckon.'

Makes it all worthwhile. And there are some nice pieces to choose from.

Love Note to a Playwright

PHYLLIS McGINLEY

This first one was sent to me by Stephen Sondheim who, along with Michael Mayne, introduced me to the works of Phyllis McGinley.

Richard Brinsley Sheridan was born into a theatrical family (his father was an actor) in Dublin in 1751. He went to Harrow school, and by the time he was twenty-six he had already written *The Rivals* (in which Captain Absolute appears), *The Duenna* and *A Trip to Scarborough*. He acquired the lease of the Theatre Royal, Drury Lane, where *The School for Scandal* had its first performance in 1777. Soon afterwards he became an MP and was an ardent campaigner for women's rights.

> Perhaps the literary man
>   I most admire among my betters
> Is Richard Brinsley Sheridan,
>   Who, viewing life as more than letters,
> Persisted, like a stubborn Gael,
> In not acknowledging his mail.
>
> They say he hardly ever penned
>   A proper 'Yrs. Received & noted,'
> But spent what time he had to spend
>   Shaping the law that England voted,
> Or calling, on his comic flute,
> The tune for Captain Absolute.
>
> Though chief of the prodigious wits
>   That Georgian taverns set to bubblin',

He did not answer Please Remits
  Or scoldings from his aunts in Dublin
Or birthday messages or half
The notes that begged an autograph.

I hear it sent his household wild —
  Became a sort of parlor fable —
The way that correspondence piled,
  Mountainous, on his writing table,
While he ignored the double ring
And wouldn't answer *anything*;

Not scrawls from friends or screeds from foes
  Or scribble from the quibble-lover
Or chits beginning 'I enclose
  Manuscripts under separate cover,'
Or cards from people off on journeys,
Or formal statements from attorneys.

The post came in. He let it lie.
  (All this biographers agree on.)
Especially he did not reply
  To things that had R.S.V.P. on.
Sometimes for months he dropped no lines
To dear ones, or sent Valentines;

But, polishing a second act
  Or coaxing kings to license Freedom,
Let his epistles wait. In fact,
  They say he didn't even read'm.
The which, some mornings, seems to me
A glorious blow for Liberty.

Brave Celt! Although one must deplore
  His manners, and with reason ample,
How bright from duty's other shore,
  This moment, seems his bold example!
And would I owned in equal balance

His courage (and, of course, his talents),

Who, using up his mail to start
   An autumn fire or chink a crevice,
Cried, 'Letters longer are than art;
   But *vita* is extremely *brevis!*'
Then, choosing what was worth the candle,
Sat down and wrote *The School for Scandal*.

The Boy Actor

NOËL COWARD

I doubt if there is an actor or actress who would not respond to
every line of this poem, and say, 'Yes, that's it ... yes ... that's
how it is.' Of course certain things have changed: children don't
wear Eton suits, gentlemen don't carry pince-nez, and sticks of
Leichner have gone out of fashion. But the doubts, the agonies
and the joys are still exactly as described.

Mercifully we don't have cue-scripts any more. I saw them only
once, when I played small-boy parts at the Frank H. Fortescue
rep. in Stockport, while I was still at school. You weren't given
the whole play to read, you were given your part only, and in
between each of your speeches there were dots followed by the
last four words of your cue. In my memory, it didn't even tell you
who spoke them.

I was introduced to this poem by the young actor Tim Heath,
who did it memorably at a Christmas concert some years ago. It
welcomes a little bit of acting, and is another of those poems
which is easier to do if you have a goodish knowledge of the lines.

I can remember. I can remember.
The months of November and December
Were filled for me with peculiar joys
So different from those of other boys
For other boys would be counting the days
Until end of term and holiday times
But I was acting in Christmas plays
While they were taken to pantomimes.
I didn't envy their Eton suits,

Their children's dances and Christmas trees.
My life had wonderful substitutes
For such conventional treats as these.
I didn't envy their country larks,
Their organized games in panelled halls:
While they made snow-men in stately parks
I was counting the curtain calls.

I remember the auditions, the nerve-racking auditions:
Darkened auditorium and empty, dusty stage,
Little girls in ballet dresses practising 'positions',
Gentlemen with pince-nez asking you your age.
Hopefulness and nervousness struggling within you,
Dreading that familiar phrase, 'Thank you dear, no more'.
Straining every muscle, every tendon, every sinew
To do your dance much better than you'd ever done before.
Think of your performance. Never mind the others,
Never mind the pianist, talent must prevail.
Never mind the baleful eyes of other children's mothers
Glaring from the corners and willing you to fail.

I can remember. I can remember.
The months of November and December
Were more significant to me
Than other months could ever be
For they were the months of high romance
When destiny waited on tip-toe,
When every boy actor stood a chance
Of getting into a Christmas show,
Not for me the dubious heaven
Of being some prefect's protégé!
Not for me the Second Eleven.
For me, two performances a day.

Ah those first rehearsals! Only very few lines:
Rushing home to mother, learning them by heart,
'Enter Left through window!' – Dots to mark the cue lines:

'Exit with the others' – Still it *was* a part.
Opening performance; legs a bit unsteady,
Dedicated tension, shivers down my spine,
Powder, grease and eye-black, sticks of make-up ready
Leichner number three and number five and number nine.
World of strange enchantment, magic for a small boy
Dreaming of the future, reaching for the crown,
Rigid in the dressing-room, listening for the call-boy
'Overture Beginners – Everybody Down!'

I can remember. I can remember.
The months of November and December,
Although climatically cold and damp,
Meant more to me than Aladdin's lamp.
I see myself, having got a job,
Walking on wings along the Strand,
Uncertain whether to laugh or sob
And clutching tightly my mother's hand,
I never cared who scored the goal
Or which side won the silver cup,
I never learned to bat or bowl
But I heard the curtain going up.

From *Star Quality*

NOËL COWARD

This excerpt from one of Coward's best short stories was chosen by Penelope Keith. 'It's a very jolly piece,' she said. 'I read it at Cedric Messina's memorial service.'

Lorraine Barrie, the star whose quality is so wickedly described, has agreed to be in a new play called *Sorrow in Sunlight* by Brian Snow, whose only previous play, *The Unconquered*, enjoyed a week's run at a fringe theatre in Bayswater. Here she meets him for the first time at her pink mews house near Knightsbridge. Her snappy dog is called Bothwell (which I suppose rhymes with Boswell), and a previous director is named as Doodie Rawlings, no far cry from Dadie (George) Rylands, who was exactly as described, except he was at Cambridge. He surfaces once more in this book as the host of the luncheon Virginia Woolf attended at King's College in 1928.

A moment later Lorraine reappeared carrying a teapot and a hot-water jug on a small tray.

'It's China tea,' she said. 'If you prefer Indian, there's masses in the kitchen and you can have a little pot all to yourself.' Bryan rose to his feet and relieved her of the tray and was about to reply that he was devoted to China tea when she cut him short by saying abruptly, 'You know you're quite different from what I thought you'd be. I can't imagine why, but I expected someone much older and drier – in fact, I can tell you now that I was really quite nervous. I've always had a dreadful inferiority complex about authors. To me there's something incredible about people being able to sit down and write plays and books. It's torture to me to have to write so much as a postcard. I'm just physically incapable of stringing three words together on paper. I suppose it's never having been to school properly and having to earn my living ever since I was tiny. I'm completely uneducated, you know; I used to drive poor Doodie Rawlings quite frantic when he was directing me in *The Cup That Clears*. He was an Oxford don, you know, with a passion for the theatre and, of course, madly intellectual, and he was astounded that anyone in the world could know as little as I did. He was a darling, of course, but frightfully twisted up emotionally, and if I hadn't a sort of instinctive feeling for what he wanted we should never have got beyond the first week of rehearsal.

'I remember quite early on going to Clemmie – that's my agent – in absolute despair. "It's no use," I said. "I can't do it." It isn't that I don't want to be directed. I do. I want it more than anyone else in the world; I want to be told every gesture, every intonation, but this man, poor angel, doesn't *know* the theatre! He may adore it; he may write brilliant essays on the Restoration playwrights or Shakespeare and God knows who, but he doesn't really *know* – I mean, one can tell in a flash, can't one?

'I remember at the very first reading of the play, when we were all sitting round a table, he kept on getting up and walking about and *explaining* our parts to us. It really was a disaster. Finally, of course, Clemmie calmed me down, and back I went with my heart literally in my boots and went straight up to Doodie in front of the whole company and had it out with him. "It's no good," I said, "expecting me to give what I have to give before I've got the book out of my hand. God knows I'm willing to rehearse until I drop at any time of the day or night, but you must let me work it out in my own way to begin with. Later on, when I'm sure of my words and not trying to think of a million things at once and worrying about my fittings into the bargain, you can do what you like with me. You can tear me to pieces, turn me inside out, but not yet — not yet — not yet!" '

On the last 'not yet' she struck the tea table sharply with her left hand, which caused the sugar tongs to shoot out of the bowl and clatter into the fender. Bryan stooped down to retrieve them, and Bothwell charged out from behind the sofa, barking loudly.

'There I go,' said Lorraine with a gay, unaffected laugh, 'over-acting again.' She handed Bryan a cup of tea.

From *Lost Fortnight*

RAY CONNOLLY

Lost Fortnight is a radio play about the very English Raymond Chandler in Hollywood, and the part alcohol played when he was trying to complete the script of *The Blue Dahlia* for Alan Ladd and Veronica Lake against impossible demands from the studio. In this excerpt he is giving advice to a young writer who has asked him to read his first screenplay. Ray Connolly, to whom I'm grateful for a lovely part and the inclusion of this speech here, said, 'I enjoyed putting this bit in. Chandler said something very close to it, and it's what I think too!'

The young man has just said, 'Be honest with me. What do you think of my screenplay?'

Chandler (*after a slight hesitation*): Have you thought there might be too much dialogue? In one of the best scenes I ever wrote the girl just said 'aha' three times. That's all there was to it. But each way she said it was different. Dialogue gets in the way of good film-making, you know. Even brilliant dialogue has no place in a movie if it slows the story down by one frame. But Hollywood is no place for good dialogue, anyway. Most of the meatheads who pass for actors around here have no feelings for words and silences. I mean, they just *haven't*. Give them a good scene and they'll muddy the best lines with little bits of improvisation and additions which they think don't matter but which, in fact, ruin everything. To a film writer the silences are as important as the words, maybe more so, but you can be sure that someone will always try to fill every silence with some terrible cliché. That's why too many movies sound so awful.

The actors change the lines or add things to suit their own personalities. They say 'I can't say this' and 'I can't say that'. And you know, Lloyd, they get away with it because, apart from the writer, no-one cares, and there's not much he can do about it because in Hollywood the writer is about as potent a force as the fifth ranking eunuch in a tenth rate harem.

Irene Vanbrugh Memorial Matinee: the Epilogue

NOËL COWARD

The matinee in memory of Dame Irene Vanbrugh was held at the Theatre Royal, Drury Lane, on Monday November 6, 1950. Earlier that same year work had started on a new theatre for the Royal Academy of Dramatic Art, to replace the one which had been destroyed in the blitz of 1941. Sir Kenneth Barnes, RADA's long-serving Principal, wanted it to be called the Vanbrugh, in memory of his two sisters, Irene and Violet. (They must have had rather different styles: Irene's great successes were in Pinero, Barrie and Shaw, whereas Violet triumphed in Shakespeare, especially as Lady Macbeth and Queen Katherine in *Henry VIII*.)

The Vanbrugh Theatre was opened in 1954. It soon became surprisingly outmoded, and was pulled about and altered and darkened and distorted, and now is to be completely rebuilt, thanks to money from the National Lottery. Hopefully it will emerge as a more flexible and long-lasting theatre than its predecessor. But it will still be the Vanbrugh, and still be the place designed especially for 'all the young beginners who will learn their intricate and fascinating trade' there.

> Your Majesty, Ladies and Gentlemen.
> A little while ago a lady died
> A lady who, for many of us here
> Epitomized the dignity and pride
> Of our profession. Over fifty years
> Have passed since young Miss Vanbrugh's quality

Was stamped indelibly upon the hearts
Of Londoners. During those changing years
We were most privileged, not only us
Her colleagues who so loved and honoured her
But you as well, you on the other side.
Perhaps you took for granted (as you should)
The lightness of her touch in comedy;
The note of hidden laughter in her voice;
The way she used her hands to illustrate
Some subtle implication. She could charge
An ordinary line with so much wit
That even critics thought the play was good!
They, too, took her for granted (as they should).
Then on the other hand, the other mask
The mask of tragedy; she could wear that
With such authority that even we,
Her fellow actors could perceive
Through her most accurate and sure technique
Her truth, which was her talent, shining clear.
Your Majesty, Ladies and Gentlemen,
A little while ago this lady died
Apparently, only apparently,
For even though the art that she adorned
Must in its essence be ephemeral,
Players of her integrity and grace
Can never die. Although we shall not hear
That lyrical, gay voice again, nor see
The personal inimitable smile
That she bestowed on us at curtain calls
The theatre that she loved will still go on
Enriched immeasurably by the years
She gave to it. This epilogue is but
A prelude to the future she endowed
With so much legend, so much memory
For all the young beginners who will learn

Their intricate and fascinating trade
And owe perhaps, some measure of their fame
To the undying magic of her name.

Twenty Tactful Phrases to Help a Voice-Over Artiste Feel at Home

No-one I spoke to at Magmasters Sound Studios in Soho could remember who wrote these Twenty Tactful Phrases. They were much quoted in the mid 1980s, when Magmasters were still concentrating on commercials for TV and radio. Now they have added a large department for recording 'audio books'. I am very grateful to Steve Cook. who has been there, it seems, for ever, for unearthing these anonymous, but crushing remarks.

1. Ah, you must be the voice.
2. Mmm, very good. Can you do it like Hywel Bennett?
3. Well we did want Felicity Kendal, but she was too expensive.
4. That was great. Do you have any other voices?
5. Can we lose the Pakistani accent? Oh you're *Welsh*. I am sorry.
6. No no, I loved it. Really. (Pause) What do you think?
7. Didn't you used to be an actor?
8. Absolutely spot on. That's a print. Could we just do one more?
9. Can you make it sound more real?
10. Over by a second I'm afraid and it's rather rushed, so could you go quicker but sound slower?
11. We've still got point three of a second to play with actually. You can spread it over the whole read if you like.
12. Would it help if I read it for you?
13. Do you think you could breathe a bit less?
14. It's quite simple, just try to imagine you're a beefburger.

15. We thought it might be fun if you all just absorbed the concept and then improvised.
16. Do you always sound like that?
17. Oh I see I thought you had a cold.
18. OK, we'd like to swap you all round now. Just to be on the safe side.
19. I'm sorry, I was on the phone. Can we play that one back?
20. Don't worry. I'm sure we can cut something together.

From *Sheppey*

W. SOMERSET MAUGHAM

This piece was sent to me by Ruth Rendell. 'I've recited it myself
at various of the sort of functions you mention,' she wrote, 'and
it never fails to get a gasp and a shiver from the audience. It is
Death's speech to Sheppey when she comes for him in Act III,
you probably know it.' Well, I didn't, so I read it. It's an odd play.
A plausible Act I in a men's hairdressing saloon in Jermyn Street
is spoiled by an implausible Act II and ruined by a preposterous
Act III in Sheppey's house in Camberwell. Preposterous, that is,
until half-way through, when the actress who has been playing
Bessie Legros, a cockney tart with a heart of gold, has to transform
herself into Death with 'a long black cloak and ordinary English'.
But it's then that the miracle happens: the claptrap and the postur-
ings of the unlikeliest characters suddenly cease, and there is a
most serene exchange between Sheppey and Death. It is, in its
way, like the closing moments of *The Taming of the Shrew*, when
all the hurly-burly's done and Katherine, tamed, speaks from her
heart. Here, Death tells Sheppey a story.

There was a merchant in Baghdad who sent his servant to
market to buy provisions and in a little while the servant
came back, white and trembling, and said:

'Master, just now when I was in the market-place I was
jostled by a woman in the crowd and when I turned I saw
it was death that jostled me. She looked at me and made a
threatening gesture; now, lend me your horse, and I will ride
away from this city and avoid my fate. I will go to Samarra
and there death will not find me.'

The merchant lent him his horse, and the servant mounted it, and he dug his spurs in its flanks and as fast as the horse could gallop he went. Then the merchant went down to the market-place and he saw me standing in the crowd and he came to me and said:

'Why did you make a threatening gesture to my servant when you him this morning?'

'That was not a threatening gesture,' I said, 'it was only a start of surprise. I was astonished to see him in Baghdad, for I had an appointment with him tonight in Samarra.'

Emergency Lines

NICHOLAS CRAIG

I have lifted this hilarious couple of pages straight out of his recent book, *I, An Actor*.

An hour spent committing these to memory will save you a hundred hours of excruciating embarrassment:

Where are they, the bastards?
'I'll just go and check if there are any murderers outside.'
'Et tu iterum, Cassius?' (And you again, Cassius?) 'Ubique procreatus Brute?' (Where the fuck is Brutus?)
'When shall I meet the other two again?'
'Westmoreland comes late upon the hour, methinks I'll take mine ease behind yon wall until he do approach.'

Oh no, pissed again!
'Mark ye how the King is sore distracted by affairs of state and cannot stand.'
'Your burps inform me ye would as lief be damned to hell as see me crowned. Nay, I'll not fight with thee. See, with my own usurper's sword I slay myself.'
'Methinks the noble Lord would fain part the news from France, which I'll wager is as follows. . . .'

You'd better bloody buy me a pint afterwards.
'Though ye say naught, thy visage tells me ye would exile me to France.'
'I can see in your eyes, m'lud, that you mean me to be taken from here to a place of execution, where I shall be hanged

by the neck until I am dead. But I didn't do it, d'you hear? I'm innocent, damn you!'
'Perchance my Lord Hamlet is wondering whether or not it is all worth it. Whether 'tis nobler in the mind . . .' (and so on, as far as necessary)

Damn! It's in the dressing-room
'Would great Caesar vouchsafe me his dagger for a moment?'
'And thus, with this poisoned empty scabbard, I do end my miserable life.'
'Why then, we'll fight with shields alone!'

Bloody props!
'Aha. The silencer works perfectly.'
'It's one of those new phones with a very quiet ring.'
'I've got a gun that works out in the car, damn you. Come with me and I'll shoot you like a dog!'
'Ho! Bring me a dishcloth and another draught of poison.'

It's stuck!
'Never mind, Algy, we can easily get to the garden through the fireplace.'
'Cynthia! I thought you were in Paris. Have you been listening up the chimney all this time?'
'Look here, I'm sick of Champagne. Let's celebrate this happy day by shaking hands instead.'

Fringe Crises
'Because of Thatcher, we're too poor to afford a radio that works, you'd better paint some more placards while I go and see if there's any talk about the strike on the streets.'
'Bloody men! Typical of them to manufacture a kettle that won't boil.'

Hamlet's Advice to the Players

WILLIAM SHAKESPEARE

This is one of my favourite party pieces, and it's what I did at the theatre benefit at the Yvonne Arnaud I mentioned earlier. It is one of those rare speeches which is probably more telling away from the turmoil of the play from which it comes. You can slow it down — it's such a long play that it's always taken at something of a lick — and you can therefore concentrate on it more, and realise yet again that its detailed and interesting advice is as fresh and apt as ever.

I've joined the three speeches up, omitting short lines from the players. It's probably better if you know it by heart, so you can talk to the audience like a teacher and put some gestures in, but it's not essential.

The splendid actress and teacher Fabia Drake introduced me to it when I was a student at RADA. The exercise she set us was to do it with five gestures. 'Five,' she said, looking us all straight in the eye. 'No more, no less. Five good, different, expressive gestures. And when you're not gesturing, don't fiddle!' It's an impeccably good exercise, and I pinched it from her when I taught at RADA some years later.

A sentence in the middle paragraph which sometimes goes wrong is the one which begins 'Now this overdone. . . .' The word 'one' needs especial emphasis: it is, after all, one person's opinion as against that of 'a whole theatre of others'.

'Speak the speech, I pray you, as I pronounc'd it to you, trippingly on the tongue; but if you mouth it, as many of your players do, I had as lief the town-crier spoke my lines.

195

Nor do not saw the air too much with your hand, thus, but use all gently; for in the very torrent, tempest, and, as I may say, whirlwind of your passion, you must acquire and beget a temperance that may give it smoothness. O, it offends me to the soul to hear a robustious periwig-pated fellow tear a passion to tatters, to very rags, to split the ears of the ground-lings, who, for the most part, are capable of nothing but inexplicable dumb shows and noise. I would have such a fellow whipp'd for o'erdoing Termagant; it out-herods Herod. Pray you avoid it.

'Be not too tame neither, but let your own discretion be your tutor. Suit the action to the word, the word to the action; with this special observance, that you o'erstep not the modesty of nature; for anything so o'erdone is from the purpose of playing, whose end, both at the first and now, was and is to hold, as 'twere, the mirror up to nature; to show virtue her own feature, scorn her own image, and the very age and body of the time his form and pressure. Now, this overdone or come tardy off, though it makes the unskilful laugh, cannot but make the judicious grieve, the censure of the which one must, in your allowance, o'erweigh a whole theatre of others. O, there be players that I have seen play – and heard others praise, and that highly – not to speak it profanely, that, neither having th' accent of Christians, nor the gait of Christian, pagan, nor man, have so strutted and bellowed that I have thought some of Nature's journeymen had made men, and not made them well, they imitated humanity so abominably.

'O, reform it altogether. And let those that play your clowns speak no more than is set down for them; for there be of them that will themselves laugh, to set on some quantity of barren spectators to laugh too, though in the meantime some necessary question of the play be then to be considered. That's villainous, and shows a most pitiful ambition in the fool that uses it. Go, make you ready.'

Instructions to an Actor

EDWIN MORGAN

The poet imagines Shakespeare directing the boy actor who first
played Hermione in *The Winter's Tale*.

Now, boy, remember this is the great scene.
You'll stand on a pedestal behind a curtain,
the curtain will be drawn, and you don't move
for eighty lines; don't move, don't speak, don't breathe.
I'll stun them all out there, I'll scare them,
make them weep, but it depends on you.
I warn you eighty lines is a long time,
but you don't breathe, you're dead,
you're a dead queen, a statue,
you're dead as stone, new-carved,
new-painted and the paint not dry
 — we'll get some red to keep your lip shining —
and you're a mature woman, you've got dignity,
some beauty still in middle-age, and
you're kind and true, but you're dead,
your husband thinks you're dead,
the audience thinks you're dead,
and you don't breathe, boy, I say
you don't even blink for eighty lines,
if you blink you're out!
Fix your eye on something and keep watching it.
Practise when you get home. It can be done.
And you move at last — music's the cue.
When you hear a mysterious solemn jangle

of instruments, make yourself ready.
Five lines more, you can lift a hand.
It may tingle a bit, but lift it –
slow, slow –
O this is where I hit them
right between the eyes, I've got them now –
I'm making the dead walk –
you move a foot, slow, steady, down,
you guard your balance in case you're stiff,
you move, you step down, down from the pedestal,
control your skirt with one hand, the other hand
you now hold out –
O this will melt their hearts if nothing does –
to your husband who wronged you long ago
and hesitates in amazement
to believe you are alive.
Finally he embraces you, and there's nothing
I can give you to say, boy,
but you must show that you have forgiven him.
Forgiveness, that's the thing. It's like a second life.
I know you can do it. – Right then, shall we try?

When I Read Shakespeare

D. H. LAWRENCE

This odd poem is, I suppose, good for a laugh. It goes quite well.
And it's brief.

Note: a 'chough' is a red-legged crow.

When I read Shakespeare I am struck with wonder
that such trivial people should muse and thunder
in such lovely language.

Lear, the old buffer, you wonder his daughters
didn't treat him rougher,
the old chough, the old chuffer!

And Hamlet, how boring, how boring to live with,
so mean and self-conscious, blowing and snoring
his wonderful speeches, full of other folks' whoring!

And Macbeth and his Lady, who should have been choring,
such suburban ambition, so messily goring
old Duncan with daggers!

How boring, how small Shakespeare's people are!
Yet the language so lovely! Like the dyes from gas-tar.

Social Grace

NOËL COWARD

A gift if you like doing this sort of thing.

I expect you've heard this a million times before
But I absolutely adored your last play
I went four times – and now to think
That here I am actually talking to you!
It's thrilling! Honestly it is, I mean,
It's always thrilling isn't it to meet someone really celebrated?
I mean someone who really does things.
I expect all this is a terrible bore for you.
After all you go everywhere and know everybody.
It must be wonderful to go absolutely everywhere
And know absolutely everybody and – Oh dear –
Then to have to listen to someone like me,
I mean someone absolutely ordinary just one of your public.
No one will believe me when I tell them
That I have actually been talking to the great man himself.
It must be wonderful to be so frightfully brainy
And know all the things that you know
I'm not brainy a bit, neither is my husband,
Just plain humdrum, that's what we are.
But we do come up to town occasionally
And go to shows and things. Actually my husband
Is quite a critic, not professionally of course,
What I mean is that he isn't all that easily pleased.
He doesn't like everything. Oh no not by any means.
He simply hated that thing at the Haymarket

Which everybody went on about. 'Rubbish' he said,
Straight out like that, 'Damned Rubbish!'
I nearly died because heaps of people were listening.
But that's quite typical of him. He just says what he thinks.
And he can't stand all this highbrow stuff –
Do you know what I mean? – All these plays about people
being miserable
And never getting what they want and not even committing
suicide
But just being absolutely wretched. He says he goes to the
theatre
To have a good time. That's why he simply loves all your
things,
I mean they relax him and he doesn't have to think.
And he certainly does love a good laugh.
You should have seen him the other night when we went to
that film
With what's-her-name in it – I can't remember the title.
I thought he'd have a fit, honestly I did.
You must know the one I mean, the one about the man who
comes home
And finds his wife has been carrying on with his best friend
And of course he's furious at first and then he decides to
teach her a lesson.
You must have seen it. I wish I could remember the name
But that's absolutely typical of me, I've got a head like a sieve,
I keep on forgetting things and as for names – well!
I just cannot for the life of me remember them.
Faces yes, I never forget a face because I happen to be
naturally observant
And always have been since I was a tiny kiddie
But names! – Oh dear! I'm quite hopeless.
I feel such a fool sometimes
I do honestly.

Value for Money

MICHAEL FRAYN

The same gushing voice would be ideal for this. Though not strictly theatrical, it is by one of our finest comic playwrights and was first performed by Eleanor Bron in a 1972 TV series called *Beyond a Joke*.

Oh, you live in the North, do you? How super. What fun. You don't by any chance know the Uzzards? They live in the North somewhere. He's in some terrific chemical thing up there, and she's *hideously* pretty. I mean, I hardly know them, but I do remember someone saying they lived up in that part of the world. You *must* meet them, they're *frightful* sweeties. Well, I say they're up in the North, but of course at the moment they aren't because he's doing . . . what is he doing? How is it that one can never remember what people are doing? I think he's doing five years. I *think* I'm right in saying five. There was some terrible confusion about some money thing he was mixed up with. Such a pity, because he's such good value. And she's so madly sensible about it all. And the absolutely unforgivably ghastly thing is that I've forgotten what *she's* doing, but I think what she's doing is life. There was some kind of dreadful muddle about her au pair getting sort of murdered. *Such* rotten luck. And of course just when she needed the girl most! Maddening when you get a good one, and off she goes. Because the tragic thing was, the girl was an absolute marvel. I think that's why David got involved in this terrible confusion about the money thing. I *think* so. There was some ghastly mix-up over sort of fur coats and abortion sort of things. I *think* that was it. Then Sue heard that David had got involved in this muddle about the money thing and she thought, wow, and *she* got into this muddle about the murder thing. So absolutely awful when everyone involved is so awfully nice. And such killingly good value. But you've never met them? And now they're not up in the North any more! How sickening. Such a dreadful waste, somehow. No, I mean of the North. Still, I get the impression it's frightful fun living up there.

TV. OD.

ANDREW MACLEAN

The overdose of the title is like an injection of a drug: the commercials go straight to the head.

I first heard this extraordinary piece at a West End showcase given by students who were about to leave the Mountview Theatre School. The audience at that lunchtime performance in Her Majesty's Theatre was made up almost entirely of agents, casting directors and producers, and this piece, performed wittily and very fast by Gilly Campbell, got the loudest laughs of the afternoon. It comes from a play called *See Base of Can* which was later performed, to considerable acclaim, at the Edinburgh Festival of 1996.

Note: 'Synapses' are places where nerve-cells join.

First rush. Sensational, electrical tingle flows through me, rising and SMACKS the BACK of my skull. CRACK! The golden axe bites deep. A million magic messages chatter crackle and pop! Synapses fuse in a confused static muse. The opium of the ether is beamed in. Filling my dreams with dreams. Selling the secrets of success. Telling me . . . Selling me what I want . . . And I want a lot!

I am entitled to:

A trip to MFI.

A satellite for Sky.

A holiday on the Planet Zanussi.

A breakfast bowl of new, improved muesli.

A freezer full of Lean Cuisine.

Woman's World and *Hello* magazine.

Soft hands.

Shining pans . . .
LOVELY thighs . . .
 . . . Natrel highs
Direct debit.
Unlimited credit.
A germ-free home.
A cordless phone
A phoneless chord.
A genuine Third Reich smoke alarm!
A Renault Clio! Two Clios! A whole herd of Clios. They're almost giving them away.
Nicole? Papa? . . .
I want breasts like Nicole. Do they come with the car? Do I come IN the car? (*Starts a mini orgasm which slides into:*) Mmmmmmmm LOVELY coffee! (*Makes coffee bean shaking motion with her hand.*) I want a date with the Nescafe Goddess!! I want sex with Ronald MacDonald!!!
I can't change the world. I can't change poverty. I can't mend the Ozone Layer . . . But I can change my burger to a Burger King Burger! . . . And that's a Comfort . . . I can't stop acting on Impulse . . . I want to get on. Get off. Get ahead. A head of healthy hair! Because day after day your hair loses elements VITAL to its protection.
Chocolate???
Maltesers!
But I do care. I do. I care about life. Important stuff like, do I smell nice? Do I look nice? I care about feeling nice. A perfect form. A perfect form is perfect content in this crazy, mixed-up, old world of ours. I care my kids are clean and white and full of food!! I care about the future. So do Mr Bradford and Mr Bingley. I trust them with my future. I want every mouthful to be an experience, every experience to be a mouthful.
I care . . .
Because BOOTS CARES!

Mrs Worthington, Don't Put Your Daughter On The Stage

A Song

NOËL COWARD

Just as some speeches can be more telling away from their plays, so some songs can bite harder away from their music. These words are funnier without the tinkly tune because the rising contempt and eventual anger they contain can be more fully realised. You can make more of 'She was lovely as Peer Gynt,' and 'She's a big girl,' and all the other felicities, so that when you get to 'Christ! Mrs Worthington,' you can be beside yourself, and really quite loud.

Though I have to admit Peter Greenwell raised many a laugh when he sang it, at the piano, à la Noël Coward, at the evening at the Yvonne Arnaud.

Regarding yours, dear Mrs Worthington,
Of Wednesday the 23rd,
Although your baby,
May be,
Keen on a stage career,
How can I make it clear,
That this is not a good idea.
For her to hope,
Dear Mrs Worthington,
Is on the face of it absurd.
Her personality

Is not in reality
Inviting enough,
Exciting enough
For this particular sphere.

Don't put your daughter on the stage, Mrs Worthington,
Don't put your daughter on the stage,
The profession is overcrowded
And the struggle's pretty tough
And admitting the fact
She's burning to act,
That isn't quite enough.
She has nice hands, to give the wretched girl her due,
But don't you think her bust is too
Developed for her age.
I repeat
Mrs Worthington,
Sweet
Mrs Worthington,
Don't put your daughter on the stage.

Don't put your daughter on the stage, Mrs Worthington,
Don't put your daughter on the stage,
She's a bit of an ugly duckling
You must honestly confess,
And the width of her seat
Would surely defeat
Her chances of success,
It's a loud voice, and though it's not exactly flat,
She'll need a little more than that
To earn a living wage.
On my knees
Mrs Worthington,
Please! Mrs Worthington,
Don't put your daughter on the stage.

Don't put your daughter on the stage, Mrs Worthington,
Don't put your daughter on the stage,
Though they said at the school of acting
She was lovely as Peer Gynt,
I'm afraid on the whole
An ingénue role
Would emphasize her squint.
She's a big girl, and though her teeth are fairly good
She's not the type I ever would
Be eager to engage,
No more buts,
Mrs Worthington,
NUTS,
Mrs Worthington,
Don't put your daughter on the stage.

Don't put your daughter on the stage, Mrs Worthington,
Don't put your daughter on the stage,
One look at her bandy legs should prove
She hasn't got a chance,
In addition to which
The son of a bitch
Can neither sing nor dance,
She's a *vile* girl and uglier than mortal sin,
One look at her has put me in
A tearing bloody rage,
That sufficed,
Mrs Worthington,
Christ!
Mrs Worthington,
Don't put your daughter on the stage.

Church Concerts

Fund raising concerts for churches are usually, thank heaven, on a less grand scale than those for theatres, so you can relax and enjoy them more easily. And there are lots of pieces to choose from. It's particularly pleasant to hear laughter in a church: it's less likely, somehow, and sounds louder because of the echo. So the funny ones here are my favourites.

Jokes are not really within the brief I have set myself for this book. But they can be useful as part of any introductory remarks you may care to make. Like this one:

A Bishop was visiting a primary school. 'I'll give a penny to the boy or girl who can tell me who I am,' he said to the gathered children.

A small boy piped up, 'Please sir, you are God.'

The Bishop replied, 'Well, no, I'm not, but here's tuppence.'

One of Our St Bernard Dogs is Missing

N. F. SIMPSON

Packed with its conversational clichés, this story of a poor lost soul, obviously on his last legs, arriving at a monastery in the mountains longing for succour, but being cruelly sent away to look for an equally lost dog, is one of several gems sent to me by Peter Jeffrey, with whom I had a happy year in Michael Frayn's *Donkeys' Years* at the Globe Theatre, now the Gielgud.

N. F. Simpson's plays, including *A Resounding Tinkle*, *One Way Pendulum*, and *The Hole*, were part of the Theatre of the Absurd, and how gloriously Absurd here is the final paragraph with hopes stubbornly rising against all the odds!

A moot point
Whether I was going to
Make it.
I just had the strength
To ring the bell.

There were monks inside
And one of them
Eventually
Opened the door.

Oh
He said.
This is a bit of a turn-up
He said

For the book.
Opportune
He said
Your arriving at this particular
As it were
Moment.

You're dead right
I said
It was touch and go
Whether I could have managed
To keep going
For very much longer.

No
He said
The reason I used the word opportune
Is that
Not to put too fine a point on it
One of our St Bernard dogs is
Unfortunately
Missing.

Oh dear
I said
Not looking for me I hope.

No
He said
It went for a walk
And got lost in the snow.

Dreadful thing
I said
To happen.

Yes
He said
It is.

To
Of all creatures
I said
A St Bernard dog
That has devoted
Its entire
Life
To doing good
And helping
Others.

What I was actually thinking
He said
Since you happen to be
In a manner of speaking
Out there already
Is that
If you could
At all
See your way clear
To having a scout
Around
It would save one of us
Having to
If I can so put it
Turn out.

Ah
I said
That would
I suppose
Make a kind of sense.

Before you go
He said
If I can find it
You'd better

Here it is
Take this.

What is it?
I said.

It's a flask
He said
Of brandy.

Ah
I said.

For the dog
He said.

Good thinking
I said.

The drill
He said
When you find it
If you ever do
Is to lie down.

Right
I said
Will do.

Lie down on top of it
He said
To keep it warm
Till help arrives.

That was a week ago, and my hopes are rising all the time. I feel
with ever-increasing confidence that once I can safely say that I
am within what might be called striking distance of knowing
where, within a square mile or two, to start getting down to
looking, my troubles are more or less, to all intents and purposes,

apart from frostbite, with any luck, once help arrives, at long last, God willing, as good as over. It is good to be spurred on with hope.

Blame the Vicar

JOHN BETJEMAN

Of the many poems John Betjeman wrote about churches, the most amusing are in *Poems in the Porch*, which was published in 1958 by the Society for Promoting Christian Knowledge. This and the one which follows are full of jokes and charm about the golden age of village church life. It is not only the value of the pound which has plummetted in the intervening years! In the Introductory Note to the book, Betjeman wrote, 'These verses do not pretend to be poetry. They were written for speaking on the wireless.'

When things go wrong it's rather tame
To find we are ourselves to blame,
It gets the trouble over quicker
To go and blame things on the Vicar.
The Vicar, after all, is paid
To keep us bright and undismayed.
The Vicar is more virtuous too
Than lay folks such as me and you.
He never swears, he never drinks,
He never *should* say what he thinks.
His collar is the wrong way round,
And that is why he's simply bound
To be the sort of person who
Has nothing very much to do
But take the blame for what goes wrong
And sing in tune at Evensong.
    For what's a Vicar really for

Except to cheer us up? What's more,
He shouldn't ever, ever tell
If there is such a place as Hell,
For if there is it's certain he
Will go to it as well as we.
The Vicar should be all pretence
And never, never give offence.
To preach on Sunday is his task
And lend his mower when we ask
And organise our village fêtes
And sing at Christmas with the waits
And in his car to give us lifts
And when we quarrel, heal the rifts.
To keep his family alive
He should industriously strive
In that enormous house he gets,
And he should always pay his debts,
For he has quite six pounds a week,
And when we're rude he should be meek
And always turn the other cheek.
He should be neat and nicely dressed
With polished shoes and trousers pressed,
For we look up to him as higher
Than anyone, except the Squire.
    Dear People, who have read so far,
I know how really kind you are,
I hope that you are always seeing
Your Vicar as a human being,
Making allowances when he
Does things with which you don't agree.
But there are lots of people who
Are not so kind to him as you.
So in conclusion you shall hear
About a parish somewhere near,
Perhaps your own or maybe not,
And of the Vicars that it got.

One parson came and people said,
'Alas! Our former Vicar's dead!
And this new man is far more "Low"
Than dear old Reverend so-and-so,
And far too earnest in his preaching,
We do not really like his teaching,
He seems to think we're simply fools
Who've never been to Sunday Schools.'
That Vicar left and by and by
A new one came, 'He's much too "High",'
The people said, 'too like a saint,
His incense makes our Mavis faint.'
So now he's left and they're alone
Without a Vicar of their own.
The living's been amalgamated
With the one next door they've always hated.
    Dear readers, from this rhyme take warning,
And if you heard the bell this morning
Your Vicar went to pray for you,
A task the Prayer Book bids him do.
'Highness' or 'Lowness' do not matter,
You are the Church and must not scatter,
Cling to the Sacraments and pray
And God be with you every day.

Electric Light and Heating

JOHN BETJEMAN

Alternately the fogs and rains
Fill up the dim November lanes,
The Church's year is nearly done
And waiting Advent not begun,
Our congregations shrink and shrink,
We sneeze so much we cannot think.
We blow our noses through the prayers,
And coughing takes us unawares;
We think of funerals and shrouds.
Our breath comes out in steamy clouds
Because the heating, we are told,
Will not be used *until it's cold*.
With aching limbs and throbbing head
We wish we were at home in bed.
    Oh! Brave November congregation
Accept these lines of commendation;
You are the Church's prop and wall,
You keep it standing for us all!
    And now I'll turn to things more bright.
I'll talk about electric light.
Last year when Mr Sidney Groves
Said he'd no longer do the stoves
It gave the chance to Mrs Camps
To say she would not do the lamps,
And that gave everyone the chance
To cry 'Well, let us have a dance!'
And so we did, we danced and danced

Until our funds were so advanced
That, helped by jumble sales and whist,
We felt that we could now insist
 – So healthy was the cash position –
On calling in the electrician.
We called him in and now, behold,
Our church is overlit and cold.
We have two hundred more to pay
Or go to gaol next Quarter Day.
    Despite the most impressive prices
Of our electrical devices,
And though the Bishop blessed the switches
Which now deface two ancient niches,
We do not like the electric light,
It's far too hard and bare and bright.
As for the heat, the bills are hot.
Unluckily the heating's not.
    They fell'd our elms to bring the wire,
They clamped their brackets on the spire
So that the church, one has to own,
Seems to be on the telephone.
Inside, they used our timbered roof,
Five centuries old and weather proof,
For part of their floodlighting scheme,
With surgical basins on each beam.
And if the bulbs in them should fuse
Or burst in fragments on the pews,
The longest ladder we possess
Would not reach up to mend the mess.
Talking of messes – you should see
The Electrician's artistry,
His Clapham-Junction-like creation
Of pipes and wires and insulation
Of meters, boxes, tubes and all
Upon our ancient painted wall.
    If Sidney Groves and Mrs Camps

Had only done the stoves and lamps
These shameful things we would not see
Which rob our church of mystery.

Cathedral Builders

JOHN ORMOND

Another from Peter Jeffrey's rich haul, this meticulous poem illustrates vividly all the dreams one has ever had, while looking up at the towers of Lincoln, or Canterbury, or wherever, and wondering, 'How did they do it?' The poem makes one thing abundantly clear: it took years and years and years.

Besides writing poems of great eloquence, John Ormond made documentary films about Welsh painters and writers for BBC Wales. He died in 1990.

They climbed on sketchy ladders towards God,
With winch and pulley hoisted hewn rock into heaven,
Inhabited sky with hammers, defied gravity,
Deified stone, took up God's house to meet Him,

And came down to their suppers and small beer;
Every night slept, lay with their smelly wives,
Quarrelled and cuffed the children, lied,
Spat, sang, were happy or unhappy,

And every day took to the ladders again;
Impeded the rights of way of another summer's
Swallows; grew greyer, shakier, became less inclined
To fix a neighbour's roof of a fine evening,

Saw naves sprout arches, clerestories soar,
Cursed the loud fancy glaziers for their luck,
Somehow escaped the plague, got rheumatism,
Decided it was time to give it up,

To leave the spire to others; and stood in the crowd
Well back from the vestments at the consecration,
Envied the fat bishop his warm boots,
Cocked up a squint eye and said, 'I bloody did that.'

From *The Towers of Trebizond*

ROSE MACAULAY

A brilliant summary of the plusses and minusses of the Christian
Church, this excerpt is as apt today as ever it was; and it applies
to all other religions and their dogmas with an equal, or even
greater, force.

Note: 'Obscurantism,' in the final sentence, means 'disincli-
nation to explain or reform,' and the emphasis is on the third
syllable.

Many people are troubled by the quarrels and the wars and
the rivalries that raged for centuries round the Holy Sepulchre, between different sets of Christians; my mother, for
instance, thought all this was a dreadful pity and disgrace,
and that the whole history of the Christian Church was
pretty shocking. Of course from one point of view she
was right about the Church, which grew so far, almost at
once, from anything which can have been intended, and
became so blood-stained and persecuting and cruel and war-
like and made small and trivial things so important, and tried
to exclude everything not done in a certain way and by
certain people, and stamped out heresies with such cruelty
and rage. And this failure of the Christian Church, of every
branch of it in every country, is one of the saddest things
that has happened in all the world. But it is what happens
when a magnificent idea has to be worked out by human
beings who do not understand much of it but interpret it in
their own way and think they are guided by God, whom they
have not yet grasped. And yet they had grasped something, so

that the Church has always had great magnificence and much courage, and people have died for it in agony, which is supposed to balance all the other people who have had to die in agony because they did not accept it, and it has flowered up in learning and culture and beauty and art, to set against its darkness and incivility and obscurantism and barbarity and nonsense, and it has produced saints and martyrs and kindness and goodness, though these have also occurred freely outside it, and it is a wonderful and most extraordinary pageant of contradictions, and I, at least, want to be inside it, though it is foolishness to most of my friends.

The Holy Well

ANONYMOUS

This sweet old poem works best when taken at a brisk pace. Not
rushed, but certainly not slow.

> As it fell out one May morning,
>   And upon one bright holiday,
> Sweet Jesus asked of his dear mother,
>   If he might go to play.
>
> 'To play, to play, sweet Jesus shall go,
>   And to play pray get you gone;
> And let me hear of no complaint
>   At night when you come home.'
>
> Sweet Jesus went down to yonder town,
>   As far as the Holy Well,
> And there did see as fine children
>   As any tongue can tell.
>
> He said, 'God bless you every one,
>   And your bodies Christ save and see:
> Little children, shall I play with you,
>   And you shall play with me?'
>
> But they made answer to him, 'No:
>   They were lords and ladies all;
> And he was but a maiden's child,
>   Born in an ox's stall.'

Sweet Jesus turned him around,
And he neither laughed nor smiled,
But the tears came trickling from his eyes
To be but a maiden's child.

Sweet Jesus turned him about,
To his mother's dear home went he,
And said, 'I have been in yonder town,
As far as you can see.

'I have been down in yonder town
As far as the Holy Well,
There did I meet as fine children
As any tongue can tell.

'I bid God bless them every one,
And their bodies Christ save and see:
Little children, shall I play with you,
And you shall play with me?

'But they made answer to me, No:
They were lords and ladies all;
And I was but a maiden's child,
Born in an ox's stall.' —

'Though you are but a maiden's child,
Born in an ox's stall,
Thou art the Christ, the King of heaven,
And the Saviour of them all.

'Sweet Jesus, go down to yonder town
As far as the Holy Well,
And take away those sinful souls,
And dip them deep in hell.'

'Nay, nay,' sweet Jesus said,
'Nay, nay, that may not be;
For there are too many sinful souls
Crying out for the help of me.'

Fidele's Grassy Tomb

SIR HENRY NEWBOLT

Another from Peter Jeffrey, this surprisingly conversational and easy story needs clear shaping, with new starts for new paragraphs, as at the beginnings of the fourth, sixth, seventh, tenth and thirteenth stanzas. Then it just seems to flow along.

Peter Newbolt, Sir Henry's grandson, told me that the story is a true one. Orchardleigh was a very grand house, now much altered, near Frome, in Somerset. In the grounds is a lake with an island in the middle where the church still stands. Sir Henry and Lady Newbolt are buried there.

Note: Peter Jeffrey pronounces the dog's name Fīday′lӳ, but apparently Sir Henry said Fīdē′lӳ.

The Squire sat propped in a pillowed chair,
His eyes were alive and clear of care,
But well he knew that the hour was come
To bid good-bye to his ancient home.

He looked on garden, wood, and hill,
He looked on the lake, sunny and still:
The last of earth that his eyes could see
Was the island church of Orchardleigh.

The last that his heart could understand
Was the touch of the tongue that licked his hand:
'Bury the dog at my feet', he said,
And his voice dropped, and the Squire was dead.

Now the dog was a hound of the Danish breed,

228

Staunch to love and strong at need:
He had dragged his master safe to shore
When the tide was ebbing at Elsinore.

From that day forth, as reason would,
He was named 'Fidele', and made it good:
When the last of the mourners left the door
Fidele was dead on the chantry floor.

They buried him there at his master's feet,
And all that heard of it deemed it meet:
The story went the round for years,
Till it came at last to the Bishop's ears.

Bishop of Bath and Wells was he,
Lord of the lords of Orchardleigh;
And he wrote to the Parson the strongest screed
That Bishop may write or Parson read.

The sum of it was that a soulless hound
Was known to be buried in hallowed ground:
From scandal sore the Church to save
They must take the dog from his master's grave.

The heir was far in a foreign land,
The Parson was wax to my Lord's command:
He sent for the Sexton and bade him make
A lonely grave by the shore of the lake.

The Sexton sat by the water's brink
Where he used to sit when he used to think:
He reasoned slow, but he reasoned it out,
And his argument left him free from doubt.

'A Bishop', he said, 'is the top of his trade;
But there's others can give him a start with the spade:
Yon dog, he carried the Squire ashore,
And a Christian couldn't ha' done no more.'

The grave was dug; the mason came

And carved on stone Fidele's name;
But the dog that the Sexton laid inside
Was a dog that never had lived or died.

So the Parson was praised, and the scandal stayed,
Till, a long time after, the church decayed,
And, laying the floor anew, they found
In the tomb of the Squire the bones of a hound.

As for the Bishop of Bath and Wells
No more of him the story tells;
Doubtless he lived as a Prelate and Prince,
And died and was buried a century since.

And whether his view was right or wrong
Has little to do with this my song;
Something we owe him, you must allow;
And perhaps he has changed his mind by now.

The Squire in the family chantry sleeps,
The marble still his memory keeps:
Remember, when the name you spell,
There rest Fidele's bones as well.

For the Sexton's grave you need not search,
'Tis a nameless mound by the island church:
An ignorant fellow, of humble lot —
But he knew one thing that a Bishop did not.

From *The Book of Daniel*
CHAPTER 3

This ringing story of the burning fiery furnace, with King Nebu-chadnezzar as ferociously violent at the end of it as he is at the beginning, though with the boot on the other foot, is a perfect party piece, and I am indebted to Alec McOwen for suggesting it. It's one of his favourites and no wonder: the repeated lists of dignitaries and musical instruments and names give it a most awesome, ceremonial grandeur. Charles Laughton loved it, too: but, says Alec, 'it must be the Authorised Version.'

So be it.

Here are just a few notes:

1. 'Cubit': approximately eighteen inches, originally the length of the forearm, from the elbow to the tip of the middle finger.
2. 'The province of Babylon': the great valley of the Rivers Euphrates and Tigris, known also as the Land of the Chaldees, and more or less equivalent to present-day Iraq. Babylon was sixty miles south of Baghdad.
3. 'Sackbut': a stringed instrument of the harp family.
4. 'Psaltery': a stringed instrument like a zither, played by plucking with the fingers or a plectrum.
5. 'Astonied': archaic for astonished.

Nebuchadnezzar the king made an image of gold, whose height was three-score cubits, and the breadth thereof six cubits: he set it up in the plain of Dura, in the province of Babylon. Then Nebuchadnezzar the king sent to gather together the princes, the governors, and the captains, the judges, the treasurers, the counsellors, the sheriffs, and all the rulers of the provinces, to come to the dedication of the image which Nebuchadnezzar the king had set up. Then the princes, the governors, and captains, the judges, the treasurers, the counsellors, the sheriffs, and all the rulers of the provinces, were gathered together unto the dedication of the image that Nebuchadnezzar the king had set up; and they stood before the image that Nebuchadnezzar had set up.

Then an herald cried aloud, To you it is commanded, O people, nations, and languages, that at what time ye hear the sound of the cornet, flute, harp, sackbut, psaltery, dulcimer, and all kinds of musick, ye fall down and worship the golden image that Nebuchadnezzar the king hath set up: And whoso falleth not down and worshippeth shall the same hour be cast into the midst of a burning fiery furnace. Therefore at that time, when all the people heard the sound of the cornet, flute, harp, sackbut, psaltery, and all kinds of musick, all the people, the nations, and the languages, fell down and worshipped the golden image that Nebuchadnezzar the king had set up.

Wherefore at that time certain Chaldeans came near, and accused the Jews. They spake and said to the king Nebuchadnezzar, O king, love for ever. Thou, O king, hast made a decree, that every man that shall hear the sound of the cornet, flute, harp, sackbut, psaltery, and dulcimer, and all kinds of musick, shall fall down and worship the golden image: And whoso falleth not down and worshippeth, that he should be cast into the midst of a burning fiery furnace. There are certain Jews whom thou hast set over the affairs of the province of Babylon, Shadrach, Meshach, and Abed-nego; these men, O king, have not regarded thee: they serve not thy gods, nor worship the golden image which thou hast set up.

Then Nebuchadnezzar in his rage and fury commanded to bring Shadrach, Meshach, and Abed-nego. Then they brought these men before the king. Nebuchadnezzar spake and said unto them, Is it true, O Shadrach, Meshach, and Abed-nego, do not ye serve my gods, nor worship the golden image which I have set up? Now if ye be ready that at what time ye hear the sound of the cornet, flute, harp, sackbut, psaltery, and dulcimer, and all kinds of musick, ye fall down and worship the image which I have made; well: but if ye worship not, ye shall be cast the same hour into the midst of a burning fiery furnace; and who is that God that shall deliver you out of my hands? Shadrach, Meshach, and Abed-nego, answered and said to the king, O Nebuchadnezzar, we are not careful to answer thee in this matter. If it be so, our God whom we serve is able to deliver us from the burning fiery furnace, and he will deliver us out of thine hand, O king. But if not, be it known unto thee, O king, that we will not serve thy gods, nor worship the golden image which thou hast set up.

Then was Nebuchadnezzar full of fury, and the form of his visage was changed against Shadrach, Meshach, and Abed-nego: therefore he spake, and commanded that they should heat the furnace one seven times more than it was wont to be heated. And he commanded the most mighty men that were in his army to bind Shadrach, Meshach, and Abed-nego, and to cast them into the burning fiery furnace. Then these men were bound in their coats, their hosen, and their hats, and their other garments, and were cast into the midst of the burning fiery furnace. Therefore because the king's commandment was urgent, and the furnace exceeding hot, the flames of the fire slew those men that took up Shadrach, Meshach, and Abed-nego. And these three men, Shadrach, Meshach, and Abed-nego, fell down bound into the midst of the burning fiery furnace.

Then Nebuchadnezzar the king was astonied, and rose up in haste, and spake, and said unto his counsellors, Did not we cast three men bound into the midst of the fire? They answered and said unto the king, True, O king. He answered and said, Lo, I see four men loose, walking in the midst of the fire, and they have no hurt; and the form of the fourth is like the Son of God.

Then Nebuchadnezzar came near to the mouth of the burning fiery furnace, and spake, and said, Shadrach, Meshach, and Abed-nego, ye servants of the most high God, come forth, and come hither. Then Shadrach, Meshach, and Abed-nego, came forth of the midst of the fire. And the princes, governors, and captains, and the king's counsellors, being gathered together, saw these men, upon whose bodies the fire had no power, nor was an hair of their head singed, neither were their coats changed, nor the smell of fire had passed on them.

Then Nebuchadnezzar spake, and said, Blessed be the God of Shadrach, Meshach, and Abed-nego, who hath sent his angel, and delivered his servants that trusted in him, and have changed the king's word, and yielded their bodies, that they might not serve nor worship any god, except their own God. Therefore I make a decree, That every people, nation, and language, which speak any thing amiss against the God of Shadrach, Meshach, and Abed-nego, shall be cut in pieces, and their houses shall be made a dunghill: because there is no other God that can deliver after this sort. Then the king promoted Shadrach, Meshach, and Abed-nego, in the province of Babylon.

Sinner and Saint

G. A. STUDDERT KENNEDY

Subtitled 'A Sermon in a Billet,' this is another Woodbine Willie
poem sent to me by Alan Burroughs.
Note: 'A daisy to scrap' means 'a first-class fighter'.

> Our Padre, 'e says I'm a sinner,
>   And John Bull says I'm a saint,
> And they're both of 'em bound to be liars,
>   For I'm neither of them, I ain't.
> I'm a man, and a man's a mixture,
>   Right down from 'is very birth,
> For part ov 'im comes from 'eaven,
>   And part ov 'im comes from earth.
> There's nothing in man that's perfect,
>   And nothing that's all complete;
> E's nubbat a big beginning,
>   From 'is 'ead to the soles of 'is feet.
> There's summat as draws 'im uppards,
>   And summat as drags 'im down,
> And the consekence is, 'e wobbles,
>   'Twixt muck and a golden crown.
> Ye remember old Billy Buggins,
>   That sargint what lorst 'is stripes?
> Well, 'e were a bloomin' 'ero,
>   A daisy to scrap, but cripes!
> That bloke were a blinkin' mixture,
>   Of all that were good and bad,
> For 'e fairly broke 'is mother's 'eart,

The best friend ever 'e 'ad.
But 'e died at Loos to save a pal,
  And that were the other side;
'E killed 'is mother and saved 'is pal,
  That's 'ow 'e lived and died.
And that's 'ow it is, it's 'uman,
  It's 'eaven and 'ell in one.
There's the 'ell of a scrap in the 'eart of a man,
  And that scrap's never done.
The Good and the Bad's at war, ye see,
  Same as us boys and the Boche,
And when both gets goin' with all their guns,
  There's the Saturday night of a squash.
And it's just the same wi' the nations,
  As it is wi' a single man,
There's 'eaven and 'ell in their vitals,
  A scrappin' as 'ard as they can.
And England, she 'as it in 'er,
  Just same as all o' the rest,
Old England same as us Englishmen,
  A mixture o' bad and best.
And that's what I reckon these parsons mean
  Wi' their Mission o' 'Pentance and 'Ope,
They want us to wash old England's face clean,
  Wi' the grace of Gawd for soap.
And it ain't a bad stunt neither,
  For England she oughter be clean,
For the sake of the boys what 'ave fought and died
  And their kiddies as might 'a' been.
We can't let it be for nothin'
  That our pals 'ave fought and bled,
So, lads, let's look to this washin' up
  For the sake o' Christ — and our dead.

Paterfamilias

PHYLLIS McGINLEY

Another poem from *The Love Letters of Phyllis McGinley,* this potted history of Saint Thomas More was sent to me by Michael Mayne.

At first More was greatly favoured by Henry VIII and was given many important political posts, including Speaker of the House of Commons. He was knighted in 1521 and later became Lord Chancellor. However, as a devout Roman Catholic he could not support Henry's breakaway from Rome, and was imprisoned in the Tower of London and executed in 1535. He was canonised in 1935.

Notes:

1. Desiderius Erasmus was for a time the Lady Margaret Professor of Divinity at Cambridge. He called his friend More 'the English Socrates'.
2. William Lily was the first High Master of St Paul's School.
3. William Roper was married to Margaret, one of More's three daughters.

> Of all the saints who have won their charter –
> Holy man, hero, hermit, martyr,
> Mystic, missioner, sage, or wit –
> Saint Thomas More is my favourite.
> For he loved these bounties with might and main:
> God and his house and his little wife, Jane,
> And four fair children his heart throve on,
> Margaret, Elizabeth, Cecily, and John.
>
> That More was a good man everybody knows.

He sang good verses and he wrote good prose,
Enjoyed a good caper and liked a good meal
And made a good Master of the Privy Seal.
A friend to Erasmus, Lily's friend,
He lived a good life and he had a good end
And left good counsel for them to con,
Margaret, Elizabeth, Cecily, and John.

Some saints are alien, hard to love,
Wild as an eagle, strange as a dove,
Too near to heaven for the mind to scan.
But Thomas More was a family man,
A husband, a courtier, a doer and a hoper
(Admired of his son-in-law, Mr Roper),
Who punned in Latin like a Cambridge don
With Margaret, Elizabeth, Cecily, and John.

It was less old Henry than Anne Boleyn
Haled him to the Tower and locked him in.
But even in the Tower he saw things brightly.
He spoke to his jailers most politely,
And while the sorrowers turned their backs
He rallied the headsman who held the axe,
Then blessed, with the blessing of Thomas More,
God and his garden and his children four.

And I fear they missed him when he was gone –
Margaret, Elizabeth, Cecily, and John.

Do I Believe

NOËL COWARD

If ever a poem was made to sound like talking, to sound like thinking it out and, even with its sassy rhymes and rhythms, not at all like a reading, this is it.

Do I believe in God?
Well yes, I suppose, in a sort of way.
It's really terribly hard to say.
I'm sure that there must be of course
Some kind of vital, motive force,
Some power that holds the winning cards
Behind life's ambiguous façades
But whether you think me odd or not
I can't decide if it's God or not.

I look at the changing sea and sky
And try to picture Eternity
I gaze at immensities of blue
And say to myself 'It can't be true
That somewhere up in that abstract sphere
Are all the people who once were here
Attired in white and shapeless gowns
Sitting on clouds like eiderdowns
Plucking at harps and twanging lutes
With cherubim in their birthday suits,
Set in an ageless, timeless dream
Part of a formulated scheme
Formulated before the Flood

Before the amoeba left the mud
And, stranded upon a rocky shelf
Proceeded to sub-divide itself.'

I look at the changing sea and sky
And try to picture Infinity
I gaze at a multitude of stars
Envisaging the men on Mars
Wondering if they too are torn
Between their sunset and their dawn
By dreadful, night-engendered fears
Of what may lie beyond their years
And if they too, through thick and thin,
Are dogged by consciousness of Sin.
Have they, to give them self-reliance,
A form of Martian Christian Science?
Or do they live in constant hope
Of dispensations from some Pope?

Are they pursued from womb to tomb
By hideous prophecies of doom?
Have they cathedral, church or chapel
Are they concerned with Adam's apple?
Have they immortal souls like us
Or are they less presumptuous?

Do I believe in God?
I can't say No and I can't say Yes
To me it's anybody's guess
Buf if all's true that we once were told
Before we grew wise and sad and old
When finally Death rolls up our eyes
We'll find we're in for a big surprise.

Miracles

WALT WHITMAN

This rhapsody, which affects audiences greatly, can be taken
thoughtfully, at a most leisurely speed.

Note: 'The whole referring' means 'they are all part of the
whole thing.'

Why, who makes much of a miracle?
As to me I know of nothing else but miracles,
Whether I walk the streets of Manhattan,
Or dart my sight over the roofs of houses toward the sky,
Or wade with naked feet along the beach just in the edge of
the water,
Or stand under trees in the woods,
Or talk by day with any one I love, or sleep in the bed at
night with any one I love,
Or sit at table at dinner with the rest,
Or look at strangers opposite me riding in the car,
Or watch honey-bees busy around the hive of a summer
fore-noon,
Or animals feeding in the fields,
Or birds, or the wonderfulness of insects in the air,
Or the wonderfulness of the sundown, or of stars shining so
quiet and bright,
Or the exquisite delicate thin curve of the new moon in
spring;
These with the rest, one and all, are to me miracles,
The whole referring, yet each distinct and in its place.
To me every hour of the light and dark is a miracle,

Every cubic inch of space is a miracle,
Every square yard of the surface of the earth is spread with
the same,
Every foot of the interior swarms with the same.

To me the sea is a continual miracle,
The fishes that swim – the rocks – the motion of the waves
– the ships with men in them,
What stranger miracles are there?

Ithaca

C. P. CAVAFY

The Lestrygonians (cannibals), the Cyclopes (savage one-eyed giants) and the angry Poseidon (god of the sea) impeded the path of Odysseus as he journeyed back to his native Ithaca, a Greek island in the Ionian Sea. Many followers were killed and many ships were sunk. But eventually he arrived.

For Cavafy, Ithaca becomes a goal of life, a Heaven, a Mecca, a Jerusalem, a Trebizond: whatever you like to call it. The importance of having such a goal is the journey it imposes on you: it is the journey, not the arrival, that matters. We are all voyagers, we all face perils; but there are many pleasures along the way and we should make the most of them.

This remarkable poem is worth explaining a little to an audience: they can then follow its argument with an easier delight. Tricia Eddington, Paul's widow, chose it for his memorial service, where it was movingly read by Dorothy Tutin.

Constantin Cavafy was born in Alexandria in 1863, and spent the greater part of his life there. He died in 1933. The translator is Rae Dalven.

Note: 'Cyclopes' is pronounced sī'klōpēz.

When you start on your journey to Ithaca,
then pray that the road is long,
full of adventure, full of knowledge.
Do not fear the Lestrygonians
and the Cyclopes and the angry Poseidon.
You will never meet such as these on your path,
if your thoughts remain lofty, if a fine

emotion touches your body and your spirit.
You will never meet the Lestrygonians,
the Cyclopes and the fierce Poseidon,
if you do not carry them within your soul,
if your soul does not raise them up before you.

Then pray that the road is long.
That the summer mornings are many,
that you will enter ports seen for the first time
with such pleasure, with such joy!
Stop at Phoenician markets,
and purchase fine merchandise,
mother-of-pearl and corals, amber and ebony,
and pleasurable perfumes of all kinds,
buy as many pleasurable perfumes as you can;
visit hosts of Egyptian cities,
to learn and learn from those who have knowledge.

Always keep Ithaca fixed in your mind.
To arrive there is your ultimate goal.
But do not hurry the voyage at all.
It is better to let it last for long years;
and even to anchor at the isle when you are old,
rich with all that you have gained on the way,
not expecting that Ithaca will offer you riches.

Ithaca has given you the beautiful voyage.
Without her you would never have taken the road.
But she has nothing more to give you.

And if you find her poor, Ithaca has not defrauded you.
With the great wisdom you have gained, with so much
    experience,
you must surely have understood by then what Ithacas mean.

How Long, O Lord . . .?

KEITH WATERHOUSE

It was Simon Williams who gave me a shortened and much altered version of this piece. He said it was a great favourite with his late mother-in-law, Celia Johnson. She had read it in the BBC radio programme, *With Great Pleasure*, but hadn't been able to trace its authorship, so she called it Anonymous; Simon later discovered it was by Keith Waterhouse, who has very kindly sent me this original, complete and 'authorised version', as he calls it. 'It started life in a newspaper column, then became a poster, and is the only piece of mine which has ever been reproduced on a tea towel,' he said. It is now in his book, *Waterhouse at Large*.

And God said unto Noah, Make thee an ark of gopher wood; rooms shalt thou make in the ark, and the length of the ark shall be 300 cubits.

And of every living thing of all flesh, two of every sort shalt thou bring into the ark, to keep them alive with thee.

And Noah said, Sign here, and leavest Thou a deposit.

And the Lord signed there, and left He a deposit.

And Noah was 600 years old when the flood of waters was upon the Earth.

And the Lord said unto Noah, Where is the ark, which I commanded thee to build?

And Noah said unto the Lord, Verily, I have had three carpenters off ill.

The gopher wood supplier hath let me down – yea, even though the gopher wood hath been on order for nigh upon

245

twelve months. The damp-course specialist hath not turned up. What can I do, O lord?

And God said unto Noah, I want that ark finished even after seven days and seven nights.

And Noah said, It will be so.

And it was not so.

And the Lord said unto Noah, What seemeth to be the trouble this time?

And Noah said unto the Lord, Mine sub-contractor hath gone bankrupt. The pitch which Thou commandest me to put on the outside and on the inside of the ark hath not arrived. The plumber hath gone on strike.

Noah rent his garments and said, The glazier departeth on holiday to Majorca – yea, even though I offerest him double time. Shem, my son, who helpeth me on the ark side of the business, hath formed a pop group with his brothers Ham and Japheth. Lord, I am undone.

And God said in his wrath, Noah, do not thou mucketh Me about.

The end of all flesh is come before me; for the Earth is filled with violence through them; and behold, I will destroy them with the Earth. How can I destroy them with the Earth if thou art incapable of completing the job that thou wert contracted to do?

And Noah said, Lo, the contract will be fulfilled.

And Lo, it was not fulfilled.

And Noah said unto the Lord, The gopher wood is definitely in the warehouse. Verily, and the gopher wood supplier waiteth only upon his servant to find the invoices before he delivereth the gopher wood unto me.

And the Lord grew angry and said, Scrubbeth thou round the gopher wood. What about the animals?

Of fowls after their kind, and of cattle after their kind, of every creeping thing of the Earth after his kind, two of every sort have I ordered to come unto thee, to keep them alive.

Where for example, are the giraffes?

And Noah said unto the Lord, They are expected today.

And the Lord said unto Noah, And where are the clean beasts, the male and the female; to keep their seed alive upon the face of all the Earth?

And Noah said, The van cometh on Tuesday; yea and yea, it will be so.

And the Lord said unto Noah, How about the unicorns?

And Noah wrung his hands and wept, saying, Lord, Lord, they are a discontinued line. Thou canst not get unicorns for love nor money.

And God said, Come thou, Noah, I have left with thee a deposit, and thou hast signed a contract.

Where are the monkeys, and the bears, and the hippopotami, and the elephants, and the zebras and the hartebeests, two of each kind; and of fowls also of the air by sevens, the male and the female?

And Noah said unto the Lord, They have been delivered unto the wrong address, but should arriveth on Friday; all save the fowls of the air by sevens, for it hath just been told unto me that fowls of the air are sold only in half-dozens.

And God said unto Noah, Thou hast not made an ark of gopher wood, nor hast thou lined it with pitch within and without; and of every living thing of all flesh, two of every sort hast thou failed to bring into the ark. What sayest thou, Noah?

And Noah kissed the Earth and said, Lord, Lord, thou knowest in thy wisdom what it is like with delivery dates.

And the Lord in his wisdom said, Noah, my son, I knowest. Why else dost thou think I have caused a flood to descend upon the Earth?

The Secret

RALPH SPAULDING CUSHMAN

A little serious for a concert, but the last two lines have a nice
ring to them, and it might come in useful for the right occasion.

> I met God in the morning
>   When my day was at its best,
> And His presence came like sunrise,
>   Like a glory in my breast.
>
> All day long the Presence lingered,
>   All day long He stayed with me,
> And we sailed in perfect calmness
>   O'er a very troubled sea.
>
> Other ships were blown and battered,
>   Other ships were sore distressed,
> But the winds that seemed to drive them
>   Brought to us a peace and rest.
>
> But I thought of other mornings,
>   With a keen remorse of mind,
> When I too had loosed the moorings,
>   With the Presence left behind.
>
> So I think I know the secret.
>   Learned from many a troubled way:
> You must seek Him in the morning
>   If you want Him through the day!

Charity Do's

The charity do's I have been to have invariably been run by good people determined to do the best they can in spite of insuperable problems. 'We can't have the hall until an hour before the concert, there aren't enough helpers to put out the stackable chairs, and the refreshments for the interval have only just arrived; the printers were late with the programmes and the raffle tickets haven't gone at all well.' They all sound exactly like poor Noah in Keith Waterhouse's piece.

But everyone works very hard and in spite of everything the evening is pronounced afterwards as having been a great success.

The amateurishness is endearing. The choir and a local tenor sing groups of songs, there is a speech of welcome at the beginning and a speech of thanks at the end. This small group of pieces starts with examples of two such speeches.

An Occasion of This Nature

MICHAEL FRAYN

I did this at a fund-raising concert organised by the Friends of the Royal Free Hospital in Hampstead, and I'm glad to say they raised rather more than the amount suggested here by Michael Frayn (though it has to be remembered that this piece was first performed by Eleanor Bron in 1972).

Fortunately it is long enough for you to cut bits of it if you think they don't apply either to the occasion or to the hall you happen to be in. I cut a few chunks of it, including the section about sandwiches in the heating vents; and I finished the last paragraph with 'I'm going to sit down and,' and then I introduced the next item. I've indicated the cuts I made with brackets.

The organiser of the concert thought it was 'hilarious', but said it made the speech of thanks she had to do at the end 'very difficult'.

There always, I'm afraid, comes the dread moment at an occasion of this nature when someone gets up on his or her hind legs and makes a speech. That moment has now come! I know that the last thing anyone here wants to do is to listen to a speech, just when everyone was enjoying themselves, and the last thing *I* want to do is to make a speech, believe me, but I do think that we cannot let an occasion of this nature go by without stopping for just a moment to say a few words about how worthwhile and enjoyable an occasion of this nature is. We all take things for granted only too easily – I know I do – and I think if no one took the trouble to just stand up for a moment and put it into words, we might just possibly all sit here and not realise quite what a worthwhile and enjoyable time we were in fact having.

It cannot, I think, be said too often that an occasion of this nature doesn't just happen of its own accord. Let's all have a good time and enjoy ourselves, by all means. But let's try to bear in mind as we do so all the hard work and long hours and personal sacrifice that have gone into it. [And I must just say here, before I forget, that Mr Pettigrew tells me there are still a great many tickets unsold for the Grand Lucky Draw. So can we all put our backs into it and make one last effort? There are some splendid prizes to be won, and anyway the prizes are not what counts. Oh yes, and would people *please* not put unwanted sandwiches or other matter into the heating vents? I know how easy it is for little fingers to do – perhaps even for fingers that *aren't* quite so little! – but getting small pieces of decaying fishpaste out again with knitting needles and surgical forceps, as we had to do last year, does waste a lot of the limited time available for committee meetings.]

I should just like to say a word of thanks to the many people involved in making today a success, [I'm sure that having their name mentioned was the last thing they had in mind in the first place, and they'll probably never forgive me, but I hope they'll forgive me if there are any names I forget to mention.]

First and foremost, of course, our heartiest thanks are due once again to Mrs Paramount. I'm sure I don't have to tell you that without Mrs Paramount an occasion of this nature simply could not take place. [This is, in a very special sense, her baby – and has been so ever since the late Lord Combermere on his death bed first planted the seed.

Our thanks are also due, in no less measure, to Mr Huddle for his unfailing cheerfulness, and his apparent readiness in emergencies to dash almost anywhere in the middle of the night, clad in old army boots and Manchester United scarf.]

And I should like to say a special word of thanks to Mr Hapforth, who came along here tonight against doctor's orders, and in spite of being in considerable pain. I think perhaps we might remember that when we see him struggling to entertain us all once again.

Last but not least I should like to thank all of you for coming along here today, and working so hard to enjoy the entertainment that all these good people have worked so hard to provide. It's particularly gratifying to see so many young faces. We often think of young people today as simply out for a good time. Well, that certainly can't be said of these young people. It's no less gratifying to see all the people here who aren't quite so young. I know how easy it is to think, 'Oh let someone else go out this time and get themselves entertained.' I must say, it's remarkable how an occasion of this nature seems to bring out the best in people. Everyone rallies round, and cheerfully tries to make the best of it. It's like the War all over again! I'd just like to say this: it's people like you who make an occasion of this nature the sort of occasion that it is. I'm sure you'll be pleased to hear that as a result of everyone's efforts today and over the past year we have raised the very gratifying total of £23.17.

Well you don't want to sit here listening to me talk, and I certainly don't want to stand here talking, so I'm going to sit down and [let Mr Dauntwater stand up and speak. Mr Dauntwater, I should explain, has kindly agreed at very short notice to make the speech thanking me for my speech. So, in the sudden but unavoidable absence of Mrs Hummer with gastric trouble, and to save time later on, I should just like if I might to thank Mr Dauntwater for his speech in advance. And thank you all for listening to me. And remember! Not in the heating vents!]

A Speech

JOYCE GRENFELL

This is No. 3 of 'Speeches' in her book *Turn Back the Clock*. She wrote, 'There are certain phrases that, when you hear them, strike dread in your heart. One of these is: "Do you mind if I say something?" And another is the patient lie: "I'm not going to make a speech"'.

Lady Clutch – Mr Mayor, Ladies and Gentlemen and Friends. I'm not going to make a speech but as the President of the Maisie Comley Whittaker Sunset Home Foundation Trust I know you will all want me on your behalfs – behalves – behalfs? – to thank Lady Clutch so, so much for so very kindly coming down at the very last moment and stepping into the breech, as it were, to rescue us from the abyss by opening the new wing for us today. (*Turns to her*) It is so, *so* kind of you and I can't tell you *how* grateful we are to you. We really are. It's quite wonderful. I can't tell you . . .

As you know we had hoped that Mr Fred of the Flybuttons Pop Group was to have opened the new wing for us but, alas, he has had to fly out to Helsinki to represent Great Britain at a Pop Festival and of course we wish him very well but we are so, *so* grateful to Lady Clutch for getting us out of a hole in this wonderful way.

Thank you so much.

There are a great many thank yous to be said today and we are particularly grateful to all those generous people who have given us of their old furniture, and *objets* and curtains that they no longer want in their own homes. I'm sure these are quite going to transform the new wing.

And Lady Clutch has not come empty-handed. She has brought with her what she very modestly describes as 'one of my poor little daubs'. But, at the risk of being rude and flatly contradicting her, I must say I think it is an enchanting impression, in oils, of a herbaceous border in full flower at the very height of its summer glory . . .

It's a football match?

How stupid of me.

Of course, it's *much* more fun that it should be a football match. Thank you so very much.

I must also thank Mrs Harding and her cohorts of willing helpers who have done such miracles to make today possible. They are entirely responsible for the delicious tea I'm sure we are all going to enjoy later. Thank you, Mrs Bude, Mrs Lumpley, Miss Cordle, Mrs G. Elphase, Mrs M. Elphase, Janice Bednick, Morwenna Hanks and Sister Bunn. Thank you all *so* much.

Now, I cannot pretend that we are not very disappointed that the new wing is not absolutely ready to be opened today, but we do congratulate the builders, Messrs Clutby and Son for very nearly having it ready. And we are so grateful that the recreation and TV lounge *is* very nearly ready – except for the glass in the windows, because where would we all be without it? I think none of us expected hail.

And I do have good news. Messrs Clutby and Son have promised that, when the first of the new residents arrive to move in next week, the stairs will be there.

From *A Letter of James*

CHAPTER 2, VERSES 14–26

Canon Geoffrey Brown, vicar of St Martin-in-the-Fields, asked me to read this at a thanksgiving service for a charity, at which he officiated. 'It is at the heart of what charity is all about,' I remember he said. This is *The New English Bible* translation.

My brothers, what use is it for a man to say he has faith when he does nothing to show it? Can that faith save him? Suppose a brother or sister is in rags with not enough food for the day, and one of you says, 'Good luck to you, keep yourselves warm, and have plenty to eat,' but does nothing to supply their bodily needs, what is the good of that? So with faith; if it does not lead to action, it is in itself a lifeless thing.

But someone may object: 'Here is one who claims to have faith and another who points to his deeds.' To which I reply: 'Prove to me that this faith you speak of is real though not accompanied by deeds, and by my deeds I will prove to you my faith.' You have faith enough to believe that there is one God. Excellent! The devils have faith like that, and it makes them tremble. But can you not see, you quibbler, that faith divorced from deeds is barren? Was it not by his action, in offering his son Isaac upon the altar, that our father Abraham was justified? Surely you can see that faith was at work in his actions, and that by these actions the integrity of his faith was fully proved. Here was fulfilment of the words of Scripture: 'Abraham put his faith in God, and that faith was counted to him as righteousness;' and elsewhere he is called 'God's friend.' You see then that a man is justified by deeds and not by faith in itself. The same is true of the prostitute Rahab also. Was not she justified by her action in welcoming the messengers into her house and sending them away by a different route? As the body is dead when there is no breath left in it, so faith divorced from deeds is lifeless as a corpse.

Blind Children

CHRISTOPHER FRY

Christopher Fry, whom I first met when I was in his play *The Dark is Light Enough* at the Aldwych Theatre in 1954, wrote a privately printed book called *Occasionally*, and he very kindly said I could have this poem and the following one in my similarly titled book. This one, he said, 'was written in October 1954 for *The Sight-Giver*, published by the Lavelle School for the Blind, New York.'

You are awake and playing in the dark.
　　So, in our way, are we.
Colour, clear as bells,
　　And light's wand altering
The morning world into the evening world
　　You cannot see. You only feel
The cool breath rising from the rose,
　　The warm sun resting on your brows.
And we, too, are blind
　　To visions deeper than the world
Which haunt us in the quiet of our mind.

For a Tree-Planting

CHRISTOPHER FRY

He introduces this poem thus: 'The Old Oak, at the bottom of Breakheart Hill in Ampthill Park, reputedly nearly a thousand years old, was dismembered and burnt in the winter of 1966–7. In 1826 the poet Samuel Rogers had written a celebratory poem which had been painted on a copper sheet and nailed to the tree's trunk. In 1987, twenty years after the tree's end, I was invited to write some verses for the planting of a young oak tree in its place.'

You, in the years to come, who see
The stir, the bud and burden of the tree,
The reach of boughs, the trunk's great girth,
Think then of us who put the roots in the earth,
Who set the slender wood, time going by,
To spread green wings and overtake the sky.

Whatever the manworld suffers or achieves
Between our day and yours, an answer of leaves
Will follow a winter question, spring after spring,
In the certain hope that April birds will sing.
And when the heavy foliage breathes with a giant's breath
Think how the hour of planting outlives the hour of death.

Musical Evenings

These pieces about music always go down well when you share a platform for an evening with musicians. The musicians themselves like it because it means you're joining in.

I always hope, at such evenings, that the singer or pianist or violinist or whoever will not want to do groups of pieces: 'And now, three songs by . . .' But they usually do. It's all right at a recital, when they are on their own, but at a shared concert it is curiously enervating: it means pauses, and a little bit of tuning, and changing the music. Why can't they just do one thing at a time? Keep the ball in the air?

At *The Four Seasons, But Not Vivaldi* concert I referred to in the Introduction the singers and I did one thing at a time and it really worked. There had been doubts about the frequent standing and sitting of the singers, but it really worked. 'It had pace,' someone said afterwards. 'It was like a conversation between you and the singers.'

Atheist's Hymn

ANONYMOUS

Robin Hawdon sent me this little-known poem which, he says,
'I have kept for many years.' It makes a lovely introduction to the
next piece of music in your shared concert.

> Lord, Lord, I don't believe in you,
> I only believe in me.
> Lord, your miracles I've never seen,
> Only your earth and sea.
> Lord, I know not your Heaven or Hell,
> Only those which burn in me.
> Lord, I wish to stand and shout from the hills,
> Not mutter on bended knee.
> Lord, Lord, I have only one prayer,
> Which I cry irreverently:
> Let me make music all my life long
> Which reminds men of thee.

Playing the Harmonium

F. P. HARTON

This letter, written to John Betjeman's wife, Penelope, by the rector of their local church near Wantage in Berkshire, was sent to me by Geoffrey Palmer. He had read it at a Platforms performance at the National Theatre years ago. The Reverend F. P. Harton went on to be the Very Reverend, and the Dean of Wells.

Baulking Vicarage

My dear Penelope,

I have been thinking over the question of the playing of the harmonium on Sunday evenings here and have reached the conclusion that I must now take it over myself.

I am very grateful to you for doing it for so long and hate to have to ask you to give it up, but, to put it plainly, your playing has got worse and worse and the disaccord between the harmonium and the congregation is become destructive of devotion. People are not very sensitive here, but even some of them have begun to complain, and they are not usually given to doing that. I do not like writing this, but I think you will understand that it is my business to see that divine worship is as perfect as it can be made. Perhaps the crankiness of the instrument has something to do with the trouble. I think it does require a careful and experienced player to deal with it.

Thank you ever so much for stepping so generously into the breach when Sibyl was ill; it was the greatest possible help to me and your results were noticeably better then than now.

Yours ever,
F. P. Harton

At a Recital

PAUL TORTELIER

This is another piece for which I am indebted to Canon Frank Wright. I read it, more than once, I remember, in his *Meditation* programmes for Granada Television. Much more recently I did it at a concert at the Royal Free Hospital, at which I shared the platform with the cellist Felix Schmidt and his pianist wife Annette Cole, so it was especially apt! Pau was Tortelier's wife, and the extract comes from his autobiography.

Pau and I gave a recital at Marlborough College in Wiltshire on a particularly pleasant autumn evening. Already during the Brahms E Minor Sonata, which opened the programme, I noticed a slight shadow that flickered from time to time across the brightly lit floor. And when I began playing my own Cello Sonata I was aware of something coming towards me from above, and then floating away again. It was there, and yet not there, like an apparition. While playing, I had little time to give my attention to it, but by the time I reached the middle movement of my sonata I was able to identify my mysterious stage companion. It was a butterfly – a beautifully coloured, rather big butterfly. It began to circle around me and, as it did so, it seemed almost to be tracing arabesques to the music I was playing, its wings moving in harmony with my bow.

The audience's attention had now been drawn to this wholly unrehearsed ballet. Closer and closer the butterfly would come, almost touch me, and then fly away. It was having a flirtation with me, or perhaps I with it. The slow movement of my sonata concludes quietly on a sustained harmonic. At that moment I closed my eyes, my bow barely moving on the string. I did not want to disturb the atmosphere of peace and calm. As I slowly drew the note to an end I opened my eyes again and there, perched on my left hand, was the butterfly. It had alighted so gently that I hadn't felt its presence. For a moment or two we looked at each other. It didn't move; I didn't move. It was so lovely, so ethereal, that I couldn't bring myself to shake it off. It had chosen the ideal moment for repose, I thought, settling there at the end of the slow movement; it seemed not to want to fly away. What could I do? Almost without thinking, I slowly brought my hand, with the butterfly still perched on it, up to my lips. I was sure it would fly away, but it didn't. I kissed it very tenderly, but it still didn't move. Not everyone has been able to kiss a butterfly. I never thought I would do so, least of all on the concert stage. Finally I shook my hand very gently, and it floated off into the air. That was just before the interval. After the interval we played Beethoven's A Major Sonata, and there was the butterfly again, dancing all the way through, only coming down to rest from time to time on Pau's music, as if wanting to have a look at what she was doing. The piece came to an end and the butterfly was nowhere to be seen. 'Aha,' I thought, 'it has left us to join the other butterflies in the fields.' Not at all. It was perched on my foot, and as the audience applauded it flapped its wings.

Who can judge what forces of spirit or nature guide our actions and bring harmony to seemingly disparate things? Such forces are there, that's all I need know. The audience that day knew it also. We had all lived a fairy tale.

From *Full Circle*

JANET BAKER

Dame Janet Baker kept a journal during her last year as an opera singer. Her final performance, in Gluck's *Orfeo* at Glyndebourne, was in the summer of 1982. From now on she was going to concentrate on the concert platform.

I heard her sing Mahler's *Das Lied von der Erde* at a Prom the following year, and I remember thinking that she was one of the few singers who made singing sound as natural as talking. In this revealing journal she wrote, 'I put my "all" into theatre work; I put the same "all" into the concert platform, and although to the outward eye the singer is only standing there, the process is just as demanding in a different way as an opera, if not more so. Performers come and go. The music is what matters – the music is for always.'

Saturday 5 December
If someone asked if my career has been 'worth it', in other words worth the sacrifices made by me and members of my family, worth the separations, the agony of performing, of trying to keep perfectly fit, the undying battle against nerves, the strains and pitfalls of being a public figure, my honest answer would have to be 'No'.

This sounds a terrible comment to make on a career which, in terms of the world, has been a highly successful one. I have done everything any singer could dream of, yet the moments when the musical rewards have equalled the price one has to pay for them have been few.

But if someone were to ask me how I would choose to

be born in order to learn about life, I would unquestionably reply, 'As an artist.' If it is, as many people suggest, a rather special privilege to be born one, the privilege lies in the opportunities such an existence provides for the individual to learn about himself; in the questions artistic life forces one to ask and try to answer; in the struggle to come to terms with performing and everything implied by an act of heroism, which demands the baring of the soul before strangers, and public judgement of this act; in the choices to be made as a result of loving something more than oneself and serving that something with the greatest integrity one is capable of. Yes, in these terms, my career *has* been 'worth it', a thousand times over. I am lucky to be born with one outstanding talent; it makes the direction of my life clearer; but I do sincerely believe that every human being is an 'artist' in the sense that everyone can make of his life a 'work of art', it all depends on the way we look at so-called 'ordinary' things. The ideal of Zen Buddhism is to make every single action a perfect meditation and this is exactly what I mean.

It has always intrigued me in the Parable of the Talents that the man with ten (the greatly gifted) and the man with five (the gifted in a diverse way) end up with *exactly* the same reward. The man with one talent would have received just what the other two did if he hadn't been such a clot.

Whatever our ambitions are, they surely all add up to the desire for happiness and fulfilment. It may even be easier to have both these qualities living the life of an 'ordinary' person because success has its own problems; but regardless of the responsibility caused by a gift, in my case, a voice, I thank God on my bended knees that I *am* an artist.

From *Duet For One*

TOM KEMPINSKI

I still think of *Duet for One* as one of the most affecting plays I have ever seen. I went many times and wept many times. The performances by Frances de la Tour as Stephanie, a violinist who developed multiple sclerosis, and David de Keyser as Dr Feldmann, a German psychiatrist whom she visits for help, were astounding in their depth and spontaneity.

Stephanie (*slowly at first*) Well – music. (*Pause*) Music. Music, Dr Feldmann, is the purest expression of humanity that there is. Because, you see, it's magic; but real magic, true mystery, not trickery. You can say it is sound, as speech is sound, as bird-song is sound, but it isn't. It's itself. A piece of music which expresses pain or sorrow, or loneliness, it sounds nothing like what a lonely man says or does, but it expresses it, and even better than the person does. Magic. You see, there's no God, you know, Dr Feldmann, but I know where they got the idea; they got it from music. It is a kind of heaven. It's unearthly. It lifts you out of life to another place. That was my prize, that's what I won.

Lunches and Dinners

Many other pieces in this book could be appropriate for reading at a formal lunch or dinner, depending on its purpose. These, however, get straight to the point.

From *A Room of One's Own*

VIRGINIA WOOLF

Published in 1929, *A Room of One's Own* was based on a series of lectures Virginia Woolf had given at Girton College, Cambridge, the previous year. Her audience, of 'starved but valiant young women,' heard of their need for independence, money and a room of their own, to enable them to function and write properly. 'Feminist propaganda,' wrote Desmond MacCarthy in *The Sunday Times*. The extract here is about a lunch hosted by George Rylands, on October 21, 1928, in his rooms at King's College, Cambridge. Leonard Woolf, Maynard Keynes and Lytton Strachey were also there.

Note: 'We are all going to heaven and Vandyck is of the company,' were the dying words of Sir Thomas Gainsborough. They were uttered to Sir Joshua Reynolds as part of a final reconciliation between the two men.

It is a curious fact that novelists have a way of making us believe that luncheon parties are invariably memorable for something very witty that was said, or for something very wise that was done. But they seldom spare a word for what was eaten. It is part of the novelist's convention not to mention soup and salmon and ducklings, as if soup and salmon and ducklings were of no importance whatsoever, as if nobody ever smoked a cigar or drank a glass of wine. Here, however, I shall take the liberty to defy that convention and to tell you that the lunch on this occasion began with soles, sunk in a deep dish, over which the college cook had spread a counterpane of the whitest cream, save that it was branded here and there with brown spots like the spots on the flanks of a doe. After that came the partridges, but if this suggests a couple of bald, brown birds on a plate you are mistaken. The partridges, many and various, came with all their retinue of sauces and salads, the sharp and the sweet, each in its order; their potatoes, thin as coins but not so hard; their sprouts, foliated as rosebuds but more succulent. And no sooner had the roast and its retinue been done with than the silent serving-man, the Beadle himself perhaps in a milder manifestation, set before us, wreathed in napkins, a confection which rose all sugar from the waves. To call it pudding and so relate it to rice and tapioca would be an insult. Meanwhile the wineglasses had flushed yellow and flushed crimson; had been emptied; had been filled. And thus by degrees was lit, half-way down the spine, which is the seat of the soul, not that hard little electric light which we call brilliance, as it pops in and out upon our lips, but the more profound, subtle and subterranean glow which is the rich yellow flame of rational intercourse. No need to hurry. No need to sparkle. No need to be anybody but oneself. We are all going to heaven and Vandyck is of the company — in other words, how good life seemed, how sweet its rewards, how trivial this grudge or that grievance, how admirable friendship and the society of one's kind, as, lighting a good cigarette, one sunk among the cushions in the window-seat.

Advertisement

WENDY COPE

If you are speaking at a lunch or dinner this poem, by one of the
wittiest of writers, might well come in useful. It is from her first
book of poems and parodies, published in 1986, *Making Cocoa for
Kingsley Amis*.

> The lady takes *The Times* and *Vogue*,
> Wears Dior dresses, Gucci shoes,
> Puts fresh-cut flowers round her room
> And lots of carrots in her stews.
>
> A moss-green Volvo, morning walks,
> And holidays in Guadeloupe;
> Long winter evenings by the fire
> With Proust and cream of carrot soup.
>
> Raw carrots on a summer lawn,
> Champagne, a Gioconda smile;
> Glazed carrots in a silver dish
> For Sunday lunch. They call it style.

From *The Stage Favourites' Cook Book*

ELIZABETH CRAIG

Four hundred actresses contributed their favourite recipes to this book, published in 1923, and Edward Petherbridge has chosen four of them. The insistence on champagne and flower petals reeks of these well-to-do actresses in their heyday.

Truffes au vin de champagne   by Mrs Patrick Campbell Brown one or two slices of veal and of ham in melted bacon fat in a casserole; cover them with peeled truffles, and add a bouquet garni, salt, pepper and a layer of peeled and roughly chopped mushrooms. Then cover this time with thin slices of bacon, moisten nicely with champagne, put on lid and allow contents to cook very slowly till tender, when serve with its own sauce strained and skimmed.

Salade des Roses   by Marie Dainton Gather half a pint of fresh pink scented rose-petals, pick them over carefully to see they are perfectly fresh, then add them to half a pint of thick cream and bruise them with a wooden spoon. When cream is delicately flavoured and fragrantly scented, pile up some large sound hulled strawberries in a crystal dish, sprinkle them with castor sugar, strain over the juice of a lemon and pour over two glasses of sherry, chablis or grave. Whip the cream, sweeten slightly with castor sugar, and pile up rockily on top.

Fraises au champagne   by Ruby Miller

This makes a delicious after-the-theatre surprise. Chill a
bottle of champagne in cracked ice, then pour it over a big
basin of strawberries. Add a few slices of orange, then serve.
In Normandy they vary this recipe in this way: they sweeten
the strawberries and soak them in cider.

Pêches Ophelia   by Ellen Terry

Carefully peel twelve ripe peaches, cut them in halves, stone,
and sprinkle with one tablespoon castor sugar and two table-
spoons maraschino. Allow peaches to stand for 15 minutes,
turning them occasionally; then beat three gills cream to a
stiff froth, add one oz. castor sugar and six drops vanilla
essence, and beat lightly again. Then pile up in the centre of
a pretty glass dish. Arrange peaches round the base, dust
lightly with crushed violets, and serve very cold.

Christmas Cheating

NANETTE NEWMAN

What could be better for a Christmas lunch, or a Christmas dinner or, indeed, a Christmas concert? I've done it at one, and the audience um'd and ah'd and laughed and made notes. It's from her *Christmas Cookbook*.

Buy the very best Christmas pudding available and prick it all over with a skewer, then pour plenty of brandy or rum into it and wrap it tightly in cooking foil. If you have time repeat this process over a few days.

The best quality bought Christmas cake can be treated in the same way as the Christmas pudding. Turn the cake upside down and pierce it all over with a skewer, then trickle plenty of brandy over the surface. Wrap the cake in cooking foil and repeat if you have time.

Shop-bought mincement can be enlivened by adding brandy or rum and some grated orange or lemon rind. If you are really stuck for time, buy the best mince pies you can find. Carefully lift off their lids and spoon a little brandy over the filling. Serve home-made brandy or rum butter with the warmed pies.

If you don't have time to prepare your own mayonnaise, then buy the best available and add a little double cream just as you are using it.

Simple casseroles can be varied and made more elaborate by adding interesting ingredients: try dried apricots, halved walnuts or shredded orange or lemon rind. You can freeze a simple meat or poultry casserole well in advance, then by adding something extra about 15 minutes before serving you can transform it into a nice meal just when you're in a panic.

Remember to freeze any dregs of wine by pouring it into ice-making trays. This way it will be ready for use in individual cubes for casseroles and sauces.

Frozen puff pastry can be improved to a high standard by rolling it out as thinly as possibly, then brushing it with melted butter and folding it in half. Continue brushing the pastry with butter and folding it until it is about the same size as it was when you started, then roll it out for use.

Make a large batch of home-made tomato sauce and keep it in the freezer – or even in the refrigerator for a few days. It is useful for a quick spaghetti, to have with meatloaf, to fill an omelette or to fill tiny pastry cases and bake for serving with drinks.

Recipe For a Salad

SYDNEY SMITH

Sydney Smith (1771–1845) was an author, clergyman, renowned talker and *bon viveur*. This recipe, however, is one of the least mouth-watering I have ever read. Anchovy sauce *and* double salt?

> To make this condiment, your poet begs
> The pounded yellow of two hard-boiled eggs;
> Two boiled potatoes, passed through kitchen-sieve,
> Smoothness and softness to the salad give;
> Let onion atoms lurk within the bowl,
> And, half-suspected, animate the whole.
> Of mordant mustard add a single spoon,
> Distrust the condiment that bites so soon;
> But deem it not, thou man of herbs, a fault,
> To add a double quantity of salt.
> And, lastly, o'er the flavored compound toss
> A magic soup-spoon of anchovy sauce.
> Oh, green and glorious! Oh, herbaceous treat!
> 'T would tempt the dying anchorite to eat;
> Back to the world he'd turn his fleeting soul,
> And plunge his fingers in the salad bowl!
> Serenely full, the epicure would say,
> Fate can not harm me, I have dined to-day!

From *Ecclesiasticus*

CHAPTERS 31 AND 32

Alec McCowen suggested this. 'A good, unexpected piece,' he said, 'for a dinner party or grand occasion can be made from verses 12 to 31 and 1 to 13 of these two chapters in *The Apocrypha*. They need a little judicious cutting and, oh yes!, it must be the *New English Bible* translation.'

If you are sitting at a grand table, do not lick your lips and exclaim, 'What a spread!' Eat what is set before you like a gentleman; do not munch and make yourself objectionable. If you are dining in a large company, do not reach out your hand before others. A man of good upbringing is content with little. The moderate eater enjoys healthy sleep; he rises early, feeling refreshed. But sleeplessness, indigestion, and colic are the lot of the glutton. If you cannot avoid overeating at a feast leave the table and find relief by vomiting.

Do not try to prove your manhood by drinking, for wine has been the ruin of many. Wine puts life into a man if he drinks it in moderation. What is life to a man who is deprived of wine? Was it not created to warm men's hearts? Wine brings gaiety and high spirits if a man knows when to drink and when to stop; but wine in excess makes for bitter feelings and leads to offence and retaliation.

If they choose you to preside at a feast, do not put on airs; behave to them as one of themselves. Let their enjoyment be your pleasure, and you will win the prize for good manners. Speak, if you are old – it is your privilege – but come to the point and do not interrupt the music. Where entertainment is provided, do not keep up a stream of talk; it is the wrong time to show off your wisdom.

Speak, if you are young, when the need arises, but twice at the most, and only when asked. Be brief, say much in few words, like a man who knows and can still hold his tongue. Among the great do not act as their equal or go on chattering when another is speaking. Leave in good time and do not be the last to go; go straight home without lingering. And one thing more: give praise to your Maker, who has filled your cup with his blessings.

Letter the Second
From Miss C. Lutterell to Miss M. Lesley in answer

JANE AUSTEN

Equally surprising is this extract from *Lesley Castle, an Unfinished Novel in Letters*, sent to me by Tim Heath. Charlotte is the Christian name of the unspeakable girl who wrote this letter about the feast she was preparing for the wedding of her sister, Eloisa, to Mr Henry Hervey.

Glenford Febry 12

I have a thousand excuses to beg for having so long delayed thanking you my dear Peggy for your agreable Letter, which beleive me I should not have deferred doing, had not every moment of my time during the last five weeks been so fully employed in the necessary arrangements for my sisters wedding, as to allow me no time to devote either to you or myself. And now what provokes me more than anything else is that the Match is broke off, and all my Labour thrown away. Imagine how great the Dissapointment must be to me, when you consider that after having laboured both by Night and by Day, in order to get the Wedding dinner ready by the time appointed, after having roasted Beef, Broiled Mutton, and Stewed Soup enough to last the new-married Couple through the Honey-moon, I had the mortification of finding that I had been Roasting, Broiling and Stewing both the Meat and Myself to no purpose. Indeed my dear Freind,

I never remember suffering any vexation equal to what I experienced on last Monday when my sister came running to me in the store-room with her face as White as a Whipt syllabub, and told me that Hervey had been thrown from his Horse, had fractured his Scull and was pronounced by his surgeon to be in the most emminent Danger. 'Good God! (said I) you dont say so? Why what in the name of Heaven will become of all the Victuals! We shall never be able to eat it while it is good. However, we'll call in the Surgeon to help us. I shall be able to manage the Sir-loin myself, my Mother will eat the soup, and You and the Doctor must finish the rest.' Here I was interrupted, by seeing my poor Sister fall down to appearance Lifeless upon one of the Chests, where we keep our Table linen. I immediately called my Mother and the Maids, and at last we brought her to herself again; as soon as ever she was sensible, she expressed a determination of going instantly to Henry, and was so wildly bent on this Scheme, that we had the greatest Difficulty in the World to prevent her putting it in execution; at last however more by Force than Entreaty we prevailed on her to go into her room; we laid her upon the Bed, and she continued for some Hours in the most dreadful Convulsions. My Mother and I continued in the room with her, and when any intervals of tolerable Composure in Eloisa would allow us, we joined in heartfelt lamentations on the dreadful Waste in our provisions which this Event must occasion, and in concerting some plan for getting rid of them. We agreed that the best thing we could do was to begin eating them immediately, and accordingly we ordered up the cold Ham and Fowls, and instantly began our Devouring Plan on them with great Alacrity. We would have persuaded Eloisa to have taken a Wing of a Chicken, but she would not be persuaded. She was however much quieter than she had been; the convulsions she had before suffered having given way to an almost perfect Insensibility. We endeavoured to rouse her by every means in our power, but to no purpose. I talked to her of Henry.

'Dear Eloisa (said I) there's no occasion for your crying so much about such a trifle. (for I was willing to make light of it in order to comfort her) I beg you would not mind it – You see it does not vex me in the least; though perhaps *I* may suffer most from it after all; for I shall not only be obliged to eat up all the Victuals I have dressed already, but must if Henry should recover (which however is not very likely) dress as much for you again; or should he die (as I suppose he will) I shall still have to prepare a Dinner for you whenever you marry any one else. So you see that tho' perhaps for the present it may afflict you to think of Henry's sufferings, Yet I dare say he'll die soon, and then his pain will be over and you will be easy, whereas my Trouble will last much longer for work as hard as I may, I am certain that the pantry cannot be cleared in less than a fortnight.' Thus I did all in my power to console her, but without any effect, and at last as I saw that she did not seem to listen to me, I said no more, but sent William to ask how Henry did. He was not expected to live many Hours; he died the same day.

Christenings

There's not a great call for readings at christenings, which is just as well, because there's not a lot to choose from! But they are mostly very short and can therefore be slotted easily into the usually very short service.

Infancy

W. H. DAVIES

This is from *The Bird of Paradise*, a poem about the delusions of a
dying prostitute, but there's no need to tell that to mummy and
daddy and their friends.

> Born to the world with my hands clenched,
>   I wept and shut my eyes;
> Into my mouth a breast was forced,
>   To stop my bitter cries.
> I did not know – nor cared to know –
>   A woman from a man;
> Until I saw a sudden light,
>   And all my joys began.
>
> From that great hour my hands went forth,
>   And I began to prove
> That many a thing my two eyes saw
>   My hands had power to move:
> My fingers now began to work,
>   And all my toes likewise;
> And reaching out with fingers stretched,
>   I laughed, with open eyes.

Baby Song

THOM GUNN

This is from *Jack Straw's Castle* and was sent to me by Michael
Mayne.

From the private ease of Mother's womb
I fall into the lighted room.

Why don't they simply put me back
Where it is warm and wet and black?

But one thing follows on another.
Things were different inside Mother.

Padded and jolly I would ride
The perfect comfort of her inside.

They tuck me in a rustling bed
– I lie there, raging, small, and red.

I may sleep soon, I may forget,
But I won't forget that I regret.

A rain of blood poured round her womb,
But all time roars outside this room.

Infant Joy

WILLIAM BLAKE

Two delights from *Songs of Innocence.*

> 'I have no name;
> I am but two days old'.
> What shall I call thee?
> 'I happy am;
> Joy is my name.'
> Sweet joy befall thee!
>
> Pretty joy!
> Sweet joy but two days old,
> Sweet joy I call thee.
> Thou dost smile;
> I sing the while.
> Sweet joy befall thee.

The Lamb

WILLIAM BLAKE

Little Lamb who made thee?
  Dost thou know who made thee?
Gave thee life and bid thee feed
By the stream and o'er the mead;
Gave thee clothing of delight,
Softest clothing woolly bright;
Gave thee such a tender voice,
Making all the vales rejoice.
  Little Lamb who made thee?
  Dost thou know who made thee?

Little Lamb I'll tell thee,
  Little Lamb I'll tell thee:
He is called by thy name,
For he calls himself a lamb.
He is meek and he is mild;
He became a little child.
I a child and thou a lamb,
We are called by his name.
  Little Lamb God bless thee.
  Little Lamb God bless thee.

When I Was Young
TRACY SAUNDERS, aged 11

I found this in *From Cover to Cover*, an anthology of poems by schoolchildren, compiled for Kent Arts and Libraries by Maggi Waite and Michael Curtis. 'The award-winning *From Cover to Cover* project gave 12,000 children opportunities to work with writers, poets, storytellers and illustrators in schools and libraries all over Kent.'

> When I was young I used to crawl along the floor.
> When I was young I used to call mommy instead of mummy.
> When I was young I used to say wogout instead of yoghurt.
> When I was young every time my dad went out I started to
>   cry.
> When I was young the only thing that would get me to sleep
>   was a drop of whisky.
> When I was young I was a little angel
> And I still am.

Why?

NICOLA SIMS, aged 8

Another anthology from Kent Arts and Libraries is called *Time to Write*. This little piece, reeking of a child's voice, warns the parents what they are in for. Soon.

Why can't I have a dog?
Why do I always have to
Feed our rabbit?
Why do I have to eat
Vegetables?
Why can't I eat chips
Every day?
Why do I have to go to
School?
Why can't I have a
Birthday every day?

My Baby Brother

SHALAMAR SMITH, aged 12

This is from *Connexions*, a book of poems, in English and French, by children from both sides of the Channel. It is published by Eurotunnel.

I have a baby brother
He always cries and squeals
He wakes me in the morning
Because he wants his meals.

He has all kinds of coloured toys
Boats and cars and bricks
He likes to chew and nibble them
But sometimes he just licks.

He has a lovely mobile
With suns and moons so bright
He stares at it all evening
Then dreams all through the night.

Inevitable

ELLA WHEELER WILCOX

A mother's point of view, from *Poems of Life*.

To-day I was so weary and I lay
    In that delicious state of semi-waking,
When baby, sitting with his nurse at play,
    Cried loud for 'mamma,' all his toys forsaking.

I was so weary and I needed rest,
    And signed to nurse to bear him from the room.
Then, sudden, rose and caught him to my breast,
    And kissed the grieving mouth and cheeks of bloom.

For swift as lightning came the thought to me,
    With pulsing heart-throes and a mist of tears,
Of days inevitable, that are to be,
    If my fair darling grows to manhood's years.

Days when he will not call for 'mamma,' when
    The world with many a pleasure and bright joy,
Shall tempt him forth into the haunts of men
    And I shall lose the first place with my boy;

When other homes and loves shall give delight,
    When younger smiles and voices will seem best.
And so I held him to my heart tonight,
    Forgetting all my need of peace and rest.

What A Grandmother Is

This is an essay by an eight-year-old spotted years ago by Alan Burroughs in the magazine, called *Contact*, of the Bexhill-on-Sea Congregational Church, now a United Reform Church.

A grandmother is a lady who has no children of her own, so she likes other people's little girls and boys. A grandfather is a man grand-mother. He goes for walks with the boys and they talk about fishing and tractors.

Grandmothers don't have to do anything but be there. They are old, so they shouldn't play hard or run. They should never say 'Hurry up'. Usually they are fat, but not too fat to tie children's shoes.

They wear glasses and funny underwear, and they can take their teeth and gums off.

They don't have to be smart, only answer questions like why dogs hate cats and why God isn't married.

They don't talk baby-talk like visitors. When they read to us, they don't skip bits, or mind if it is the same story over again.

Everybody should have one, especially if you don't have television, because grandmothers are the only grown-ups who have the time.

The New School

ANNABEL GULLETT, aged 11

Another poem in *From Cover to Cover*, this time about the agonies
which lie ahead for the christened child.

Are my socks the right colour?
Is my skirt too long?
How will I ever carry my bag?
What do I do when I get there?
How will I know where to go?
What will the teachers be like?
And lunchtime, what then?
I'm bound to get lost!

Monday morning,
Will it ever come?
Hope not!
It can't be true.
The new school – it's so huge,
And full of Big Girls,
Big enough to push and jostle me,
Telling jokes,
Laughing and teasing.

I'll have a locker –
One of my own.
But it might get broken into
Or I might lose the key.
And then there's homework.
Oh help!

What if I lose it?
Or forget to bring it in?
Or it gets chewed by the cat?

Walking there on Monday mornings,
Will it ever be me?

Weddings

A reading at a wedding reception is a very rare thing. Weddings are for families and dressing up and photographers and smiling a lot. And drinking champagne and eating fine food. And everyone likes it if the speeches of the Best Man and the Bridegroom are funny, though with a bit of wisdom, advice and reminiscence thrown in. Maybe a morsel of that wisdom and advice could include a short reading, say from *The Prophet*. So I'll start with that. But most of the other pieces are *about* weddings and probably best performed away from them!

From *The Prophet*

KAHLIL GIBRAN

This excerpt was suggested to me by James Roose-Evans, writer, director, teacher and priest. I've cut just a word or two at the beginning so as to arrive at the great line, 'But let there be spaces in your togetherness,' as soon as possible.

Then Almitra spoke again and said, And what of Marriage,
    master?
And he answered saying:
Together you shall be for evermore.
But let there be spaces in your togetherness.
And let the winds of the heavens dance between you.

Love one another, but make not a bond of love.
Let it rather be a moving sea between the shores of your
    souls.
Fill each other's cup but drink not from one cup.
Give one another of your bread but eat not from the same
    loaf.
Sing and dance together and be joyous, but let each one of
    you be alone,
Even as the strings of a lute are alone though they quiver
    with the same music.

Give your hearts, but not into each other's keeping.
For only the hand of Life can contain your hearts.
And stand together yet not too near together:
For the pillars of the temple stand apart,
And the oak tree and the cypress grow not in each other's
    shadow.

Sonnet 116

WILLIAM SHAKESPEARE

'Love is not love which alters when it alteration finds' is straight
to the heart of the matter for the bride and bridegroom facing,
hopefully, a long and happy life together.

Notes:
1. 'Or bends with the remover to remove': or alters course if
   the loved one turns elsewhere.
2. 'bark': boat or ship.

> Let me not to the marriage of true minds
> Admit impediments. Love is not love
> Which alters when it alteration finds,
> Or bends with the remover to remove:
> O, no! it is an ever-fixed mark,
> That looks on tempests and is never shaken;
> It is the star to every wandering bark,
> Whose worth's unknown, although his height be taken.
> Love's not Time's fool, though rosy lips and cheeks
> Within his bending sickle's compass come;
> Love alters not with his brief hours and weeks,
> But bears it out even to the edge of doom.
>   If this be error and upon me proved,
>   I never writ, nor no man ever loved.

Untitled

AUTHOR UNKNOWN

Yet another piece from the prolific Alan Burroughs, who said, 'All
I can remember is that I cut it out of a newspaper years ago and I
think it might have been the Dundee Post. It's not good poetry,
but it's bound to raise a laugh at a wedding.'

> He criticised her puddings and he
> didn't like her cake
> He wished she'd make the
> biscuits that his mother used to bake
> She didn't wash the dishes and
> she didn't make the stew
> She didn't mend his stockings like
> his mother used to do
> Oh, well she was not perfect,
> though she tried to do her best,
> Until at last she thought it was
> time she had a rest
> So one day when he said the
> same old rigmarole all through
> She turned and boxed his ears –
> just as his mother used to do

The Father of the Bride

KEITH WATERHOUSE AND WILLIS HALL

I first heard of this speech from Michael Redington, and I'm very grateful to Keith Waterhouse for sending it to me. 'Willis Hall and I wrote it for dear Roy Kinnear,' he said. And that gives a clue as to the sort of part the bride's father is!

The opening stage direction says, 'The father of the Bride stands by a table on which there is a large wedding cake. He wears morning dress and holds a glass of champagne. He is proposing a toast at the wedding reception.'

As the father of the bride I would now like to reply to the best man's toast and propose the health of the happy couple.

This indeed is a proud day for me. I have often dreamed of the moment when Marlene would come to me and say: 'Daddy, I'm in love with George Witherspoon. He's been promoted to manager of the bank and now he wants my hand in marriage.' As things turned out George Witherspoon married the chief bridesmaid, but then you can't have everything. What we do have is Rodney, and it is with humble pleasure that I welcome him to our family circle. We represent a number of honourable professions in my family. My father was a respected retail tobacconist, my brother is a distinguished solicitor, and as you know I have the honour of being manager of a chain of grocery shops. We have not had a window cleaner in the family before and I sincerely welcome this new blood.

It's true that Rodney has had some bad luck lately and is

temporarily out of employment owing to that unfortunate misunderstanding over Mrs Parkinson's jewellery. I myself entirely accept his explanation that the brooch and necklace must have fallen into his pocket when he knocked them with his chamois leather. In any event my brother assures me that he has a good chance and that he is likely to get off with a heavy fine, which will be my small wedding present to the happy couple.

They have a fine start in life – a fine home and fine prospects. My Marlene should learn a great deal from living in one room over a plumber's shop, and of course it will be very handy for the radiant couple if they ever think of getting hot water installed. Both Marlene and Rodney know that my house is at their disposal whenever they want a bath, and the sooner Rodney avails himself of the invitation the better.

Now I want to recall a conversation which I was having with Rodney's father in the vestry before the vicar separated us. Rodney's father reckons that in the heat of the moment I referred to his son as a half-baked twit. Let me assure Rodney's father that I never speak in the heat of the moment, particularly on such an auspicious day as this. The way I look upon it I am not losing a daughter but gaining a son. In fact I am also gaining a grandson. The credit for that is entirely Rodney's. He admits it and she admits it and we won't go into all that again thank you very much Rodney's mother. I admire Rodney for the way in which he has stood by my Marlene. When the paternity case came up a lesser man would have skipped his bail. Not Rodney. He came all the way back from holiday in Dublin to face his responsibilities like a man, and also gave myself, my brother and my three sons an opportunity of visiting the great Irish capital.

Finally, before proposing the toast, I have a message from the catering manager about twelve fish-knives and a silver-plated cruet. He says that Rodney's family will know what he means and that he is prepared to accept it as a joke if the missing items are on the table when we leave. Now I ask you all to charge your glasses, and be upstanding for the happy couple. Marlene — could you help Rodney's father to his feet, there's a love. The happy couple.

And Yet I Don't Know

BOB WESTON AND BERT LEE

Bob Western and Bert Lee wrote many successful songs, including
'Goodbyee,' a great hit during the First World War. They wrote
this song in 1919 for a popular entertainer called Ernest Hastings,
who accompanied himself at the piano. I haven't found the music,
but it goes very well without it, and there can be a bit more
acting around all the indecisions. I am grateful to my friend and
neighbour, the actor John Cunningham, for introducing me to
this piece.

> Now, my sister's daughter Elizabeth May
> Is going to get married next Sunday, they say.
> Now, what shall I buy her? She's such a nice gel!
> I think a piano would do very well.
> I saw one today, only ninety-five pound:
> A decent piano, I'll have it sent round.
>
> And yet I don't know! And yet I don't know!
> I think she's the rottenest player I know.
> And if she keeps thumping out that 'Maiden's Pray'r'
> The husband might kill his young bride, and so there!
> I won't buy the piano! It's not that I'm mean;
> I think I'd best buy her a sewing machine.
>
> And yet I don't know! And yet I don't know!
> A sewing machine is a 'tenner' or so!
> A tenner would buy lots of needles and thread,
> And things that are hand-made are best, so it's said.
> So it's not that I'm mingy, although I'm half Scotch –

I know what I'll buy her: an Ingersoll watch!

And yet I don't know! And yet I don't know!
In five or six years they're too fast or too slow.
And when she's turn'd seventy, that's if she's spar'd,
'Twill have cost her a fortune in being repair'd.
Or else she'll have pawn'd it, and lost it, so there!
I know what I'll buy her: a jumper to wear!

And yet I don't know! And yet I don't know!
The girls won't wear jumpers in ten years or so.
Besides she might start getting fat before long.
And fat girls in jumpers show too much ong bong!
And open work jumpers give ladies the 'flu.
I'll buy her some handkerchiefs, that's what I'll do!

And yet I don't know! And yet I don't know!
Good hankies cost twelve bob a dozen or so.
And twelve bob's too much for her poor Uncle John.
Why, anything does just to blow your nose on.
And talking of noses, hers looks red enough!
I know what I'll buy her: a nice powder puff.

She can't powder her nose with a grand piano,
Nor yet with a sewing machine.
She can't powder her nose with an Ingersoll watch:
Well, it's silly! You see what I mean!

She can't powder her nose with a jumper:
She would find it a little bit rough;
So I'll go round to Woolworth's tonight, God bless her!
And buy her a powder puff.

And yet I don't know! And yet I don't know!
Sixpence ha'p'nies don't grow in backyards,
So I don't think I'll send her a powder puff,
I'll send her — my kindest regards!

Funerals and Memorial Services

Whereas there is little call for readings at christenings and weddings, there's a huge demand for them at funerals and memorial services, both religious and humanist, and fortunately there are lots of wonderful pieces about death and dying and loving and remembering to choose from.

In the Introduction to his admirable anthology, *Remembrance*, Ned Sherrin writes, 'A memorial service is not only a chance to pay respects and to celebrate a person's life. It is often a happy way to put a period to a time of mourning. Funerals arrive too soon.' His book contains all the hymns, music, prayers, readings, poems and Bible readings that anyone who has to plan a memorial service could wish for, and they are arranged in the order of their popularity. So I thought I would start here with some of his winners ('Death is nothing at all' by Canon Scott Holland, 'To everything there is a season' from Ecclesiastes, and two marvellous pieces by Shakespeare) and then drift off for a time into my own storehouse of less well known pieces. The winners are winners because they are superb: they contain a lot of beauty and strike right home. But it's nice to have a surprise or two.

Death Is Nothing At All

HENRY SCOTT HOLLAND

I received this accurate version from the Reverend Philip Buckler, vicar of Hampstead. He said, 'This is a copy I made several years ago from a book in the library at St Paul's Cathedral, where Scott Holland had been a Canon Residentiary. It is part of a sermon called "The King of Terrors." It has been used widely and in various forms. I have seen it presented as a poem, but more often it is written in prose and usually edited in one way or another.'

As far as I've been able to tell, it's not the most popular piece with clergymen. Indeed, one said to me, 'There are sentences which stick, and I always cut them: "It does not count," "Nothing has happened." "Everything remains exactly as it was." "What is this death but a negligible accident?" You get the message, and the picture, more clearly and comfortably without them.'

The passage which comes immediately before this famous piece is interesting, and puts it into a clearer context: 'There is another aspect altogether which death can wear for us. It is that which first comes to us, perhaps, as we look down upon the quiet face, so cold and white, of one who has been very near and dear to us. There it lies in possession of its own secret. It knows it all. So we seem to feel. And what the face says in its sweet silence to us as a last message from the one whom we loved is:

'Death is nothing at all. It does not count. I have only slipped away into the next room. Nothing has happened. Everything remains exactly as it was. I am I, and you are you, and the old life that we lived so fondly together is untouched, unchanged. Whatever we were to each other, that we are

313

still. Call me by the old familiar name. Speak of me in the easy way which you always used. Put no difference into your tone. Wear no forced air of solemnity or sorrow. Laugh as we always laughed at the little jokes that we enjoyed together. Play, smile, think of me, pray for me. Let my name be ever the household word that it always was. Let it be spoken without an effort, without the ghost of a shadow upon it. Life means all that it ever meant. It is the same as it ever was. There is absolute and unbroken continuity. What is this death but a negligible accident? Why should I be out of mind because I am out of sight? I am but waiting for you, for an interval, somewhere very near, just around the corner. All is well.'

From *Ecclesiastes*

CHAPTER 3, VERSES 1–8

To everything there is a season, and a time to every purpose under the heaven: a time to be born and a time to die; a time to plant, and a time to pluck up that which is planted; a time to kill, and a time to heal; a time to break down, and a time to build up; a time to weep and a time to laugh; a time to mourn, and a time to dance; a time to cast away stones, and a time to gather stones together; a time to embrace, and a time to refrain from embracing; a time to seek, and a time to lose; a time to keep, and a time to cast away; a time to rend, and a time to sew; a time to keep silence, and a time to speak; a time to love, and a time to hate; a time for war, and a time for peace.

From *Cymbeline*

WILLIAM SHAKESPEARE

This beautiful and famous song is in Act 4, Scene 2.

> Fear no more the heat o' th' sun
>   Nor the furious winter's rages;
> Thou thy worldly task hast done,
>   Home art gone, and ta'en thy wages.
> Golden lads and girls all must,
> As chimney-sweepers, come to dust.
>
> Fear no more the frown o' th' great;
>   Thou art past the tyrant's stroke.
> Care no more to clothe and eat;
>   To thee the reed is as the oak.
> The sceptre, learning, physic, must
>   All follow this and come to dust.
>
> Fear no more the lightning flash
>   Nor th'all-dreaded thunder-stone;
> Fear not slander, censure rash;
>   Thou hast finished joy and moan.
> All lovers young, all lovers must
> Consign to thee and come to dust.
>
> No exorciser harm thee!
> Nor no witchcraft charm thee!
> Ghost unlaid forbear thee!
> Nothing ill come near thee!

Quiet consummation have,
And renowned be thy grave!

From *The Tempest*

WILLIAM SHAKESPEARE

In Act 4, Scene 1, Prospero dismisses 'certain Nymphs' and 'certain Reapers, properly habited' in the middle of their graceful dance. Then, turning to his daughter Miranda and her newly betrothed Ferdinand, he says:

> Our revels now are ended. These our actors,
> As I foretold you, were all spirits, and
> Are melted into air, into thin air;
> And, like the baseless fabric of this vision,
> The cloud-capp'd towers, the gorgeous palaces,
> The solemn temples, the great globe itself,
> Yea, all which it inherit, shall dissolve,
> And, like this insubstantial pageant faded,
> Leave not a rack behind. We are such stuff
> As dreams are made on; and our little life
> Is rounded with a sleep.

From *An Essay*

WILLIAM HAZLITT

This was read at the memorial service for Dennis Potter. Peter
Jeffrey, who sent it to me, told me that shortly before he died
Dennis Potter had telephoned Kenith Trodd, with whom he had
enjoyed a rather spiky friendship, to say, 'I've got bad news, I'm
afraid. I've been to the quack and he says I haven't got long to
live. Shall we meet? I'd love to see you.' They met in a wine bar
and drank and drank. When they were on their third bottle,
Dennis Potter said, 'You know, Ken, there's something that worries
me about dying: the fact that you might be asked to speak at my
memorial service.' Which he was. And did.

No young man ever thinks he shall die. He may believe that
others will, or assent to the doctrine that 'all men are mortal'
as an abstract proposition, but he is far enough from bringing
it home to himself individually. If, in a moment of idle
speculation, we indulge in this notion of the close of life as
a theory, it is amazing at what a distance it seems; what a
long, leisurely interval there is between. We eye the farthest
verge of the horizon, and think what a way we shall have to
look back upon, ere we arrive at our journey's end – and
without our in the least suspecting it, the mists are at our
feet, and the shadows of age encompass us. The two divisions
of our lives have melted into each other: the extreme points
close and meet with none of that romantic interval stretching
out between them that we had reckoned upon. The pains by
their repeated blows have worn us out, and have left us
neither spirit nor inclination to encounter them again in

retrospect. We do not want to rip up old grievances, nor to renew our youth like a phoenix, nor to live our lives twice over. Once is enough. As the tree falls, so let it lie. Shut up the book and close the account for all!

The most rational cure after all for the inordinate fear of death is to set a just value on life. If we merely wish to continue on the scene to indulge our headstrong humours and tormenting passions, we had better begone at once; and if we only cherish a fondness for existence according to the good we derive from it, the pang we feel at parting with it will not be very severe!

Perhaps the best cure for the fear of death is to reflect that life has a beginning as well as an end. There was a time when we were not: this gives us no concern — why, then, should it trouble us that a time will come when we shall cease to be? To die is only to be as we were before we were born; yet no one feels any remorse, or regret, or repugnance, in contemplating this last idea. It seems to have been a holiday-time with us then: we were not called to appear upon the stage of life, to wear robes or tatters, to laugh or cry, be hooted or applauded; we had lain snug all this while, out of harm's way; and had slept out our thousands of centuries without wanting to be waked up; at peace and free from care, wrapped in the softest and finest dust. And the worst that we dread is, after a short, fretful, feverish being, after vain hopes and idle fears, to sink to final repose again, and forget the troubled dream of life!

My Days Among the Dead are Passed

ROBERT SOUTHEY

Yet another poem by the wonderful Robert Southey. With its unusually strong statement of the ever-presence of the dead in the minds of the living, it strikes immediate chords, and is as succinct as any you'll find.

Southey had a huge collection of books, over 14,000 of them, and it was their musty presence in Greta Hall that inspired this poem. 'The shelves extended over the walls in every room of his large, dismal house in Keswick,' wrote Shelley. 'They were in the bedrooms and even down the stairs.'

Notes:

1. The first line needs emphasis on the word 'dead' and none at all on the word 'passed', otherwise 'passed' becomes 'past'!
2. 'Weal' means 'good fortune.' 'Weal and woe' used to be a well known phrase or saying.

> My days among the Dead are passed;
>   Around me I behold,
> Where'er these casual eyes are cast,
>   The mighty minds of old;
> My never-failing friends are they,
> With whom I converse day by day.
>
> With them I take delight in weal,
>   And seek relief in woe;
> And while I understand and feel
>   How much to them I owe,

My cheeks have often been bedewed
With tears of thoughtful gratitude.

My thoughts are with the Dead; with them
   I live in long-past years,
Their virtues love, their faults condemn,
   Partake their hopes and fears,
And from their lessons seek and find
Instruction with an humble mind.

My hopes are with the Dead; anon
   My place with them will be,
And I with them shall travel on
   Through all Futurity;
Yet leaving here a name, I trust,
That will not perish in the dust.

We Are Seven

WILLIAM WORDSWORTH

Indeed, the theme of many poems which are suitable for funerals
and memorial services is: the dead are still living when we carry
them around in our hearts. And what more beautiful illustration
of that could there be than in this poem by Wordsworth?

> – A simple Child,
> That lightly draws its breath,
> And feels its life in every limb,
> What should it know of death?
>
> I met a little cottage Girl:
> She was eight years old, she said;
> Her hair was thick with many a curl
> That clustered round her head.
>
> She had a rustic, woodland air,
> And she was wildly clad:
> Her eyes were fair, and very fair;
> – Her beauty made me glad.
>
> 'Sisters and brothers, little maid,
> How many may you be?'
> 'How many? Seven in all,' she said.
> And wondering looked at me.
>
> 'And where are they? I pray you tell.'
> She answered, 'Seven are we;
> And two of us at Conway dwell,
> And two are gone to sea.

'Two of us in the church-yard lie,
My sister and my brother;
And, in the church-yard cottage, I
Dwell near them with my mother.'

'You say that two at Conway dwell,
And two are gone to sea.
Yet ye are seven! I pray you tell,
Sweet Maid, how this may be.'

Then did the little Maid reply,
'Seven boys and girls are we;
Two of us in the church-yard lie.
Beneath the church-yard tree.'

'You run about, my little Maid,
Your limbs they are alive;
If two are in the church-yard laid,
Then ye are only five.'

'Their graves are green, they may be seen,'
The little Maid replied,
'Twelve steps or more from my mother's door,
And they are side by side.

'My stockings there I often knit,
My kerchief there I hem;
And there upon the ground I sit,
And sing a song to them.

'And often after sun-set, Sir,
When it is light and fair,
I take my little porringer,
And eat my supper there.

'The first that died was sister Jane;
In bed she moaning lay,
Till God released her of her pain;
And then she went away.

'So in the church-yard she was laid;
And, when the grass was dry,
Together round her grave we played,
My brother John and I.

'And when the ground was white with snow,
And I could run and slide,
My brother John was forced to go,
And he lies by her side.'

'How many are you, then,' said I,
'If they two are in heaven?'
Quick was the little Maid's reply,
'O Master! we are seven.'

'But they are dead: those two are dead!
Their spirits are in heaven!'
'Twas throwing words away; for still
The little Maid would have her will,
And said, 'Nay, we are seven!'

He Wishes For the Cloths of Heaven

W. B. YEATS

This very different poem on the same theme was given to me by
Thelma Holt, who said, 'I last read it at the memorial service for
Toby Rowland. I really love it.'

> Had I the heavens' embroidered cloths,
> Enwrought with golden and silver light,
> The blue and the dim and the dark cloths
> Of night and light and the half light,
> I would spread the cloths under your feet:
> But I, being poor, have only my dreams;
> I have spread my dreams under your feet;
> Tread softly because you tread on my dreams.

Untitled

AUTHOR UNKNOWN

This was sent to me by Mark Shivas, who told me, 'I got it from a Swedish/Australian neighbour of mine, Ruth Larson. She can't remember who sent it to her, or who wrote it, but she received it when her mother died.'

> Though I am dead, grieve not for me with tears,
> Think not of death with sorrowing and fears
> I am so near that every tear you shed
> Touches and torments me, though you think me dead
> But when you sing and laugh in glad delight
> My soul is uplifted to the light
> Laugh and be glad for all that life is giving
> And I, though dead, will share your joy in living

From *The Prophet*

KAHLIL GIBRAN

Another extract from this beautiful book, again suggested by James Roose-Evans.

Then Almitra spoke, saying, We would ask now of Death.
And he said:
You would know the secret of death.
But how shall you find it unless you seek it in the heart of life?
The owl whose night-bound eyes are blind unto the day cannot unveil the mystery of light.
If you would indeed behold the spirit of death, open your heart wide unto the body of life.
For life and death are one, even as the river and the sea are one.

In the depth of your hopes and desires lies your silent knowledge of the beyond;
And like seeds dreaming beneath the snow your heart dreams of spring.
Trust the dreams, for in them is hidden the gate to eternity.
Your fear of death is but the trembling of the shepherd when he stands before the king whose hand is to be laid upon him in honour.
Is the shepherd not joyful beneath his trembling, that he shall wear the mark of the king?
Yet is he not more mindful of his trembling?

For what is it to die but to stand naked in the wind and to melt into the sun?

And what is it to cease breathing but to free the breath from its restless tides, that it may rise and expand and seek God unencumbered?

Only when you drink from the river of silence shall you indeed sing.

And when you have reached the mountain top, then you shall begin to climb.

And when the earth shall claim your limbs, then shall you truly dance.

When I Have Fears

NOËL COWARD

Ned Sherrin notes, with some surprise, that this piece, and the following one, could not be included in his book, *Remembrance*, because they had not been used during the period he was covering. 'I missed them,' he says. Yes.

> When I have fears, as Keats had fears,
> Of the moment I'll cease to be
> I console myself with vanished years,
> Remembered laughter, remembered tears,
> And the peace of the changing sea.
>
> When I feel sad, as Keats felt sad,
> That my life is so nearly done
> It gives me comfort to dwell upon
> Remembered friends who are dead and gone
> And the jokes we had and the fun.
>
> How happy they are I cannot know
> But happy am I who loved them so.

I'm Here For A Short Visit Only

NOËL COWARD

I'm here for a short visit only
And I'd rather be loved than hated:
Eternity may be lonely
When my body's disintegrated,
And that which is loosely termed my soul
Goes whizzing off through the infinite
By means of some vague remote control;
I'd like to think I was missed a bit.

Epitaph

(Said to have been once found in Bushey Churchyard, Hertfordshire)

'Is it still there?' I wondered, and went to St James's Church, Bushey on a very cold May morning to find out. I looked at every gravestone in the hilly churchyard and found nothing. But later, in the warm church hall, I met Margot Bliss, who told me, 'Yes it was here. In fact it was quoted in the parish magazine last December.' She got it out and showed it to me, and it said, 'Epitaph in Bushey Churchyard, before 1860, destroyed by 1916.'

Here lies a poor woman who always was tired,
For she lived in a place where help wasn't hired,
Her last words on earth were, 'Dear friends, I am going,
Where washing ain't done nor cooking nor sewing,
And everything there is exact to my wishes,
For there they don't eat, there's no washing of dishes,
I'll be where loud anthems will always be ringing
(But having no voice, I'll be out of the singing).
Don't mourn for me now, don't grieve for me never,
For I'm going to do nothing for ever and ever.'

Go Cheerful

ROSEMARY ANNE SISSON

A persistent plea in pieces for memorial services is 'Don't be sad;
be cheerful.' Rosemary Anne Sisson is a cheerful woman, and a
delight to be with, as I discovered when I was in one of the five
films she wrote for Walt Disney, *Escape from the Dark*. This poem
is collected in her book, *Rosemary for Remembrance*.

When my time has come to die,
I hope that there may be
To bid farewell to me
A brilliant, cloudlessly-blue sky.

I hope the lilac is in bloom,
And daffodils may dance,
And tulips bend and glance,
And sunlight stream into the room.

Don't draw the curtains, don't pull down the blind,
And don't wear sombre dress.
Don't think of ugliness,
If to my memory you would be kind.

Please ask the Minister to speak of me
As one who trod
Life's path with God.
Oh, let his words ring out in glorious certainty!

Plant flowers there among the grass
Whose cheerful bloom
And sweet perfume

May please the churchgoers who pass.

Oh, don't let dying make my memory false!
Put in my epitaph
How much I loved to laugh,
And that I loved to dance to an old-fashioned waltz.

Indian Prayer

I read this at the funeral of Norman Warwick, Hannah Gordon's husband. He had died in the summer of 1994 and Hannah found this among his papers. 'So in a strange way it belongs to him,' she said, 'and it is exactly what he would have said himself.'

Its extreme brevity gives the reader an opportunity to preface it with a memory of 'some moment/That is pleasant to recall.'

> When I am dead,
> Cry for me a little,
> Think of me sometimes
> But not too much.
>
> Think of me now and again
> As I was in life at some moment
> That is pleasant to recall –
> But not too long.
>
> Leave me in peace
> And I shall leave you in peace.
> And whilst you live
> Let your thoughts be with the living.

I Am Not There

AUTHOR UNKNOWN

I first heard this in Griff Rhys Jones's entertaining programme, *The Bookworm*, on BBC 1. The mother and father of a soldier who had died found a copy of it among his possessions and thought he might have written it. There was a clamour for it from the viewers and, along with thousands of others, I sent my cheque for £1 to Children in Need for my copy of it. However, a week or so later it was declared Anonymous. Since then it has turned up in Ned Sherrin's book, but with curious differences. Here are both versions, with the one from *The Bookworm* first.

Do not stand at my grave and weep.
    I am not there. I do not sleep.
I am a thousand winds that blow.
I am the diamond glints on snow.
I am the sunlight on ripened grain.
    I am the gentle autumn rain.

When you awaken in the morning's hush
    I am the swift uplifting rush
    of quiet birds in circled flight.
I am the soft stars that shine at night.

Do not stand at my grave and cry
    I am not there; I did not die.

336

Do Not Be Afraid

AMERICAN INDIAN

Do not stand at my grave and weep
I am not there, I do not sleep.
I am a thousand winds that blow,
I am the diamond glint on snow.
I am the sunlight on ripened grain,
I am the gentle autumn rain.
When you wake in the morning hush
I am the swift, uplifting rush
of quiet birds in circling flight.
I am the soft starlight at night.
Do not stand at my grave and weep
I am not there – I do not sleep.

A Song of Living

AMELIA JOSEPHINE BURR

At a memorial service for Greer Garson at St Paul's, Covent Garden in July 1996, Andrew Ray read the first version of the previous poem, and I read this. We had both been in a television recording of Royce Ryton's play, *Crown Matrimonial*, in which Greer had been Queen Mary. She was one of the most generous people I've ever met, and a real mate, and I thought there was a lot of her in this.

Because I have loved life, I shall have no sorrow to die.
I have sent up my gladness on wings, to be lost in the blue
of the sky.
I have run and leaped with the rain, I have taken the wind
to my breast.
My cheek like a drowsy child to the face of the earth I have
pressed.
Because I have loved life, I shall have no sorrow to die.

I have kissed young Love on the lips, I have heard his song
to the end.
I have struck my hand like a seal in the loyal hand of a friend.
I have known the peace of heaven, the comfort of work done
well.
I have longed for death in the darkness and risen alive out of
hell.
Because I have loved life, I shall have no sorrow to die.

I give a share of my soul to the world where my course is
run.

I know that another shall finish the task I must leave undone.

I know that no flower, nor flint was in vain on the path I trod.

As one looks on a face through a window, through life I have looked on God.

Because I have loved life, I shall have no sorrow to die.

Man's Mortality

ANONYMOUS

Doubts about the Virgin Birth, the Resurrection and the Ascension have noticeably increased in recent years, spurred on by pronouncements made by certain prominent clergymen. As a result there is, I think, a growing reluctance to include in memorial services pieces which affirm the likelihood of an Afterlife.

Nevertheless, this anonymous poem is such a happy expression of it, with its long lists of things which are transitory, as opposed to man, who 'shall live again,' that I want to include it here. It has the advantage of being eminently cuttable: you can do as many or as few of the stanzas as you want, provided you keep in the last one!

Notes:

1. 'The gourd which Jonas had': God provided a gourd (vine) to give shade from the relentless sun, but the next day allowed a worm to chew it so that it withered.

2. 'Dole,' in the fourth stanza, is a charitable gift, usually of a fixed amount.

3. Lazarus was a beggar whose sores were licked by dogs, who died, and 'was carried by the angels into Abraham's bosom.'

4. Tabitha, also called Dorcas, was sick, and died. St Peter prayed and said, 'Tabitha arise.' And she opened her eyes and sat up.

5. Jonas (Jonah) was at sea in a great storm and was swallowed by a whale. After three days 'it vomited out Jonas upon the dry land.'

Like as the damask rose you see,
Or like the blossom on the tree,
Or like the dainty flower of May,
Or like the morning to the day,
Or like the sun, or like the shade,
Or like the gourd which Jonas had —
Even such is man, whose thread is spun,
Drawn out, and cut, and so is done.
The rose withers, the blossom blasteth,
The flower fades, the morning hasteth,
The sun sets, the shadow flies,
The gourd consumes; and man he dies.

Like to the grass that's newly sprung,
Or like a tale that's new begun,
Or like the bird that's here to-day.
Or like the pearled dew of May,
Or like an hour, or like a span,
Or like the singing of a swan —
Even such is man, who lives by breath,
Is here, now there: so life, and death.
The grass withers, the tale is ended,
The bird is flown, the dew's ascended,
The hour is short, the span not long,
The swan's near death; man's life is done.

Like to the bubble in the brook,
Or, in a glass, much like a look,
Or like a shuttle in weaver's hand,
Or like a writing on the sand,
Or like a thought, or like a dream,
Or like the gliding of the stream —
Even such is man, who lives by breath,
Is here, now there: so life, and death.
The bubble's cut, the look's forgot,
The shuttle's flung, the writing's blot,

The thought is past, the dream is gone,
The water glides; man's life is done.

Like to an arrow from the bow,
Or like swift course of watery flow,
Or like the time 'twixt flood and ebb,
Or like the spider's tender web,
Or like a race, or like a goal,
Or like the dealing of a dole –
Even such is man, whose brittle state
Is always subject unto fate.
The arrow's shot, the flood soon spent,
The time no time, the web soon rent,
The race soon run, the goal soon won,
The dole soon dealt; man's life first done.

Like to the lightning from the sky,
Or like a post that quick doth hie,
Or like a quaver in short song,
Or like a journey three days long,
Or like the snow when summer's come,
Or like the pear, or like the plum –
Even such is man, who heaps up sorrow,
Lives but this day and dies to-morrow.
The lightning's past, the post must go,
The song is short, the journey's so,
The pear doth rot, the plum doth fall,
The snow dissolves, and so must all.

Like to the seed put in earth's womb,
Or like dead Lazarus in his tomb,
Or like Tabitha being asleep,
Or Jonas-like within the deep,
Or like the night, or stars by day
Which seem to vanish clean away:
Even so this death man's life bereaves,

But, being dead, man death deceives.
The seed it springeth, Lazarus standeth,
Tabitha wakes, and Jonas landeth,
The night is past, the stars remain;
So man that dies shall live again.

How Do I Love Thee?

ELIZABETH BARRETT BROWNING

It was Dame Wendy Hiller, with whom I spent a royal year in *Crown Matrimonial* at the Theatre Royal, Haymarket, who introduced me to the *Sonnets from the Portuguese* by Elizabeth Barrett Browning. She read this hauntingly at the memorial service for Dame Gwen Ffrangcon-Davies at St Martin-in-the-Fields in June 1992.

How do I love thee? Let me count the ways.
I love thee to the depth and breadth and height
My soul can reach, when feeling out of sight
For the ends of Being and ideal Grace.
I love thee to the level of every day's
Most quiet need, by sun and candlelight.
I love thee freely, as men strive for Right;
I love thee purely, as they turn from Praise.
I love thee with the passion put to use
In my old griefs, and with my childhood's faith.
I love thee with a love I seemed to lose
With my lost saints, — I love thee with the breath,
Smiles, tears, of all my life! — and, if God choose,
I shall but love thee better after death.

Heraclitus

WILLIAM JOHNSON CORY

'I have a real fondness for this,' said Donald Sinden, when he suggested it to me.

The Greek philosopher Heraclitus (c.540–475 BC) was born at Ephesus, in the province of Caria, in the mountainous south-west corner of Asia Minor. He believed that the single cause of all physical phenomena was fire. 'Everything burns,' he said, meaning, not that flames were everywhere, but that everything was in a constant state of flux. He wrote, 'To think is the greatest virtue; and wisdom consists of speaking what is true.' No wonder the conversations between him and the poet had 'tired the sun with talking'!

They told me, Heraclitus, they told me you were dead,
They brought me bitter news to hear and bitter tears to
    shed.
I wept as I remembered how often you and I
Had tired the sun with talking and sent him down the sky.

And now that thou art lying, my dear old Carian guest,
A handful of grey ashes, long, long ago at rest,
Still are thy pleasant voices, thy nightingales, awake:
For Death, he taketh all away, but them he cannot take.

If I Should Go Before the Rest of You

JOYCE GRENFELL

I received identical double choices, this and the next piece, from two friends: Robin Hawdon, the playwright, and Canon Frank Wright. Robin says of this one, 'I carry this enchanting piece around in my Filofax. I cut it out of a newspaper which had included it in an obituary piece about her.'

> If I should go before the rest of you,
> Break not a flower nor inscribe a stone.
> Nor when I'm gone speak in a Sunday voice,
> But be the usual selves that I have known.
> Weep if you must,
> Parting is hell,
> But life goes on,
> So sing as well.

Song

CHRISTINA ROSSETTI

When I am dead, my dearest,
Sing no sad songs for me;
Plant thou no roses at my head,
Nor shady cypress tree:
Be the green grass above me
With showers and dewdrops wet;
And if thou wilt, remember,
And if thou wilt, forget.

I shall not see the shadows,
I shall not feel the rain;
I shall not hear the nightingale
Sing on, as if in pain;
And dreaming through the twilight
That doth not rise nor set,
Haply I may remember,
And haply may forget.

Remember

CHRISTINA ROSSETTI

The theme of 'Do not grieve' persists in this second poem by
Christina Rossetti, sent to me by Tom Conti.

Remember me when I am gone away,
    Gone far away into the silent land;
    When you can no more hold me by the hand,
Nor I half turn to go, yet turning stay.
Remember me when no more day by day
    You tell me of our future that you planned:
    Only remember me; you understand
It will be late to counsel then or pray.

Yet if you should forget me for a while
    And afterwards remember, do not grieve:
    For if the darkness and corruption leave
    A vestige of the thoughts that once I had,
Better by far you should forget and smile
    Than that you should remember and be sad.

When Earth's Last Picture is Painted
RUDYARD KIPLING

Sent to me by Ian Richardson, this would be a splendid choice
for a memorial service for a painter!

When Earth's last picture is painted and the tubes are twisted
and dried,
When the oldest colours have faded, and the youngest critic
has died,
We shall rest, and, faith, we shall need it – lie down for an
aeon or two,
Till the Master of All Good Workmen shall put us to work
anew.

And those that were good shall be happy: they shall sit in a
golden chair;
They shall splash at a ten-league canvas with brushes of
comets' hair.
They shall find real saints to draw from – Magdalene, Peter,
and Paul;
They shall work for an age at a sitting and never be tired at
all!

And only the Master shall praise us, and only the Master shall
blame;
And no one shall work for money, and no one shall work
for fame,
But each for the joy of the working, and each, in his separate
star,
Shall draw the Thing as he sees It for the God of Things as
They are!

The Ship

BISHOP CHARLES H. BRENT

I conclude this section with two more pieces from Ned Sherrin's
book. This one paints such a vivid picture of a ship getting smaller
as it sails way, but larger as it approaches a far, welcoming shore,
that it is unmissable.

> What is dying?
> I am standing in the sea shore,
> a ship sails to the morning breeze
> and starts for the ocean.
> She is an object of beauty
> and I stand watching her
> till at last she fades
> on the horizon
> and someone at my side says,
> 'She is gone'.
> Gone! Where?
> Gone from my sight – that is all.
> She is just as large in the masts, hull and spars
> as she was when I saw her,
> and just as able to bear her load of living
> freight to its destination.
> The diminished size and total loss of sight is in me,
> not in her;
> and just at the moment when someone at my side says,
> 'She is gone'
> there are others who are watching her coming,

and other voices take up a glad shout —

'There she comes!'

— and that is dying.

How Long is a Man's Life?

BRIAN PATTEN

Cuanto vive el hombre por fin? Vive mil dias o uno solo?
Una Semana o varios siglos? Por cuanto tiempo muere el
hombre?
Que quiere decir 'para siempre'?

Pablo Neruda

And this is Ned Sherrin's 'dark horse tip.' He included it only in
his Introduction, for it hadn't been published by the time *Remembrance* came out. It is in *Armada*, a collection of poems and elegies
by Brian Patten. 'He read it on *Loose Ends* on BBC Radio 4 and
we received an unprecedented number of requests for copies,'
wrote Ned Sherrin. 'The poem speaks with such a universal voice
that I'm sure it will strike a chord.'

How long does a man live, after all?
A thousand days, or only one?
One week, or a few centuries?
How long does a man spend living or dying
and what do we mean when we say, gone forever?

Adrift in such preoccupations, we seek clarification.
We can go to the philosophers,
but they will weary of our questions.
We can go to the priests and the rabbis
but they might be too busy with administrations.

So, How long does a man live, after all?
And how much does he live while he lives?

We fret, and ask so many questions –
then when it comes to us
the answer is so simple after all.

A man lives for as long as we carry him inside us,
for as long as we carry the harvest of his dreams,
for as long as we ourselves live,
holding memories in common, a man lives.

His lover will carry his man's scent, his touch;
his children will carry the weight of his love.
One friend will carry his arguments,
another will hum his favourite tunes,
another will still share his terrors.

And the days will pass with baffled faces,
then the weeks, then the months,
then there will be a day when no question is asked,
and the knots of grief will loosen in the stomach,
and the puffed faces will calm.
And on that day he will not have ceased,
    but will have ceased to be separated by death.
How long does a man live, after all?

A man lives so many different lengths of time.

The Four Seasons

The Four Seasons, and Love, provide the reader's staple diet. Poems, prose and party pieces about them are legion, and can be used at most of the Occasions included in this book. It's always nice to have something appropriate for *when* a concert takes place: Christmas in winter, Easter in spring, Armistice Day in autumn, etc. Here are just a few.

Tree

CHERYL MARTIN, aged 12

What a tree must feel like in each of the four seasons! I found this just in time for *The Four Seasons, But Not Vivaldi* concert. I did it as the opening item. It introduced the theme, set the tone and, because it starts with summer and ends fortuitously with spring, it heralded the first song with a flourish.

It's another poem in *From Cover to Cover*, published by Kent Arts and Libraries.

> Summer.
> My luscious leaves
> Shimmer in the sunlight.
> They quiver in the gentle breeze.
> Under my huge structure it is cool and shady.
>
> Autumn.
> My leaves shine gold,
> Red, brown, orange.
> The strong gusts of chilly wind
> Strip my priceless treasure from me.
> They go twisting and twirling
> Out of my reach,
> Leaving me naked.
>
> Winter.
> My dull brown skeleton stands alone.
> My long fingers stretch up to the sky.
> The snowflakes flutter silently to the ground,
> Creating a white, silky blanket.

357

Long, spiky icicles hang
From my bare branches.

Spring.
The March wind caresses my branches,
And April rain helps the tiny, delicate buds
Sprout from my body.
I am soon covered in juicy green leaves.
I feel excited and full of energy.
Colour has returned to the world.

The First Spring Day

CHRISTINA ROSSETTI

It is the deep and tender longing for spring, both in nature and the human heart, that gives this poem such a personal voice.

I wonder if the sap is stirring yet,
If wintry birds are dreaming of a mate,
If frozen snowdrops feel as yet the sun
And crocus fires are kindling one by one:
    Sing, robin, sing;
I still am sore in doubt concerning Spring.

I wonder if the springtide of this year
Will bring another Spring both lost and dear;
If heart and spirit will find out their Spring,
Or if the world alone will bud and sing:
    Sing, hope, to me;
Sweet notes, my hope, soft notes for memory.

The sap will surely quicken soon or late,
The tardiest bird will twitter to a mate;
So Spring must dawn again with warmth and bloom,
Or in this world, or in the world to come:
    Sing, voice of Spring,
Till I too blossom and rejoice and sing.

The Fight of the Year

ROGER McGOUGH

Good for a bit of acting, this: you're the radio commentator.

'And there goes the bell for the third month
and Winter comes out of its corner looking groggy
Spring leads with a left to the head
followed by a sharp right to the body
    daffodils
    primroses
    crocuses
    snowdrops
    lilacs
    violets
    pussywillow
Winter can't take much more punishment
and Spring shows no signs of tiring
    tadpoles
    squirrels
    baalambs
    badgers
    bunny rabbits
    mad march hares
    horses and hounds
Spring is merciless
Winter won't go the full twelve rounds
    bobtail clouds
    scallywaggy winds
    the sun

a pavement artist
in every town
A left to the chin
and Winter's down!
  1 tomatoes
  2 radish
  3 cucumber
  4 onions
  5 beetroot
  6 celery
  7 and any
  8 amount
  9 of lettuce
  10 for dinner
Winter's out for the count
Spring is the winner!'

Home Thoughts From Abroad

ROBERT BROWNING

I am including some terrifically well-known pieces in this book simply because they are so terrifically good: wonderful to speak and interesting to work on. Writing from his self-imposed exile in Italy, Browning compared the 'gaudy melon-flower', which he saw there, to the sights and sounds of a remembered English spring.

The poem provides interesting examples of what you could call 'getting rid of bits of it'. In the first stanza the essential words, from the second line to the sixth, are: 'And whoever wakes in England – Sees . . . That the lowest boughs and the brushwood sheaf . . . are in tiny leaf.' So you could stress those and skate over all the others. Similarly, in the second stanza, slightly harder to do because of rather more skating, the essential words, this time from the third line to the sixth, are: 'Hark! . . . That's the wise thrush.'

I

Oh, to be in England
Now that April's there,
And whoever wakes in England
Sees, some morning, unaware,
That the lowest boughs and the brush-wood sheaf
Round the elm-tree bole are in tiny leaf,
While the chaffinch sings on the orchard bough
In England – now!

II

And after April, when May follows,

And the whitethroat builds, and all the swallows —
Hark! where my blossomèd pear-tree in the hedge
Leans to the field and scatters on the clover
Blossoms and dewdrops — at the bent spray's edge —
That's the wise thrush; he sings each song twice over,
Lest you should think he never could recapture
The first fine careless rapture!
And though the fields look rough with hoary dew,
All will be gay when noontide wakes anew
The buttercups, the little children's dower,
— Far brighter than this gaudy melon-flower!

The Poem I'd Like To Write

CLIVE SANSOM

I'd like to write a poem about daffodils.
I'd like to say
How beautiful they look on a March day,
Their green stems rising
Into those large, incredibly surprising
Trumpets of pure gold;
And how, after frost and cold,
They bring
Such colour and such warmth to everything,
They shake us into Spring.

I'd like to write it, but I know
That Wordsworth wrote it long ago.

A Nursery Rhyme
as it might have been written by
William Wordsworth

WENDY COPE

Hardly a Four Seasons poem, but it makes an amusing companion
piece to the preceding one.

> The skylark and the jay sang loud and long,
> The sun was calm and bright, the air was sweet,
> When all at once I heard above the throng
> Of jocund birds a single plaintive bleat.
>
> And, turning, saw, as one sees in a dream,
> It was a Sheep had broke the moorland peace
> With his sad cry, a creature who did seem
> The blackest thing that ever wore a fleece.
>
> I walked towards him on the stony track
> And, pausing for a while between two crags,
> I asked him, 'Have you wool upon your back?'
> Thus he bespake, 'Enough to fill three bags.'
>
> Most courteously, in measured tones, he told
> Who would receive each bag and where they dwelt;
> And oft, now years have passed and I am old,
> I recollect with joy that inky pelt.

Springtime

TIM SHACKLETON

I took this straightforward but charming piece from the cover of the presentation pack of the Royal Mail Mint Stamps for spring, 1995. The stamps themselves were photographs of tiny sculptures, by Andy Goldsworthy, made out of dandelions, sweet chestnut and garlic leaves and spring grass.

It's possible to overlook the change of the seasons in cities – it just gets colder, it gets warmer, it rains. In the country, however, you can't ignore springtime; it's all around. One day the fields are empty, the next they're lush with new green shoots. There's an old country saying: 'It's not spring until you can plant your foot upon twelve daisies.' The earth itself changes colour and so, as their water content dries out, do the stones in walls and buildings. The smells are different too, sweet and fresh. Birds are in fine voice as their courtship begins. Spring is a feast for the senses; things are changing at last.

This sense of change and regrowth has been celebrated for centuries. Traditions such as dancing round the maypole are relics of ancient spring celebrations. Even the Old English word for springtime, *lencten*, means 'lengthening' – how the days so clearly change following the spring equinox.

From *The Weald of Youth*

SIEGFRIED SASSOON

Siegfried Sassoon writes here of peaceful summers in Kent when
he was in his early twenties. He lived at Matfield, near Brenchley,
and the garden sloped down to the north, giving an uninterrupted
view of Paddock Wood and the Weald beyond. It was just a year
or two before the First World War.

In summer I didn't often wake early. But when I did, and
had the gumption to get up and see the sunrise, I was always
glad of it afterwards. In fact a few such 'getting-ups' have
dwelt in my remembrance ever since.

Out on the lawn the Eden freshness was like something
never breathed before. In a purified ecstasy I inhaled the
smell of dew-soaked grass, and all the goodness of being alive
now met me in a moment, as I stood on the doorstep outside
the drawing-room.

Near and far, the June landscape was vocal with the
exultant chorus of the birds, here in the terraced garden and
away down into the low-misted Weald, where my old friend
the milk-train was puffing away from Paddock Wood station.
Somehow the sound of it gave me a comfortable feeling of
the world remaining pleasantly unchanged and peaceful . . .
The white pigeons too were already up and about, sitting
idly on the gabled roof above their loft as though they didn't
quite know what to do with themselves after getting up so
early.

And now I was beholding the sun himself as his scarlet
disc rose inch by inch above the auroral orchards and the

level horizon far down the Weald. A very Kentish sun he looked, while I surmised, as had always been my habit, that he must be rising from somewhere just beyond Canterbury or the cliffs of Dover – rising out of the English Channel, in fact – this being as yet the boundary of my earthly adventures in that direction. There he was, anyhow, like some big farmer staring at his hay-fields and hop-gardens.

And here was I, unconsciously lifting my arms to welcome the glittering shafts of sunrise that went wide-winged up through the innocent blueness above the east.

But with the first rays slanting across the lawn everything somehow became ordinary again. On the tennis-court below, a busy little party of birds was after the worms. And I noticed that I'd forgotten to loosen the net when we'd finished yesterday evening's game. I yawned; felt a bit lonely; and then went indoors to see if I could find myself something to eat.

Summer

JOHN BETJEMAN

Betjeman was thirteen and a half when he wrote this as an exercise for prep. He was a happy schoolboy at the Dragon School in Oxford, and his poem was later published in its magazine, *The Draconian*.

Whatever will rhyme with Summer?
There only is 'plumber' and 'drummer':
Why! the cleverest bard
Would find it quite hard
To connect with the Summer – a plumber!

My Mind's getting glummer and glummer
Hooray! there's a word besides drummer;
Oh, I will think of some
Ere the prep's end has come
But the rhymes will get rummer and rummer.

Ah! If the bee hums, it's a hummer;
And the bee showeth signs of the Summer;
Also holiday babels
Make th'porter gum labels,
And whenever he gums, he's a gummer!

The cuckoo's a goer and comer
He goes in the hot days of Summer;
But he cucks ev'ry day
Till you plead and you pray
That his voice will get dumber and dumber!

From the *Evening Standard*

The headline was 'Official: it's the hottest August ever.'

And the leading paragraph said, 'At midnight tonight it comes to an end – one of the hottest, driest summers of the last 200 years. This month is the hottest August ever recorded, with an average 24-hour temperature of 67.9°F, and an average daily maximum of nearly 80°F.'

The article which followed was written by Valentine Low and Simon Perry, who remembered some of the details of that extraordinary summer.

British seaside resorts had a boom year as people decided to take their holidays at home. In Blackpool some 30,000 more deckchairs were hired out than last summer, and Bournemouth reported business up 20 per cent on last year. Kathy Chellew of the British Tourist Authority said, 'One of my colleagues went to Bournemouth and said it looked like California with all those bronzed bodies on the beach.'

300 sheep and 80 cattle had to be shipped off the Isle of Lundy to the north Devon village of Appledore, 13 miles away, because of a shortage of water on the island.

Free bottles of water were delivered to thousands of homes by Welsh Water after tapwater from the reservoir at Llandegfed turned green.

The spectre of drought orders hung over millions of water users for much of August. More than 17 million people were hit by hosepipe bans – one third of the population of England and Wales.

The sleepy hamlet of Telscombe Cliffs between Newhaven and Brighton was split in two by the hot weather. Most of the village is served by Southern Water, which had a hosepipe ban, but some families on the Eastbourne side of the village get their supplies from South East Water, which did not. Gardeners in the 'dry' half of the village turned green with envy as they watched their neighbours sprinkle their gardens.

Swarms of ladybirds drove sunbathers off beaches in the west country. They even bit people in their search for moisture.

Rare insects which turned up to enjoy the sun included Camberwell Beauty butterflies, which were blown in from the Low Countries on their way down from Scandinavia. Hummingbird hawk moths also paid a visit from their normal habitat of Southern Europe and North Africa.

At London Zoo, rhinos Jos and Rosie had to have sun cream rubbed into their hides to stop them from burning. Originally from East Africa, they are unused to so much direct sunlight because their natural habitat provides them with shelter.

Moorlands got so dry that officials in three National Parks warned they were at greater risk of ecological disaster than at any time since 1976. Fire burned slowly beneath the surface of peat moors near Wensleydale, and five fire engines had to soak the ground to stop it spreading. Cannock Chase was closed to the public on the advice of the Fire Brigade, and more than 80 square miles of moorland in the Peak National Park was closed.

Weather forecasters on Radio 4's *Today* programme got tired of saying the same thing every morning, and wondered how they would fill the bulletin when the whole country was sun, sun, sun. Not TV's Ian McCaskill, however. He said, 'It's not a bit boring for us, because records are tumbling right and left. This is sheer naked excitement for weathermen!'

371

Prayer For Michaelmas

VIOLA GARVIN

Michaelmas Day, no longer heralded in our pocket diaries, is the
Festival of St Michael and All Angels, observed on 29 September,
and one of the English quarter days. I found this charming prefer-
ence for an earthly autumn over a shining paradise in a book
called *Uncommon Prayers*, edited by Cecil Hunt.

Good Saint Michael, if we must
Leave our bodies here to dust,
Grant our souls a heaven where we
Still your Michaelmas may see.
Do not make me quire and sing
With radiant angels in a ring,
Nor idly tread a pearl-paved street
With my new unearthly feet;
Do not shut me in a heaven
Golden bright from morn to even,
Where no shadows and no showers
Dim the tedious, shining hours.
Grant that there be autumn still,
Smoke-blue dusk, brown crisp and chill,
And let the furrowed plough-land bare
Curve strongly to the windswept air;
Make the leafy beechwoods burn
Russet, yellow, bronze by turn,
And set the hedgerow and the briar
Thick with berries red as fire.
Let me search and gather up

Acorns green, with knobbed cup,
And prickly chestnuts, plumping down
To show a glossy kernel brown.
Splendid cities like me ill,
And for song I have no skill;
Then let me, in an autumn wood,
Sweep, and pick up sticks for God.

Autumn 1964
(For Karen)

JOHN BETJEMAN

Red apples hang like globes of light
   Against this pale November haze,
And now, although the mist is white,
   In half-an-hour a day of days
Will climb into its golden height
   And Sunday bells will ring its praise.

The sparkling flint, the darkling yew,
   The red brick, less intensely red
Than hawthorn berries bright with dew
   Or leaves of creeper still unshed,
The watery sky washed clean and new,
   Are all rejoicing with the dead.

The yellowing elm shows yet some green,
   The mellowing bells exultant sound:
Never have light and colour been
   So prodigally thrown around;
And in the bells the promise tells
   Of greater light where Love is found.

Back From Australia

JOHN BETJEMAN

Betjeman wrote this poem in 1971, soon after his return to Treen, his house in Trebetherick in North Cornwall: he'd been filming for a four-part series for television called *Betjeman in Australia.*

Trebetherick is at the mouth of the River Camel. Stepper Point is across the water, and Bray (or Brea) Hill is just to the south of the village. The tiny Norman church of St Enodoc, where Betjeman is buried, nestles beneath it.

> Cocooned in Time, at this inhuman height,
>   The packaged food tastes neutrally of clay.
>   We never seem to catch the running day
> But travel on in everlasting night
> With all the chic accoutrements of flight:
>   Lotions and essences in neat array
>   And yet another plastic cup and tray.
> 'Thank you *so* much. Oh no, I'm quite all right'.
>
> At home in Cornwall hurrying autumn skies
>   Leave Bray Hill barren, Stepper jutting bare,
>   And hold the moon above the sea-wet sand.
> The very last of late September dies
>   In frosty silence and the hills declare
>   How vast the sky is, looked at from the land.

Ode to Autumn

JOHN KEATS

The trouble with a well-known poem is that you think you know it when you don't. You know a generalised, and often sentimentalised, reduction of it. It has an all-over colour, rather than a pattern.

It was only when I was studying this poem for *The Four Seasons* concert that I realised I didn't know it at all. I had never clearly identified the three different aspects of autumn described in the three stanzas: in the first, its weather, fruits and flowers; in the second, its personification as a languid young man with long hair, lying about the place; and in the third, its songs and sounds. At the concert I introduced it thus, and at least one person came up afterwards and said she'd understood it for the first time. 'Join the gang,' I confessed, gratefully.

Yes. A little explanation can go a long way.

But the trouble with a little explanation is that, once you've received it, it all seems so obvious that you're surprised a little explanation was thought necessary in the first place!

Season of mists and mellow fruitfulness,
    Close bosom-friend of the maturing sun;
Conspiring with him how to load and bless
    With fruit the vines that round the thatch-eaves run;
To bend with apples the moss'd cottage-trees,
    And fill all fruit with ripeness to the core;
        To swell the gourd, and plump the hazel shells
    With a sweet kernel; to set budding more,
And still more, later flowers for the bees,

Until they think warm days will never cease;
    For summer has o'erbrimm'd their clammy cells.

Who hath not seen thee oft amid thy store?
    Sometimes whoever seeks abroad may find
Thee sitting careless on a granary floor,
    Thy hair soft-lifted by the winnowing wind;
Or on a half-reap'd furrow sound asleep,
    Drows'd with the fume of poppies, while thy hook
      Spares the next swath and all its twinéd flowers;
And sometimes like a gleaner thou dost keep
    Steady thy laden head across a brook;
    Or by a cider-press, with patient look,
      Thou watchest the last oozings, hours by hours.

Where are the songs of Spring? Aye, where are they?
      Think not of them, – thou hast thy music too,
    While barréd clouds bloom the soft-dying day
      And touch the stubble-plains with rosy hue;
    Then in a wailful choir the small gnats mourn
Among the river sallows, borne aloft
      Or sinking as the light wind lives or dies;
And full-grown lambs loud bleat from hilly bourn;
    Hedge-crickets sing, and now with treble soft
    The redbreast whistles from a garden-croft,
      And gathering swallows twitter in the skies.

November

TOM HOOD

Thomas Hood (1799–1845) was a London poet and journalist
who knew about peasoupers! This can be a most effective party
piece if the first half, say up to 'No knowing 'em,' is a gradual
crescendo of awfulness, and the second a diminuendo of just – oh
– giving up, so that the last line is whispered.

No sun, no moon.
No morn, no noon.
No dawn, no dusk, no proper time of day,
No sky, no earthly view,
No distance looking blue,
No roads, no streets, no t'other side the way;
No end to any row,
No indication where the crescents go,
No top to any steeple,
No recognition of familiar people,
No courtesies for showing 'em,
No knowing 'em!
No travelling at all – no locomotion,
No inkling of the way – no notion,
'No go' – by land or ocean,
No mail, no post,
No news from any foreign coast,
No park, no ring, no afternoon gentility;
No company, no nobility,
No warmth, no cheerfulness, no healthful ease,
No comfortable feel in any member,

No shade, no shine, no butterflies, no bees,
No fruits, no flowers, no leaves, no birds,
No–Vember

Snowflakes

CLIVE SANSOM

That each snowflake is different is well known. But never can
it have been put more eloquently and serenely than in this
poem.

And did you know
That every flake of snow
That forms so high
In the grey winter sky
And falls so far,
Is a bright six-pointed star?
Each crystal grows
A flower as perfect as a rose.
Lace could never make
The patterns of a flake.
No brooch
Of figured silver could approach
Its delicate craftsmanship. And think:
Each pattern is distinct.
Of all the snowflakes floating there –
The million million in the air –
None is the same. Each star
Is newly forged, as faces are,
Shaped to its own design
Like yours and mine.
And yet . . . each one
Melts when its flight is done;
Holds frozen loveliness

A moment, even less;
Suspends itself in time –
And passes like a rhyme.

London Snow

ROBERT BRIDGES

'Yes, that's how it is,' you want to say after almost every line of this haunting poem. Or rather, 'Yes, that's how it used to be.' Gerald Isaaman sent it to me.

When men were all asleep the snow came flying,
In large white flakes falling on the city brown,
Stealthily and perpetually settling and loosely lying,
 Hushing the latest traffic of the drowsy town;
Deadening, muffling, stifling its murmurs falling;
Lazily and incessantly floating down and down:
 Silently sifting and veiling road, roof and railing;
Hiding difference, making unevenness even,
Into angles and crevices softly drifting and sailing.
 All night it fell, and when full inches seven
It lay in the depth of its uncompacted lightness,
Its clouds blew off from a high and frosty heaven;
 And all woke earlier for the unaccustomed brightness
Of the winter dawning, the strange unheavenly glare:
The eye marvelled — marvelled at the dazzling whiteness;
 The ear harkened to the stillness of the solemn air;
No sound of wheel rumbling nor of foot falling,
And the busy morning cries came thin and spare.
 Then boys I heard, as they went to school, calling,
They gathered up the crystal manna to freeze
Their tongues with tasting, their hands with snow-balling;
 Or rioted in a drift, plunging up to the knees;
Or peering up from under the white-mossed wonder,

'O look at the trees!' they cried, 'O look at the trees!'
  With lessened load a few carts creak and blunder,
Following along the white deserted way,
A country company long dispersed asunder:
  When now already the sun, in pale display
Standing by Paul's high dome, spread forth below
His sparkling beams, and awoke the stir of the day.

  For now doors open, and war is waged with the snow;
And trains of sombre men, past tale of number,
Tread long brown paths, as toward their toil they go:
  But even for them awhile no cares encumber
Their minds diverted; the daily word unspoken,
The daily thoughts of labour and sorrow slumber
At the sight of the beauty that greets them, for the charm
  they have broken.

Snow in Suburbia

DAVID LODGE

This same subject, differently put. And more like how it is now.

Sunday in the city, and there is snow.
It melts reluctantly in cold canals;
Buses plough furrows through the heavy slush;
Congregations steam gently through the first hymn.

In the quiet, residential street
Few footsteps violate the white carpet.
A kind of grace has settled on
The roofs of ugly, half-timbered houses.

It softens the bulbous shapes of cars,
Clings delicately to clotheslines, privet hedges,
Moulds itself to heaps of coal,
Spends its beauty on the meanest object.

But behind the doors of 'Ferndale',
'Belmont' and 'Sunnyside' stand men
Gum-booted and breathing quickly, their hands
Eagerly fingering the handles of spades.

Scarcely has the snow begun to falter
Before they are out, and the street resounds
To the rasp and scrape of iron on stone.
They are turning the white beauty upside down

And hurling into the gutter,
Exposing the dirty pavement and the hard

Line of the kerbstones. This done,
They brush the tops of their gates and hedges.

Then, with tools at the ready, they march up the street,
Knocking on the doors of the aged, sick and widowed,
Offering to rid more paths and pavements
Of the intolerable white plague;

Until only one semi-detached house bears
Its spotless white apron. My house.
They look reproachfully at my front door,
For I am neither aged, sick, nor widowed.

Making a spyhole in the misted window,
I peer down at the desecrated street.
The men prowl round my apron, but will not touch it.
One is shaking the snow from a sooty tree.

Dissatisfied, the men disperse, stamping their boots,
Squinting at the sky, hopeful of another fall.
Satisfied, I return to my book.
I prefer my sepulchre whited.

When the River Thames Froze

The hottest summers are now; the coldest winters were then. Global warming, we call it.

The River Thames froze nine times between the sixteenth and nineteenth centuries. *Dawk's Newletter* of January 14, 1716, describes that winter's frost.

The Thames seems now a solid rock of ice, and booths for the sale of brandy, wine, ale and other exhilarating liquors, have been for some time fixed thereon; but now it is in a manner like a town: thousands of people cross it, and with wonder view the mountainous heaps of water, that now lie congealed into ice. On Thursday, a great cook's shop was erected, and gentlemen went as frequently to dine there, as at any ordinary. Over against Westminster, Printing-presses are kept upon the ice, where many persons have their names printed, to transmit the wonders of the season to posterity. Coaches, waggons, carts etc. were driven on it; and an enthusiastic preacher held forth to a motley congregation on the mighty waters with a zeal fiery enough to have thawed himself through the ice, had it been susceptible to religious warmth. This, with other pastimes and diversions, attracted the attention of many of the nobility, and brought the Prince of Wales to visit the Frost Fair.

And in *Frostiana, or a History of the River Thames In a Frozen*

State, printed and published on the ice, there is this account of the Thames freezing again:

The winter of 1739–40 became memorable from its uncommon severity, and occurence of one of the most intense frosts that had ever been known in this country, and which, from its piercing cold and long continuance, has been recorded in our annals by the appellation of the *Great Frost*. It commenced on Christmas day and lasted until the seventeenth of the following February, when it began to break up, but was not wholly dissipated till near the end of the month. Many of the houses which at that time stood upon London Bridge, as well as the Bridge itself, received considerable damage when the thaw commenced, by the driving of ice. The distress which it occasioned among the poor and labouring classes in London, was extreme: coals could hardly be obtained for money, and water was equally scarce. Many lives were lost, destroyed by the intenseness of the cold, both on land and water.

December Stillness

SIEGFRIED SASSOON

This has long been my favourite poem about winter: dark and
mysterious. I muttered it once, in December, while I watched an
endless stream of birds flying south over Lake Ullswater.

December stillness, teach me through your trees
That loom along the west, one with the land,
The veiled evangel of your mysteries.
  While nightfall, sad and spacious, on the down
Deepens, and dusk imbues me, where I stand,
With grave diminishings of green and brown,
Speak, roofless Nature, your instinctive words;
And let me learn your secret from the sky,
Following a flock of steadfast-journeying birds
In lone remote migration beating by.
December stillness, crossed by twilight roads,
Teach me to travel far and bear my loads.

Show-off Poems

The title for this last section, which contains some remarkable stories in verse which didn't quite fit into any of the other categories, came from Ian Richardson. It sums up exactly what an ideal party piece should be: a lovely, zestful poem, requiring a deal of virtuosity in the telling. It is our equivalent to those pieces musicians save up for encores: showy, and sure of applause!

How the Water Comes Down at Lodore

ROBERT SOUTHEY

So here is Ian Richardson's choice: a dazzling show-off poem. 'It requires both diction and stamina, and it performs extremely well,' he said.

Robert Southey, who was born in Bristol in 1774, moved to the Lake District when he was twenty-seven, and lived in a house called Greta Hall in Keswick until his death in March 1843. Keswick is at the northern end of Derwent Water; the Lodore Falls are five miles away to the south. To visit them now you have to go through a turnstile at the back of a hotel called The Swiss Lodore.

> Here it come sparkling,
> And there it lies darkling.
> Here smoking and frothing,
> Its tumult and wrath in,
> It hastens along conflicting strong;
> Now striking and raging,
> As if a war waging,
> Its caverns and rocks among.
>   Rising and leaping
>   Sinking and creeping,
>   Swelling and flinging,
>   Showering and springing
>   Eddying and whisking,
>   Spouting and frisking,

Turning and twisting
        Around and around;
    Collecting, disjecting,
        With endless rebound:
        Smiting and fighting,
        A sight to delight in,
        Confounding, astounding,
Dizzying and deafening the ear with its sound.
        Receding and speeding,
    And shocking and rocking,
    And darting and parting,
    And threading and spreading,
    And whizzing and hissing,
    And dripping and skipping,
    And brightening and whitening,
    And quivering and shivering,
    And hitting and splitting,
    And shining and twining,
    And rattling and battling,
    And shaking and quaking,
    And pouring and roaring,
    And waving and raving,
    And tossing and crossing,
    And flowing and growing,
    And running and stunning,
    And hurrying and skurrying,
    And glittering and flittering,
    And gathering and feathering,
    And dinning and spinning,
    And foaming and roaming,
    And dropping and hopping,
    And working and jerking,
    And guggling and struggling,
    And heaving and cleaving,
    And thundering and floundering,
And falling and crawling and sprawling,

And driving and riving and striving,
And sprinkling and twinkling and wrinkling,
And sounding and bounding and rounding,
And bubbling and troubling and doubling,
Dividing and gliding and sliding,
And grumbling and rumbling and tumbling,
And clattering and battering and shattering,
And gleaming and streaming and steaming and beaming,
And rushing and flushing and brushing and gushing,
And flapping and rapping and clapping and slapping,
And curling and whirling and purling and twirling,
Retreating and meeting and beating and sheeting,
Delaying and straying and playing and spraying,
Advancing and prancing and glancing and dancing,
Recoiling, turmoiling, and toiling and boiling,
And thumping and plumping and bumping and jumping,
And dashing and flashing and splashing and clashing,
And so never ending but always descending,
Sounds and motions for ever and ever are blending;
All at once, and all o'er, with a mighty uproar,
And in this way the water comes down at Lodore.

Skimbleshanks: The Railway Cat

T. S. ELIOT

I walked past the New London Theatre the other day and read, in large letters, 'The longest running musical in West End and Broadway history. Now in its sixteenth phenomenal year.' Who would have thought it! But now that *Cats* is so famous, I've noticed that audiences do like to hear the poems which inspired it. This one is beautifully nimble and evocative, with its impeccable rhythms and rhymes: you can hear the clatter of the wheels as the train speeds along. And could it slow down and stop at the end of the journey? Well, you could hint at it!

There's a whisper down the line at 11.39
When the Night Mail's ready to depart,
Saying 'Skimble where is Skimble has he gone to hunt the
    thimble?
We must find him or the train can't start.'
All the guards and all the porters and the stationmaster's
    daughters
They are searching high and low,
Saying 'Skimble where is Skimble for unless he's very nimble
Then the Night Mail just can't go.'
At 11.42 then the signal's nearly due
And the passengers are frantic to a man –
Then Skimble will appear and he'll saunter to the rear:
He's been busy in the luggage van!
    He gives one flash of his glass-green eyes
      And the signal goes 'All Clear!'
    And we're off at last for the northern part
      Of the Northern Hemisphere!

You may say that by and large it is Skimble who's in charge
Of the Sleeping Car Express.
From the driver and the guards to the bagmen playing cards
He will supervise them all, more or less.
Down the corridor he paces and examines all the faces
Of the travellers in the First and in the Third;
He establishes control by a regular patrol
And he'd know at once if anything occurred.
He will watch you without winking and he sees what you
    are thinking
And it's certain that he doesn't approve
Of hilarity and riot, so the folk are very quiet
When Skimble is about and on the move.
    You can play no pranks with Skimbleshanks!
        He's a Cat that cannot be ignored;
    So nothing goes wrong on the Northern Mail
        When Skimbleshanks is aboard.

Oh it's very pleasant when you have found your little den
With your name written up on the door.
And the berth is very neat with a newly folded sheet
And there's not a speck of dust on the floor.
There is every sort of light – you can make it dark or bright;
There's a handle that you turn to make a breeze.
There's a funny little basin you're supposed to wash your
    face in
And a crank to shut the window if you sneeze.
Then the guard looks in politely and will ask you very
    brightly
'Do you like your morning tea weak or strong?'
But Skimble's just behind him and was ready to remind him,
For Skimble won't let anything go wrong.
    And when you creep into your cosy berth
        And pull up the counterpane,
    You ought to reflect that it's very nice
    To know that you won't be bothered by mice –

You can leave all that to the Railway Cat,
    The Cat of the Railway Train!

In the watches of the night he is always fresh and bright;
Every now and then he has a cup of tea
With perhaps a drop of Scotch while he's keeping on the
    watch,
Only stopping here and there to catch a flea.
You were fast asleep at Crewe and so you never knew
That he was walking up and down the station;
You were sleeping all the while he was busy at Carlisle,
Where he greets the stationmaster with elation.
But you saw him at Dumfries, where he speaks to the police
If there's anything they ought to know about:
When you get to Gallowgate there you do not have to wait –
For Skimbleshanks will help you to get out!
    He gives you a wave of his long brown tail
        Which says: 'I'll see you again!
    You'll meet without fail on the Midnight Mail
        The Cat of the Railway Train.'

The King's Breakfast

A. A. MILNE

The trick with this poem is to delineate the five characters in it
as penetratingly as you dare, while keeping the rhythm going,
fairly consistently, at a nice rollicking speed.

The King asked
The Queen, and
The Queen asked
The Dairymaid:
'Could we have some butter for
The Royal slice of bread?'
The Queen asked
The Dairymaid,
The Dairymaid
Said: 'Certainly,
I'll go and tell
The cow
Now
Before she goes to bed.'

The Dairymaid
She curtsied,
And went and told
The Alderney:
'Don't forget the butter for
The Royal slice of bread.'
The Alderney
Said sleepily:

'You'd better tell
His Majesty
That many people nowadays
Like marmalade
Instead.'

The Dairymaid
Said: 'Fancy!'
And went to
Her Majesty.
She curtsied to the Queen, and
She turned a little red:
'Excuse me,
Your Majesty,
For taking of
The liberty,
But marmalade is tasty, if
It's very
Thickly
Spread.'

The Queen said:
'Oh!'
And went to
His Majesty:
'Talking of the butter for
The Royal slice of bread,
Many people
Think that
Marmalade
Is nicer.
Would you like to try a little
Marmalade
Instead?'

The King said:
'Bother!'

And then he said:
'Oh, deary me!'
The King sobbed: 'Oh, deary me!'
And went back to bed.
'Nobody,'
He whimpered,
'Could call me
A fussy man;
I *only* want
A little bit
Of butter for
My bread!'

The Queen said:
'There, there!'
And went to
The Dairymaid.
The Dairymaid
Said: 'There, there!'
And went to the shed.
The cow said:
'There, there!
I didn't really
Mean it;
Here's milk for his porringer
And butter for his bread.'

The Queen took
The butter
And brought it to
His Majesty;
The King said:
'Butter, eh?'
And bounced out of bed.
'Nobody,' he said:
And he kissed her
Tenderly,

'Nobody,' he said,
As he slid down
The banisters,
'Nobody,
My darling,
Could call me
A fussy man –
BUT
I do like a little bit of butter to my bread!'

Look Closer

PHYLLIS McCORMACK

This and the next four poems provide wonderfully evocative party
pieces for actresses.

What do you see, nurses, what do you see?
Are you thinking, when you are looking at me,
A crabbit old woman, not very wise,
Uncertain of habit, with far away eyes,
Who dribbles her food, and makes no reply,
When you say in a loud voice, 'I do wish you'd try',
Who seems not to notice the things that you do,
And forever is losing a stocking or shoe,
Who, quite unresisting, lets you do as you will
With bathing and feeding, the long day to fill?
Is that what you're thinking, is that what you see?
Then open your eyes, you're not looking at me.
I'll tell you who I am, as I sit here so still,
As I move at your bidding, as I eat at your will,
I'm a small child of ten, with a father and mother,
Brothers and sisters, who love one another,
A young girl of sixteen with wings on her feet,
Dreaming that soon a true lover she'll meet;
A bride now at twenty — my heart gives a leap,
Remembering the vows that I promised to keep;
At twenty-five now I have young of my own,
Who need me to build a secure, happy home;
A woman of thirty, my young now grow fast,
Bound to each other with ties that should last;

At forty my young sons will soon all be gone,
But my man stays beside me to see I don't mourn;
At fifty once more babies play round my knee;
Again we know children, my loved one and me.
Dark days are upon me, my husband is dead.
I look at the future, I shudder with dread,
For my young are all busy, with young of their own,
And I think of the years and the love that I've known.
I'm an old woman now and nature is cruel,
'Tis her jest to make old age look like a fool.
The body it crumbles, grace and vigour depart,
There now is a stone where I once had a heart.
But inside this old carcase a young girl still dwells,
And now and again my battered heart swells.
I remember the joys, I remember the pain,
And I'm loving and living life over again.

I think of the years, all too few — gone too fast,
And accept the stark fact that nothing can last.
So open your eyes, nurses, open and see,
Not a crabbit old woman, look closer — see ME.

Consumer Complaint

C. MARJORIE SMITH

Shopping Then and Now! What a difference! I can remember all
the Then ingredients, listed here, in the shops in Kenton, Mid-
dlesex, where my mother and father and sister and I lived during
the 1930s.

When I was young – say, three or four –
I was not put to ride, astride,
A trolley round a Super Store.
Nor wheeled between the loaded shelves
From which the shoppers helped themselves,
Nor did I dare to raise my voice
Demanding goodies of my choice.

No! I was lifted on a stool
My dangling, gaitered legs to cool,
Bidden sit quietly – 'Not a word!
Nice children should be seen, not heard!'
Hatted and veiled, and also seated,
My Mother was with deference treated.
Our Grocer – (apron, bow-tie, wax moustache)
Was all attention to her pleasure,
Gave his opinion of the weather,
Touched civilly on this and that
While pouring sugar on to flat
Thick squares of paper – fold and twist,
Tuck in the corners – who could wish
A neater package? Then to hold the thing

He made a finger-loop of string!
(No smart machine to snip and snap
No sealing tape – or plastic wrap!)

From creamy kegs this clever chap
Sliced off two pounds of butter! Slapped
And shaped it with a wooden pat.
Then he turned and pointed at
Intricate scrolls of red and gold
On patterned tall canisters and told
What brands of tea were stored within.
Biscuits from an enormous tin
Were weighed out, loose, in paper bags –
(Oh how frustrated, now, I drag
At layers of cellophane that snag
My finger nails!) . . .
. . . Straw-boated butcher in his shop
Of hanging carcasses, would slice the chop
That took one's fancy . . .
                    Oh! for hours
One could compare the Now and Then! . . .
Murdered by customer-protection men
Those gracious days will not return again.

Time

JOYCE GRENFELL

When I was a girl there was always time,
There was always time to spare.
There was always time to sit in the sun;
And we were never done
With lazing and flirting,
And doing our embroidery,
And keeping up our memory books,
And brushing our hair,
And writing little notes,
And going on picnics,
And dancing, dancing, dancing, dancing –
When I was a girl there was always time to waste.

Thank the Lord.

When I was a young woman there was always time,
There was always time to spare.
There was always time to walk in the sun,
And we were never done
With going to weddings,
Our own and our friends',
And going to parties,
Away at weekends,
And having our children
and bringing them up,
And talking, talking, talking, talking –
When I was a young woman there was always time to enjoy
things.

Thank the Lord.

And when I was an elderly woman there was no more time,
There was no more time to spare.
There was no more time to sit in the sun,
For we were never done
With answering the telephone,
And looking at the TV,
And doing baby-sitting,
And talking to our friends,
And shopping, shopping, shopping, shopping,
And washing-up, washing-up, washing-up,
Writing letters, writing letters
Rushing, rushing, rushing,
And we were always hurried,
And we were never bored.
When I was an elderly woman
There was never time to think.

Thank the Lord.

But now I'm an old old woman,
So I want the last word:
There is no such thing as time —
Only this very minute
And I'm in it.

Thank the Lord.

Mrs Malone

ELEANOR FARJEON

Notes:
1. 'Pap': semi–liquid food for babies.
2. 'Happed them and lapped them': held them and hugged them.

Mrs Malone
Lived hard by a wood
All on her lonesome
As nobody should.
With her crust on a plate
And her pot on the coal
And none but herself
To converse with, poor soul.
In a shawl and a hood
She got sticks out-o'door,
On a bit of old sacking
She slept on the floor,
And nobody nobody
Asked how she fared
Or knew how she managed,
For nobody cared.
> Why make a pother
> About an old crone?
> What for should they bother
> With Mrs Malone?

One Monday in winter

With snow on the ground
So thick that a footstep
Fell without sound,
She heard a faint frostbitten
Peck on the pane
And went to the window
To listen again.
There sat a cock-sparrow
Bedraggled and weak,
With half-open eyelid
And ice on his beak.
She threw up the sash
And she took the bird in,
And mumbled and fumbled it
Under her chin.

    'Ye're all of a smother,
    Ye're fair overblown!
    I've room fer another,'
    Said Mrs Malone.

Come Tuesday while eating
Her dry morning slice
With the sparrow a-picking
('Ain't company nice!')
She heard on her doorpost
A curious scratch,
And there was a cat
With its claw on the latch.
It was hungry and thirsty
And thin as a lath,
It mewed and it mowed
On the slithery path.
She threw the door open
And warmed up some pap,
And huddled and cuddled it
In her old lap.

'There, there, little brother,
Ye poor skin–an'–bone,
There's room fer another,'
Said Mrs Malone.

Come Wednesday while all of them
Crouched on the mat
With a crumb for the sparrow,
A sip for the cat,
There was a wailing and whining
Outside in the wood,
And there sat a vixen
With six of her brood.
She was haggard and ragged
And worn to a shred,
And her half–dozen babies
Were only half–fed,
But Mrs Malone, crying
'My! ain't they sweet!'
Happed them and lapped them
And gave them to eat.

'You warm yerself, mother,
Ye're cold as a stone!
There's room fer another,'
Said Mrs Malone.

Come Thursday a donkey
Stepped in off the road
With sores on his withers
From bearing a load.
Come Friday when icicles
Pierced the white air
Down from the mountainside
Lumbered a bear.
For each she had something,
If little, to give –
'Lord knows, the poor critters

Must all of 'em live,'
She gave them her sacking,
Her hood and her shawl,
Her loaf and her teapot –
She gave them her all.
>   'What with one thing and t'other
>   Me fambily's grown,
>   And there's room fer another,'
>   Said Mrs Malone.

Come Saturday evening
When time was to sup
Mrs Malone
Had forgot to sit up.
The cat said meeow,
And the sparrow said peep,
The vixen, she's sleeping,
The bear, let her sleep.
On the back of the donkey
They bore her away,
Through trees and up mountains
Beyond night and day,
Till come Sunday morning
They brought her in state
Through the last cloudbank
As far as the Gate.
>   'Who is it,' asked Peter,
>   'You have with you there?'
>   And donkey and sparrow,
>   Cat, vixen, and bear

Exclaimed, 'Do you tell us
Up here she's unknown?
It's our mother, God bless us!
It's Mrs Malone,
Whose havings were few
And whose holding was small

And whose heart was so big
It had room for us all.'
Then Mrs Malone
Of a sudden awoke,
She rubbed her two eyeballs
And anxiously spoke:
'Where am I to goodness,
And what do I see?
My dear, let's turn back,
This ain't no place fer me!'
　　　But Peter said, 'Mother
　　　Go in to the Throne.
　　　There's room for another
　　　One, Mrs Malone.'

From *Miss Thompson Goes Shopping*

MARTIN ARMSTRONG

In her lone cottage on the downs,
With winds and blizzards and great crowns
Of shining cloud, with wheeling plover
And short grass sweet with the small white clover,
Miss Thompson lived, correct and meek,
A lonely spinster, and every week
On market-day she used to go
Into the little town below,
Tucked in the great downs' hollow bowl,
Like pebbles gathered in a shoal.

So, having washed her plates and cup
And banked the kitchen fire up,
Miss Thompson slipped upstairs and dressed,
Put on her black (her second best),
The bonnet trimmed with rusty plush,
Peeped in the glass with simpering blush,
From camphor-smelling cupboard took
Her thicker jacket off the hook
Because the day might turn to cold.
Then, ready, slipped downstairs and rolled
The hearthrug back; then searched about,
Found her basket, ventured out,
Snecked the door and paused to lock it
And plunged the key in some deep pocket.

Then as she tripped demurely down
The steep descent, the little town
Spread wider till its sprawling street
Enclosed her and her footfalls beat
On hard stone pavement; and she felt
Those throbbing ecstasies that melt
Through heart and mind, as, happy, free,
Her small, prim personality
Merged into the seething strife
Of auction-marts and city life.

The Glory of the Garden

RUDYARD KIPLING

And now, to finish, six show-off poems for men, starting with this great and glorious piece of Kipling.

Our England is a garden that is full of stately views,
Of borders, beds and shrubberies and lawns and avenues,
With statues on the terraces and peacocks strutting by;
But the Glory of the Garden lies in more than meets the eye.

For where the old thick laurels grow, along the thin red wall,
You find the tool- and potting-sheds which are the heart of
all;
The cold-frames and the hot-houses, the dungpits and the
tanks,
The rollers, carts and drain-pipes, with the barrows and the
planks.

And there you'll see the gardeners, the men and 'prentice boys
Told off to do as they are bid and do it without noise;
For, except when seeds are planted and we shout to scare the
birds,
The Glory of the Garden it abideth not in words.

And some can pot begonias and some can bud a rose,
And some are hardly fit to trust with anything that grows;
But they can roll and trim the lawns and sift the sand and
loam,
For the Glory of the Garden occupieth all who come.

Our England is a garden, and such gardens are not made

By singing: 'Oh, how beautiful!' and sitting in the shade,
While better men than we go out and start their working lives
At grubbing weeds from gravel-paths with broken dinner-
knives.

There's not a pair of legs so thin, there's not a head so thick,
There's not a hand so weak and white, nor yet a heart so sick,
But it can find some needful job that's crying to be done,
For the Glory of the Garden glorifieth every one.

Then seek your job with thankfulness and work till further
orders,
If it's only netting strawberries or killing slugs on borders;
And when your back stops aching and your hands begin to
harden,
You will find yourself a partner in the Glory of the Garden.

Oh, Adam was a gardener, and God who made him sees
That half a proper gardener's work is done upon his knees,
So when your work is finished, you can wash your hands and
pray
For the Glory of the Garden, that it may not pass away!
And the Glory of the Garden it shall never pass away!

At Lord's

FRANCIS THOMPSON

Francis Thompson was born in Preston in 1859, and died in 1907. Robert Powell, who sent me this poem, once played him in a dramatised documentary for BBC radio. 'I've been hooked ever since,' he said. 'I love this poem: it's by a Lancastrian, like me, about Lancashire cricket. And when I do it, I love adopting my native accent.'

W. G. Grace,' The long-whiskered Doctor,' was captain of the opposing Gloucester from 1870 to 1899. His younger brother, G. F. Grace, was also in the team. A. N. Hornby and R. G. Barlow were Lancashire's opening batsmen.

Note: 'bans,' in the third stanza, means 'curses.'

It is little I repair to the matches of the Southron folk,
Though my own red roses there may blow;
It is little I repair to the matches of the Southron folk,
Though the red roses crest the caps I know.
For the field is full of shades as I near the shadowy coast
And a ghostly batsman plays to the bowling of a ghost,
And I look through my tears on a soundless-clapping host
As the run-stealers flicker to and fro.
To and fro;
O my Hornby and my Barlow long ago!

It is Glo'ster coming North, the irresistible,
The Shire of the Graces, long ago!
It is Gloucestershire up North, the irresistible,
And new-risen Lancashire the foe!

A Shire so young that has scarce impressed its traces,
Ah, how shall it stand before all-resistless Graces?
O, little red rose, their bats are as maces
To beat thee down, this summer long ago!

This day of seventy-eight, they are come up North against
 thee,
This day of seventy-eight, long ago!
The champion of centuries, he cometh up against thee,
With his brethren, every one a famous foe!
The long-whiskered Doctor, that laugheth rules to scorn,
While the bowler, pitched against him, bans the day that he
 was born;
And G. F. with his science makes the fairest length forlorn;
They are come from the West to work thee woe!

It is little I repair to the matches of the Southron folk,
Though my own red roses there may blow:
It is little I repair to the matches of the Southron folk,
Though the red roses crest the caps I know.
For the field is full of shades as I near the shadowy coast,
And a ghostly batsman plays to the bowling of a ghost,
And I look through my tears on a soundless-clapping host,
As the run-stealers flicker to and fro,
To and fro,
O my Hornby and my Barlow long ago!

Little Aggie

Author unknown

Another Lancashire piece. I don't know where I found it, or who it's by, and I've never seen it in a book. But it was one of my regular party pieces when I was a boy. It's easy. There are easy laughs. (I've been told, since writing the foregoing, that it is indeed by Stanley Holloway. Apologies!)

When Joe Dove took his elephants out on the road
He made each one hold fast with his trunk
To t'tail of the elephant walking in front –
To stop them from doing a bunk.

There were fifteen in all, so 'twere rather a job
To get them linked up in a row:
But once he had fixed them Joe knew they'd 'old on –
For an elephant never lets go.

The pace it were set by the big 'uns in front.
'Twas surprising how fast they could stride,
And poor little Aggie – the one at the back –
Had to run till she very near died.

They were walking one Sunday from Blackpool to Crewe,
They'd started at break of day,
Joe followed behind with a bagful of buns
In case they got hungry on t'way.

They travelled along at a rattling good pace
Over moorland and valley and plain,
And poor little Aggie – the one at the back –

418

Her trunk fairly creaked with the strain.

They came to a place where the railway crossed road,
An ungated crossing it were,
And they wasn't to know as the express were due
At the moment that they landed there.

They were half-way across when Joe saw the express –
It came tearing along up the track:
Joe tried hard to stop, but it wasn't much good,
For an elephant never turns back.

He saw if he didn't do summat at once
The train looked like spoiling his troupe:
So he ran on ahead and waggled the buns
To show them they'd best hurry up.

When they caught sight of the buns they all started to run;
They soon got across at this gait
Except poor little Aggie – the one at the back –
She were one second too late.

The express came dashing along at full speed
And caught her end on, fair and square;
She bounced off the buffers, turned head over heels,
And lay with her legs in the air.

Joe thought she were dead when he saw how she lay,
With the back of her head on the line;
He knelt by her side, put his ear to her chest,
And told her to say, 'ninety-nine.'

She waggled her tail and twiggled her trunk
To show him as she were alive.
She hadn't the strength for to say, 'ninety-nine';
She managed a weak 'eighty-five.'

When driver of th'engine got down from his cab
Joe said, 'Here's a nice howd'youdo:
To see fifteen elephants ruined for life

By a clumsy great driver like you.'

Said the driver, 'There's no need to mak' all this fuss.
There's only one hit as I've seen.'
Said Joe, 'Aye, that's right, but they held on so fast
You've pulled back-end off t'other fourteen.'

Joe still walks round with his elephant troupe,
He got them patched up at the vet's;
But Aggie won't walk at the back any more,
'Cos an elephant never forgets.

Billy's Rose

GEORGE R. SIMS

Simon Brett sent me this poem, which is mercifully less well known than *Christmas Day in the Workhouse* by the same author, but thankfully just as good. If not better. And all the better for being just a bit shorter. George R. Sims was a poet, dramatist and journalist who wrote pieces called *Horrible London* for the *Daily News*!

Billy's dead, and gone to glory — so is Billy's sister Nell:
There's a tale I know about them were I poet I would tell;
Soft it comes, with perfume laden, like a breath of country air
Wafted down the filthy alley, bringing fragrant odours there.

In that vile and filthy alley, long ago one winter's day,
Dying quick of want and fever, hapless, patient Billy lay,
While beside him sat his sister, in the garret's dismal gloom,
Cheering with her gentle presence Billy's pathway to the tomb.

Many a tale of elf and fairy did she tell the dying child,
Till his eyes lost half their anguish, and his worn, wan features
   smiled:
Tales herself had heard hap-hazard, caught amid the Babel roar,
Lisped about by tiny gossips playing round their mothers' door.

Then she felt his wasted fingers tighten feebly as she told
How beyond this dismal alley lay a land of shining gold,
Where, when all the pain was over — where, when all the tears
   were shed —

He would be a white-frocked angel, with a gold thing on his
  head.

Then she told some garbled story of a kind-eyed Saviour's love,
How He'd built for little children great big playgrounds up above,
Where they sang and played at hop-scotch and at horses all the
  day,
And where beadles and policemen never frightened them away.

This was Nell's idea of Heaven — just a bit of what she'd heard,
With a little bit invented, and a little bit inferred.
But her brother lay and listened, and he seemed to understand,
For he closed his eyes and murmured he could see the Promised
  Land.

'Yes,' he whispered, 'I can see it — I can see it, sister Nell;
Oh, the children look so happy, and they're all so strong and
  well;
I can see them there with Jesus — He is playing with them, too!
Let us run away and join them if there's room for me and you.'

She was eight, this little maiden, and her life had all been spent
In the garret and the alley, where they starved to pay the rent;
Where a drunken father's curses and a drunken mother's blows
Drove her forth into the gutter from the day's dawn to its close.

But she knew enough, this outcast, just to tell the sinking boy,
'You must die before you're able all these blessings to enjoy.
You must die,' she whispered, 'Billy, and I am not even ill;
But I'll come to you, dear brother, — yes, I promise that I will.

'You are dying, little brother, — you are dying, oh, so fast:
I heard father say to mother that he knew you couldn't last.
They will put you in a coffin, then you'll wake and be up there,
While I'm left alone to suffer in this garret bleak and bare.'

'Yes, I know it,' answered Billy. 'Ah, but, sister, I don't mind,
Gentle Jesus will not beat me; He's not cruel or unkind.
But I can't help thinking, Nelly, I should like to take away

Something, sister, that you gave me, I might look at every day.

'In the summer you remember how the mission took us out
To a great green lovely meadow, where we played and ran about,
And the van that took us halted by a sweet bright patch of land,
Where the fine red blossoms grew, dear, half as big as mother's
    hand.

'Nell, I asked the good kind teacher what they called such flowers
    as those,
And he told me, I remember, that the pretty name was rose.
I had never seen them since, dear — how I wish that I had one!
Just to keep and think of you, Nell, when I'm up beyond the
    sun.'

Not a word said little Nelly; but at night, when Billy slept,
On she flung her scanty garments and then down the stairs she
    crept.
Through the silent streets of London she ran nimbly as a fawn,
Running on and running ever till the night had changed to
    dawn.

When the foggy sun had risen, and the mist had cleared away,
All around her, wrapped in snowdrift, there the open country
    lay.
She was tired, her limbs were frozen, and the roads had cut her
    feet,
But there came no flowery gardens her poor tearful eyes to greet.

She had traced the road by asking — she had learnt the way to
    go;
She had found the famous meadow — it was wrapped in cruel
    snow;
Not a buttercup or daisy, not a single verdant blade
Showed its head above its prison. Then she knelt her down and
    prayed.

With her eyes upcast to heaven, down she sank upon the ground,

And she prayed to God to tell her where the roses might be
   found.
Then the cold blast numbed her senses, and her sight grew
   strangely dim;
And a sudden, awful tremor seemed to seize her every limb.

'Oh, a rose!' she moaned, 'good Jesus – just a rose to take to
   Bill!'
And as she prayed a chariot came thundering down the hill;
And a lady sat there, toying with a red rose, rare and sweet;
As she passed she flung it from her, and it fell at Nelly's feet.

Just a word her lord had spoken caused her ladyship to fret,
And the rose had been his present, so she flung it in a pet;
But the poor, half-blinded Nelly thought it fallen from the skies,
And she murmured. 'Thank you, Jesus!' as she clasped the dainty
   prize.

. . . . .

Lo that night from out the alley did a child's soul pass away,
From dirt and sin and misery to where God's children play.
Lo that night a wild, fierce snowstorm burst in fury o'er the
   land,
And at morn they found Nell frozen, with the red rose in her
   hand.

Billy's dead, and gone to glory – so is Billy's sister Nell;
Am I bold to say this happened in the land where angels dwell: –
That the children met in heaven, after all their earthly woes,
And that Nelly kissed her brother, and said, 'Billy, here's your
   rose'?

Tarantella

HILAIRE BELLOC

A musical poem about music and dancing in an Inn in the mountains of Spain, with the tempestuous River Aragon roaring outside.

Do you remember an Inn,
Miranda?
Do you remember an Inn?
And the tedding and the spreading
Of the straw for a bedding,
And the fleas that tease in the High Pyrenees,
And the wine that tasted of the tar?
And the cheers and the jeers of the young muleteers
(Under the vine of the dark verandah)?
Do you remember an Inn, Miranda,
Do you remember an Inn?
And the cheers and the jeers of the young muleteers
Who hadn't got a penny,
And who weren't paying any,
And the hammer at the doors and the din?
And the Hip! Hop! Hap!
Of the clap
Of the hands to the twirl and the swirl
Of the girl gone chancing,
Glancing,
Dancing,
Backing and advancing,
Snapping of a clapper to the spin
Out and in —

And the Ting, Tong, Tang of the Guitar!
Do you remember an Inn,
Miranda?
Do you remember an Inn?
    Never more;
    Miranda,
    Never more.
    Only the high peaks hoar:
    And Aragon a torrent at the door.
    No sound
    In the walls of the Halls where falls
    The tread
    Of the feet of the dead to the ground
    No sound:
    But the boom
    Of the far Waterfall like Doom.

The Highwayman

ALFRED NOYES

And to end, here is another poem from the repertoire of Samuel
West. 'On the long side,' he said. But the story has such power
and rhythm and drama and panache that the time just slips by.
And it needs its length to build up to the spine-chilling coda,
when all passion is spent and a great quietness descends.

I

The wind was a torrent of darkness among the gusty trees,
The moon was a ghostly galleon tossed upon cloudy seas,
The road was a ribbon of moonlight over the purple moor,
And the highwayman came riding –
        Riding – riding –
The highwayman came riding, up to the old inn-door.

He'd a French cocked-hat on his forehead, a bunch of lace at his
   chin,
A coat of claret velvet, and breeches of brown doe-skin;
They fitted with never a wrinkle: his boots were up to the thigh!
And he rode with a jewelled twinkle,
        His pistol butts a-twinkle,
His rapier hilt a-twinkle, under the jewelled sky.

Over the cobbles he clattered and clashed in the dark inn-yard,
And he tapped with his whip on the shutters, but all was locked
   and barred;
He whistled a tune to the window, and who should be waiting
   there
But the landlord's black-eyed daughter,

Bess, the landlord's daughter,
Plaiting a dark red love-knot into her long black hair.

And dark in the old inn-yard a stable-wicket creaked
Where Tim the ostler listened; his face was white and peaked;
His eyes were hollows of madness, his hair like mouldy hay,
But he loved the landlord's daughter,
      The landlord's red-lipped daughter;
Dumb as a dog he listened, and he heard the robber say —

'One kiss, my bonny sweetheart, I'm after a prize to-night,
But I shall be back with the yellow gold before the morning
   light;
Yet, if they press me sharply, and harry me through the day,
Then look for me by moonlight,
      Watch for me by moonlight,
I'll come to thee by moonlight, though hell should bar the way.'

He rose upright in the stirrups; he scarce could reach her hand,
But she loosened her hair i' the casement! His face burnt like a
   brand
As the black cascade of perfume came tumbling over his breast;
And he kissed its waves in the moonlight,
      (Oh, sweet black waves in the moonlight!)
Then he tugged at his rein in the moonlight, and galloped away
   to the west.

II

He did not come in the dawning; he did not come at noon;
And out o' the tawny sunset, before the rise o' the moon,
When the road was a gipsy's ribbon, looping the purple moor,
A red-coat troop came marching —
      Marching — marching —
King George's men came marching, up to the old inn-door.

They said no word to the landlord, they drank his ale instead,
But they gagged his daughter and bound her to the foot of her
   narrow bed;

Two of them knelt at her casement, with muskets at their side!
There was death at every window;
                    And hell at one dark window;
For Bess could see, through her casement, the road that *he* would
    ride.

They had tied her up to attention, with many a sniggering jest;
They had bound a musket beside her, with the barrel beneath
    her breast!
'Now keep good watch!' and they kissed her.
                    She heard the dead man say —
Look for me by moonlight;
                    Watch for me by moonlight;
I'll come to thee by moonlight, though hell should bar the way!

She twisted her hands behind her; but all the knots held good!
She writhed her hands till her fingers were wet with sweat or
    blood!
They stretched and strained in the darkness, and the hours
    crawled by like years,
Till, now, on the stroke of midnight,
                    Cold, on the stroke of midnight,
The tip of one finger touched it! The trigger at least was hers!

The tip of one finger touched it; she strove no more for the rest!
Up, she stood to attention, with the barrel beneath her breast,
She would not risk their hearing; she would not strive again;
For the road lay bare in the moonlight;
                    Blank and bare in the moonlight;
And the blood of her veins in the moonlight throbbed to her
    love's refrain.

Tlot-tlot; tlot-tlot! Had they heard it? The horse-hoofs ringing
    clear;
Tlot-tlot, tlot-tlot, in the distance? Were they deaf that they did
    not hear?
Down the ribbon of moonlight, over the brow of the hill,
The highwayman came riding,

Riding, riding!
The red-coats looked to their priming! She stood up, straight
and still!

Tlot-tlot, in the frosty silence! *tlot-tlot*, in the echoing night!
Nearer he came and nearer! Her face was like a light!
Her eyes grew wide for a moment; she drew one last deep
breath,
Then her finger moved in the moonlight,
Her musket shattered the moonlight,
Shattered her breast in the moonlight and warned him — with
her death.

He turned; he spurred to the westward; he did not know who
stood
Bowed, with her head o'er the musket, drenched with her own
red blood!
Not till the dawn he heard it, and slowly blanched to hear
How Bess, the landlord's daughter,
The landlord's black-eyed daughter,
Had watched for her love in the moonlight, and died in the
darkness there.

Back, he spurred like a madman, shrieking a curse to the sky,
With the white road smoking behind him and his rapier
brandished high!
Blood-red were his spurs i' the golden noon; wine-red was his
velvet coat;
When they shot him down on the highway,
Down like a dog on the highway,
And he lay in his blood on the highway, with the bunch of lace
at his throat.

And still of a winter's night, they say, when the wind is in the trees,
When the moon is a ghostly galleon tossed upon cloudy seas,
When the road is a ribbon of moonlight over the purple moor,
A highwayman comes riding —
Riding — riding —

A highwayman comes riding, up to the old inn-door.

Over the cobbles he clatters and clangs in the dark inn-yard
And he taps with his whip on the shutters, but all is locked and barred;
He whistles a tune to the window, and who should be waiting there
But the landlord's black-eyed daughter,
   Bess, the landlord's daughter,
Plaiting a dark red love-knot into her long black hair.